The Rise and Fall of the Press Box

The Rise and Fall of the Press Box

Leonard Koppett

For information about permission to reproduce selections from this book,
please write to:

Permissions
Sport Media Publishing, Inc.,
21 Carlaw Ave.,
Toronto, Ontario, Canada, M4M 2R6
www.sportclassicbooks.com

Cover design: Paul Hodgson / pHd
Interior design: Greg Oliver

ISBN: 1-894963-04-0

Library of Congress Control Number: 2003111742

Printed in Canada

DEDICATION: To my good friends, mentors, colleagues and fellow travelers who are no longer living—Louie, Barney, Dick, three Harolds, three Bobs, three Jims, three Joes, two Arts, two Milts, Irving, Ike, Paul, Bill, Bennie, Frankie, and Sid—and Red, John, Dan, Kenny, Allison, Roscoe, Jesse, Jerry, Arch, Al and Willard, and all the others who shared that time with us.

KEY TO DEDICATION: Louis Effrat, Barney Kremenko, Dick Young, Harold Rosenthal, Harold Claassen, Harold Weissman, Bob Harron, Bob Cooke, Bob Fishel, Jim Roach, Jimmy Cannon, Jim McCulley, Joe Reichler, Joe Nichols, Joe Trimble, Arthur Daley, Art Richman, Milt Richman, Milton Gross, Irving Marsh, Ike Gellis, Paul Sann, Bill Roeder, Ben Epstein, Frank Blauschild, Sid Gray—and Red Smith, John Drebinger, Dan Daniel, Ken Smith, Allison Danzig, Roscoe McGowen, Jesse Abramson, Jerry Mitchell, Arch Murray, Al Buck and Willard Mullin.

CONTENTS

Foreword

In one of many tributes authored shortly after Leonard Koppett's death on June 23, 2003, a colleague described him as "the professor of the press box." I can't think of a better way to remember this erudite, good-natured gentleman, who was born in Russia in 1923, grew up in the shadow of Yankee Stadium in the Bronx and rose to become one of the pillars of his profession, honored by both the baseball and basketball Halls of Fame.

The author of 17 books, a number of which went through several editions, Leonard belongs to an elite group of sports writers who brought an analytical perspective to their work, elevating it to another dimension. His articles invariably were thought-provoking. He was constantly probing beneath the surface, digging for the key piece that would make sense of the puzzle.

No sports writer ever has made more sense of the myriad statistics of our games than Leonard Koppett. With his trusty satchel of reference books by his side in the press box, he could look at a box score and uncover truths hidden in the raw numbers, and place those truths in their proper perspective. Where others approached statistics as black and white, Leonard uncovered the shades of gray that gave them meaning and context. For example, he recognized that 30 home runs hit with live balls against pitching staffs diluted by expansion are hardly equivalent to 30 home runs hit in the pre-expansion, dead-ball era.

Knowledgeable, astute and innovative in his thinking, Leonard challenged his readers—and his colleagues, for that matter—to look at sports more deeply. Of the building blocks of any good news story, the one that fascinated him the most was *why*. Others could tell you *who* won, *what* the score was, *where* and *when* the game was played and *how* it was won or lost. Leonard chose to tell you *why*, and nobody did it better.

Growing up in New York City, I had the good fortune to read Leonard's work in the old *Herald Tribune,* the *Post* and *The Times,* and I shared his fascination with a struggling enterprise of that period called the National Basketball Association. Long before professional basketball took its place in the mainstream of American sports, Leonard was analyzing the game and breaking it down like no one else. His book, *24 Seconds to Shoot: The Birth and Improbable Rise of the NBA,* first published in 1968 and reissued more than 30 years later, is the seminal work about the early days of the NBA and often is cited as source material by those who have followed in his path. A later book about basketball, *The Essence of the Game Is Deception: Thinking About Basketball,* told all you needed to know about Leonard's approach to his profession. Other titles are similarly revealing: *The Thinking Fan's Guide to Baseball,* for example, or *Sports Illusion, Sports Reality.*

Leonard had been working in California for a decade by the time I became commissioner of the NBA in 1984. But whenever his travels would bring him back to New York, I'd make sure to find time to sit with him before a game at the Garden or have him over to the league offices in midtown Manhattan. During those conversations, he invariably would give a new twist or a different spin to something that was in the news or on my mind, so that I'd never look at the subject in quite the same way again. We didn't just talk sports, either. Leonard was a renaissance man, a graduate of Columbia University (of which I am a Trustee) whose interests included history, literature, theater and astronomy. He was just as likely to tease me good-naturedly on all matters of University administration as he was to explain—professor to pupil—my continuing failure to understand a particular insight of his on shooting, scoring or collective bargaining—you name it—that he would then support with statistics and historical example! Our sport—and all sports—have lost a good man, one whom I was greatly honored to know, and to call a friend.

DAVID STERN
NBA COMMISSIONER
NEW YORK, JULY 2003

Introduction

This is not a history but a memoir, with the emphasis on fallible memory (mine) and a cavalier attitude toward exactness. Although it tries to deal with a national cultural phenomenon that no longer exists in a similar form, it is necessarily biased and limited by my own perspectives.

It is too narrowly focused on New York and insufficiently informative about other equally important people and places, and is more centered on the post-World War II era than the pre-war era deserves. But that's unavoidable, since my own experience occurred where it did, when it did, and that's what I have to go on.

If I were a historian, I would try to do justice to geographical distribution and to the giants of the pre-war generation, many of whom were, by all objective measures, larger figures than my own generation produced. But I am not a historian, and do not pretend to be, and this is not a research project. It is essentially descriptive, aimed at conveying the mood, feel and context of a time gone by, a memoir—not of my own particular activities, but of what it was like to be in that milieu, as filtered through a participant's perceptions.

What follows are an amalgam of anecdote, gossip, common knowledge, imperfectly remembered incidents and a subjective sense of atmosphere. It's no less valid, in its own way, than documented narrative, but it is being offered from a strictly personal point of view.

Part One is a brief and necessarily superficial survey of the people and times that created the Golden Age of the Press Box, roughly between 1910 and 1940. Its leaders were the originators and builders of what became a powerful institution. Who they were, why they were important, what they did, how they did it, where they lived and when they worked has to be told, however sketchily, to make comprehensible the scene I moved into in the 1940s.

Part Two contains the main substance of my story. The Way It Was covers the period from 1940 through the 1960s, when print was still the predominant form of news media. From here on, the material is first-hand in the sense that all second-hand and third-hand accounts have gone through my own interpretations. To be more precise, this may not be actually The Way It Was but more like This Is The Way I Now Think I Saw It Then. The intervening years have affected my consciousness along with everyone else's. I have absorbed new subliminal attitudes with the advantage (or disadvantage?) of knowing how things turned out. So exact recollection of former viewpoints may always be suspect.

Part Three and the rest is The Way It Is, with enough history tossed in to see how and why the press box of the Golden Age no longer exists, and what has taken its place. This I have experienced first-hand also, with greater perspective than when I was younger, but I have tried hard not to let nostalgia adulterate my recognition (and acceptance) of today's realities.

Nowadays I move among people to whom the world of Part Two is ancient history, not relevant to today's concerns—understandably and properly so. But there are those who are curious about ancient history, for whatever reason. During the explosion of retrospective that marked the last year of the Twentieth Century (whichever year that was), especially on television, I found myself being sought out frequently for comment. I was one of a dwindling supply of those "who were there" when some particular event or person had become an immediate subject of recollection or commemoration.

So I might as well speak for myself to anyone interested in this particular portion of the past. But the reader must be warned: DO NOT rely on this book for factual reference. I have made no attempt to check, thoroughly or consistently, facts, dates, scores and details or the "true" version of controversial or variously reported incidents. I'm repeating stories, often received third-hand with no guarantee that I heard or understood them correctly in the first place, honed by constant repetition and thus fixed permanently in my mind. I'm sure contradictions can be found in my own published writing and certainly others have described the same occasions and personalities in a different way. But that's not the point. I'm just trying to depict the mood, attitudes, unspoken assumptions and social context of that time, as I try to recall them.

Barney Kremenko, who used to cover the New York Giants for the *Journal-American*, had an answer whenever we thought something he wrote was silly or unsubstantiated. When we'd tell him that, he liked to say: "It's *MY* little story and *I* like it."

This is mine, and I don't need any more justification for it than he did for his.

Part One

How It
Started

1

The Working Press

Once upon a time—during the Twentieth Century in the United States of America—there was a special place where millions of Americans of all ages and all segments of society yearned to be. Admission could not be purchased, its unique privileges were not available elsewhere, its particular blend of intimacy, visibility and glamour could not be artificially reproduced, and its occupants considered themselves fortunate to be there.

It was called a press box.

Every venue used for any significant sports event had one. It was a section set aside for "members of the press" in an age when daily newspapers ruled supreme as the primary medium for disseminating news. It was intended for, and restricted to, the "working press": Those reporters and columnists assigned by daily newspapers to cover that particular event (which the promoter wanted publicized as much as possible), along with the skilled telegraphers needed to transmit their stories, at first by Morse Code key and later by teletype machines.

Therefore, it was situated at the best location for observers— behind baseball's home plate, above football's midfield and racing's finish line, at boxing's ringside and basketball's courtside, or whatever. It provided essential working facilities: A seat with clear sight lines, desk space, a means of transmitting copy, separation from the rest of the crowd, and some method of communicating with appropriate officials.

"Can you get me a seat in the press box?"

That unceasing request, directed at sportswriters, and particularly at sports editors, came from all sides—the rich and the poor, the old and the young, friends and strangers, co-workers and bosses, and especially relatives, however distant and previously unheard from. If flaunting influence didn't work, wheedling and even begging were attempted without shame. Most understood it was a futile hope, but you couldn't be blamed for trying.

What made the press box so special? Of course, it had good views and sufficient comfort for its working occupants, better than the accommodations available to most ticket buyers. But that was incidental. What mattered was its exclusivity. The magic word "insider" permeated its aura. If you got in, whoever you were, you became an insider for a day.

It flourished in a world that existed before television, before universal access to "up close and personal" depictions of any and all celebrities, before we assumed that everyone could and would enjoy (or endure) 15 minutes of fame. A respect for privacy and propriety, more widely felt in "decent" society then than now, helped maintain the distance between the unapproachably famous and "ordinary" folk, even the ones who had considerable status within their own circles.

So mingling with "insiders" meant contact with that kind of glamour, as well as a visible sign that you warranted, or could obtain, inclusion in it. To a fan, this meant the best seat in the house plus the chance to eavesdrop on insider conversation, or even engage in it. To a non-sports celebrity, it meant a certification of one's importance and another chance to be noticed—along with the purer pleasure of authentic fandom, to which so many celebrities sincerely belonged.

It also implied free admission to a choice location, when getting something without paying for it had much more allure than in subsequent, far more prosperous, times. As small as $1.10 for a general admission ticket seems now, it was a significant sum before, during and for a while after the Depression. As for individuals who could well afford the most expensive seats, (as much as $6!) they gloried in the idea of free access to those special seats that were not for sale at any price.

I learned the strength of this urge very early in my career. As fifth graders in P.S. 89 on 78th Street and Amsterdam Avenue in New York City, we had been encouraged to start savings accounts in a magnificent bank building at 74th Street and Broadway. For years I dealt with the same teller, whom I remembered because he looked exactly like the then-aging Charlie Chaplin.

He never gave any sign of recognizing me until I started depositing paychecks from the *Herald Tribune*, some 13 years later.

"You work for the paper?" he asked. "What do you do?"

"I'm a sportswriter."

"Sportswriter? Can you get me free tickets?"

"Depends on what," I waffled.

"The race track," he said. "That's the only sport I'm interested in."

"I'll see," I said.

But after thinking about it, I soon decided to change banks.

In the press box, one might mingle with legends of literature like Damon Runyon, Ring Lardner and Paul Gallico, as well as with equally distinguished chroniclers who didn't also write fiction—Grantland Rice, John Kieran, Bill Corum, Fred Leib, Dan Daniel, John Drebinger, Fred Russell, Shirley Povich, Quentin Reynolds, Heywood Broun and a dozen or more of comparable status. But within it, an absolutely perfect democracy reigned. These giants of their field put on no airs, expected no special privileges and accepted as fellow workers the scores of lesser lights who surrounded them, from the rawest rookie to the oldest hack and the frequently anonymous telegraph operators. Any occupant, it was automatically assumed, was entitled to equal professional respect simply by the legitimacy of his presence. Nobody pulled rank, or even thought to try. Once admitted, you were, however temporarily, an insider.

Outside the press box, the famous and the ordinary went their separate ways, moved in different circles, and were perceived differently by the world at large. Inside, however, everyone was on an equal footing and any of the youngest could aspire to reach (some day) the celebrity, professional status and material rewards the great ones enjoyed.

And there was no doubt about it. Those at the top of the sportswriter pyramid were important folk, generally recognized as such, and the envy of those around them.

2

What
Happened To It

That press box, as a destination devoutly to be wished by so many, is gone—not exactly with the wind, but definitely with the airwaves.

Sections where the working press can do its work, better outfitted than ever, remain in use everywhere. But the symbolic value has evaporated. Glamour and exclusivity have passed on to the television booth and studio, where access is much more stringently limited and patrolled. Here the issue is not joining "insiders" but television itself, which created a universal craving to be part of what everyone else is looking at. Any time the camera pans anywhere, people aware of it start waving their arms and making faces. Odd costumes and behavior, painted body parts and especially hand-made signs, are aimed at being caught by the roving cameras, not simply to be seen by others in the vicinity. Getting your name in the paper was once a guarantee of local celebrity and attention; being *seen,* on television, however briefly, magnified that thrill tenfold and made mere printed mention of your name less worthy of notice. (After all, how many viewers pay attention to the scrolled credits?)

This reaction to the camera was so widely recognized by 1960 that it provided a running gag in the hit Broadway musical *Bye Bye Birdie.* The father of the teenage girl who swoons at rock star Birdie's presence hates everything about the outrageous music, the silly groupies, Conrad Birdie (a play on Conway Twitty) and the whole scene this represents. But the moment the cameras come to the house, he starts waving his arms and grinning like an idiot while pushing his way into every picture.

So in a television age, every broadcaster becomes, immediately and automatically, a celebrity, in ways that writers never become—unless the writer is among the few who also has regular radio and television exposure. Newspaper stories are identified by their institution. One says, "*The New York Times* said…" rather than "Joe Sheehan said…"—whether or not we note the byline on the story, which most readers don't. But we identify broadcasters by personality and appearance, as visitors to our homes, and they are promoted as such. Now it's "Tom Brokow brings you the news," even when Tom Brokaw is being replaced by a substitute. (One of my pet peeves is the standard sign-off, "I'll see you tomorrow at the same time." He won't see me, he never has; I'll see him.) In a newspaper, not even the publisher, let alone the editor-in-chief, gets that kind of top billing.

At the same time, the focus of the promoter—the provider of the facilities—has shifted. Newspapers remain an important element in delivering the free publicity his product needs, but definitely secondary. Television not only reaches more people with more immediate impact, but also pays the promoter lavishly for the privilege. The "news media" always were and always will be the essential ingredient in making commercialized sports (or any entertainment) work. Each day's stories were automatically free advertisements for the next event, and are now even more important as free advertisements for the televised event. But the primary medium now is electronic: Radio, television and, most recently, elaborate message boards and web sites. Understandably, promoters learned to concentrate their main effort, expense, cooperation and staffing on the needs of those operators.

The press box is still there, but that's all it is, a place where the print media work, alongside whomever else the promoter decides ought to be there (business associates, club employees, freelancers, politicians and so forth). Since the writers themselves are no longer celebrities (to the degree that some used to be), mingling with them is no longer the goal of the general public. Even in radio-only days, a team's broadcaster was recognizable enough to be stopped for autographs the way players were; writers weren't. But since television, this difference is greater than ever. What fan wouldn't love to be in the booth with Vin Scully or John Madden? But the press box? It may be a better seat than in the bleachers but not nearly as good as being a guest in anybody's luxury box.

Look at it this way: The bearer of news, or a story-teller, always held a special place in any society, from Homer through the troubadours through Nineteenth Century essayists. In the middle decades of the Twentieth Century, newspapers reigned supreme as the deliverers of information, and their identifiable writers were the common man's window to the world. When television took over, the news bearer became the camera, with the commentator a needed but subsidiary element. But an inanimate camera cannot be a celebrity. A commentator can.

One difference between then and now inside the press box is particularly striking: Laughter, or rather its absence.

The old press box permeated with it. Our chatter was replete with jokes, wisecracks, insults, irreverent observations and uninhibited one-liners, exchanged endlessly among the "regulars" who interacted eagerly with each other. (One major benefit, now gone, was that we got the bad jokes out of our system verbally and could keep them from cluttering up our stories; as in vaudeville, jokesters tried things out and discarded what didn't work. Today's writers miss such external discipline. We would say things we wouldn't write; today one writes anything anyone says.) We had fun, and we felt we owned the turf we were on. Dick Young's answer to random complaints (including his own) was: "How many people get to spend most of their working hours laughing?" We did, and appreciated our good luck.

Today's press box occupants seem much more solemn and silent, apparently not as intimately in touch with (or interested in) one another, each more openly concerned with his or her career progress than with enjoying what they do. They see their fellows as rivals, not colleagues. And they are all too aware that they are guests in a publicity department's realm, accepted as an unfortunately necessary evil, to be tolerated with good grace and even affection in some cases, but not entirely welcome and a reason to be wary of what one may say. Writers are also under greater pressure from their editors to "get quotes," to touch every base that radio and television happen to touch (no matter how silly and irrelevant in the writer's own judgment), rather than follow their own inclinations when those diverge from the herd.

On top of that, the relationship with players and coaches in the clubhouse is generally hostile and uncomfortable on both sides (as we'll see in a later chapter), and that carries over into the rest of the working experience.

To what extent that just reflects the outside world is a good question.

Also, today's press box population is much more diverse than it once was. A positive change is that the presence of women (as reporters and in management jobs), blacks, Latinos and Asians is taken for granted. Professionally, however, what used to be a homogenous group—newspaper writers, telegraphers and a couple of publicity men—now includes radio reporters, dot-com writers, statistic-system feeders, wire-service part-timers and freelancers, along with half a dozen P.R. department members (themselves much lower on the club's internal totem pole than the "marketing and promotion" people). The official scorer, who once had to be an active beat writer, now be may be a local high school coach. All these operate with different needs, on different agendas, with different backgrounds and viewpoints. Their work is entirely legitimate, but a unity of outlook that once existed is gone.

Admission is still limited, but exclusivity is no longer its panache.

3

Giants of the Golden Age

The Base Ball Writers Association of America, the prototype and still the most powerful of all the other sportswriter associations, was formed in 1908. By 1920, it was established as an official part of organized baseball, granted responsibility for official scoring (on which all official statistics are based) and controlling its own working press facilities.

The 1908 season had a tumultuous ending. An apparent victory by the Giants over the Cubs was called a tie game because Fred Merkle, a Giants rookie, failed to go all the way from first to touch second base with two out. So the "winning" run scoring from third was disallowed. Subsequently, the Giants and Cubs ended the regular season tied for first place, so that game had to be replayed, also in New York.

In the Polo Grounds, in those days, writers were given seats at ground level behind home plate. When they arrived for the playoff game, they found those highly desirable locations had been sold as premium seats. Legend has it that Hugh Fullerton, one of the highest-ranking Chicago writers, sat down on the lap of the occupant.

The Cubs won and went to the World Series for the third straight year. In Chicago, out-of-town writers were relegated to the last row of the grandstand. In Detroit, they had to climb a ladder to the roof of the first-base pavilion, were they had no protection from the October rain and snow.

The morning of the final game, writers from all 10 major league cities met in a hotel room and decided to organize, and to write a constitution. In December, they had their first formal meeting in New York, and won assurance from the American and National League presidents that their leagues would co-operate with the new association's goals of improving press box conditions and making scoring-rule reforms.

In their constitution, they defined the objects of the BBWAA as:

1. To encourage the square deal in baseball.

2. To simplify the rules of scoring and promote uniformity in applying them.

3. To secure better facilities for reporting baseball games and better regulation of the scorers' boxes during both the championships seasons and the World Series.

4. To bring together into a closer bond of friendship writers of baseball throughout the United States and Canada.

I learned of all the above in the 1939 edition of the *Spalding Official Base Ball Guide,* in an article written by Henry P. Edwards of Cleveland, one of the original members, marking the association's 30th anniversary.

When I first entered a major league press box in 1947, at the Polo Grounds, some of those original members, including Fullerton, were still around. From the 1920s on, the sports writing community had developed a class system. Syndicated columnists and full-time baseball writers were the nobility; all others, commoners. The columnists, of course, dealt with everything, but baseball was their staple. Ring Lardner, Paul Gallico and Damon Runyon became even more prominent as fiction writers whose stories were made into movies. Heywood Broun and Westbrook Pegler branched out into politics and social comment, while Grantland Rice stayed within the sports sphere without losing status. More closely connected primarily with baseball were legendary names (to me) like James C. Isaminger of Philadelphia, H.G. Salsinger of Detroit, Irving Vaughan, I.E. Sanborn and Fullerton (and Lardner) of Chicago, Ed Bang and Edwards of Cleveland, J. Roy Stockton of St. Louis, Shirley Povich of Washington, and a New York contingent that included Fred Lieb, Dan Daniel, Bill Slocum, Sid Murcer, Ernie Lanigan (a statistics pioneer) and John B. Foster (who edited the Spalding Guides).

Most venerated by me personally was John Kieran, *The New York Times* intellectual whose fame beyond sports was spread by *Information Please*, radio's seminal quiz show, in the 1930s.

The central characteristic of these people was that they considered writing, and baseball, important—not solemn or holy or larger than life, but important, to be taken seriously. They knew and cared about writing as such, and wanted to convey what baseball meant to the people in it.

They created and maintained the glamour of the press box, and built the structure and traditions which later generations enjoyed living off. They started out writing long-hand, became converted to typewriters as soon as that instrument was made small enough to be portable, and could produce first-rate stories under deadline pressure, in distracting surroundings.

I'm not qualified to describe their personalities and backgrounds, but anyone who wants that should get a book called *No Cheering in the Press Box*, which Jerry Holtzman wrote in 1973 after years of collecting taped interviews with many of these men (and the giants of the generation that immediately followed them, like Red Smith and Jimmy Cannon).

Before them, baseball writing was not a full-fledged profession. The common interest of daily newspapers and sports promoters was well recognized by 1880, and the alliance has been strong every since. But baseball was just one of the things general reporters were sent to, and the pre-BBWAA working conditions were abominable.

But by the time I got there, right after World War II, the press box was in full glory.

Part Two

The Way It Was

4

Press Box and Press Room

The press *box* was (and is) where writers work during a game.

The press *room* is where they can gather (and work) before and after a game.

The difference is not trivial.

In the press box, the focus really is on work. If occupied before and after the game itself, it's only by people who have something to do at that time—write, transmit or carry out some service function. During the game, for all the jokes and chatter and socializing that goes on, whatever is happening on the field and around it must be paid attention to. We take the business of reporting very seriously and it is always paramount, however relaxed our manner may be.

The press room is primarily social. It's a gathering place where hometown and visiting writers and broadcasters can meet and converse with each other, as well as with club employees, scouts and all sorts of other "legitimate" visitors connected with broadcasting, advertising, marketing and celebrity of any kind. Food and drink are provided. It also has storage space and places to write for those who still have to, but that's almost incidental. (One could always go back to the press box if necessary.) It's the main meeting place pre-game and post-game, and after a game managers and coaches can drop in for post-mortems. It is the ideal spot for informal information exchange in a relaxed atmosphere.

The "box's" purpose is to facilitate the work of those who perform the tasks so essential to the promoter: Generating free publicity through the news media. The "room" is fundamentally a hospitality suite to serve management's varied interests as it sees fit.

In the period we're talking about, from the 1930s through the 1970s, these general arrangements differed for different sports.

In baseball, the press box was behind home plate at second-deck level, where an occasional in-coming foul ball encouraged alertness. (Hugh Bradley of the *Journal-American* made the Yankees put up a small square screen in front of his regular seat.) Its governance was delegated to the local chapter of the Baseball Writers Association of America (still referred to as the BBWAA, a holdover from an earlier time when Base Ball was two words). Only in baseball did writers enjoy this degree of self-government. In other sports, we understood that the host was in charge.

The press room, which became universally elaborate only after World War II, was under the stands, more accessible to the club-houses, or in some other spot physically removed from the press box area. Its operation was clearly governed by management.

In football, the press box was centered on the 50-yard line, an enclosed section (for protection from the elements) at the top of most bowl-like college stadiums. When a baseball stadium was used for football, a special football box might be added at second-tier level, or the baseball box might be used despite its one-sided location, and the existing press room remained usable. College hospitality facilities varied according to campus layouts and the host's preferences.

For basketball in gyms, armories or commercial arenas, the working "box" was simply tables placed at floor level, courtside, in front of the first row of sold seats.

For boxing, some of the first few ringside rows were equipped with table space.

For hockey in major arenas, a press box was usually hung, like a gondola, off the front of an upper tier, or in some otherwise elevated location. This also served for indoor track meets and other events whose activity required the entire arena floor.

At race tracks (for horses or cars), a football-like layout would be built at roof height centered on the finish line.

At the indoor-sport facilities, a "press room" was simply someone's office temporarily drafted for this purpose.

In the press box, certain utterances could be heard with

ritualistic frequency:

"How'd the last man go out?"

"Who carried?"

"Who was that foul on?"

"What's today's date?"

"What number homer was that?"

And the classic request (or demand) uttered by anyone who, arriving late or having his attention distracted for several plays, returned to his score book: "Bring me up."

(Frank Finch of Los Angeles, occasionally falling into a mood of arrogance, once arrived in the fourth inning and said, "bring me up." A colleague went through the play by play for him and at one point said, "fly to eight, and put a circle around it," our score book indication for an exceptional catch. Frank bristled. "I'll be the judge of that," he declared haughtily.)

Such remarks were not directed at anyone in particular, just thrown out in the expectation that someone would supply an answer. It was part of an assumed information exchange all were willing to share, saving the time and effort it would take to look up something anyone easily could and someone probably already had.

My favorite example is attributed to Grantland Rice. A football game had just ended and the afternoon sun was setting behind the stadium rim opposite the press box. A young writer, deep into his deathless prose, looked up and pointed across the way, asking, "Is that west?"

"If it ain't," Rice told him, "you've got a *hell* of a story."

In Yankee Stadium, the baseball box used to be the first few rows of the mezzanine behind home plate. After World War II, it became a gondola hanging down from the front of the mezzanine at that location. For football, a similar gondola beyond third base was an extension of what had been a photographer's perch, roofed over, since the gridiron ran roughly parallel to the left-field line. The press room, under the stands near the home clubhouse, behind the first base dugout, was used for both.

At the Polo Grounds, the baseball box also hung down from the front of the upper stand behind home plate, following the wide curve of that stand between the dugouts. The football box was built into the roof above right field, as the gridiron ran from home to center. The press room was on an upper floor of the center-field building which contained the player clubhouses and, on the top floor, the baseball team's offices.

At Ebbets Field in Brooklyn, the baseball box originally was hung (as an afterthought) from the front of the upper stand behind home plate. Later, a much larger one was built under the second tier's roof, while the lower one was turned over to radio and television. A modest hospitality room was behind the old-box level back under the upper stand. The baseball box was used for football too. Even though it was over a corner of one end zone, it was high enough to provide a decent view.

When Shea Stadium opened for the Mets and Jets in 1964, a spacious baseball box ran along the private box "club" level behind home, with a similar (but smaller) football box on the left-field side. The press room, also ample, was in the back part of the same level, serving both.

At Madison Square Garden, whatever the event, there was no true hospitality room as such, and not much need for one. Intermission and pre-game conversation took place at courtside or in the appropriate offices on the 49th Street side of the building, or even in the Eighth Avenue lobby.

We'll come across what it was like in other cities in due course.

The liveliest venue, because of the particular writers involved, was Brooklyn's baseball box in the 1950s. That's where Carl Lundquist, of the United Press, issued his definitive comment on the great change taking place in postwar baseball.

To go to the bathroom, one had to walk to the elevator, take it down to the press room level, and come back the same way. Usually, that trek was made between innings in the sixth or seventh. But as three-hour games began to be common, Lunk found it necessary to head down while an inning, perhaps only the fifth, was still in progress.

"Well," he'd declare, "we've got ourselves another two-piss ball game."

Little did he know that by the end of the century he (and we) would be enduring three-piss ball games.

Out-of-town scores came in on a Western Union ticker, the same sort of glass-globe-topped machine then used for stock quotations, whose thin strips of paper were the original material of "ticker-tape" parades. It was at one end of the box. The official scorer, who had a telephone and microphone at his elbow, sat in the middle of the box. The phone could be used to call the public address system announcer, Tex Rickard, at his seat next to the Dodger dugout (on the first base side). Tex could relay a question to the dugout in case of injury or an unusual play, and he could also call up to the box.

One day, the Dodgers were watching the scoreboard during a close pennant race. In the out-of-town linescores, a number identified who was pitching. A number change showed that the Cubs had changed pitchers.

"Find out who's pitching now for the Cubs," they told Tex.

Tex called the box.

Sid Friedlander, that day's scorer, answered.

"They wanna know who's pitching for the Cubs," said Tex.

"Just a minute, I'll look," said Sid.

He got up, walked half the length of the box to the ticker, went through the tape until he found what he wanted, came back, and picked up the phone.

"Tex?"

"Yes?"

"Bob Rush."

"How are ya, Bob?" roared Tex, exuding cordiality but no surprise.

Who wouldn't want to be part of an environment like that?

A press box was judged by its degree of comfort for working.

A press room was rated by the quality of the refreshment provided.

The free food was a reasonable perk. Writers enter a ballpark three hours or so before a game, and leave an hour or two after it's over. In that stretch of seven to eight hours, they (especially the older ones) need access to more decent food than the hot dogs and peanuts concession stands then offered. It was impractical to go out to a nearby restaurant, nor would your paper want you to abandon your post while on the job. Once the management started to install a restaurant facility for its "Stadium Club" clientele, it was natural enough to have its kitchen provide something warm and edible to the press room, which could also be used by working club personnel. As night games became prevalent, while double-headers remained frequent, the rationale for such service became stronger.

(Eventually, Barney Kremenko, who loved soup, would call ahead to find out what the soup of the day was, to determine how early he'd come out.) During a game, some coffee, hot dogs or ice cream might be available in the press box too. (These courtesies are no longer free to the media, with an $8-10 charge presumably, but not always, reimbursed by someone's own expense account. And the main press box fare is limited to popcorn and soft drinks.)

But a well-equipped bar had an older and greater importance. The journalistic community has always had a high proportion of individuals who enjoy (or require) alcohol. During Prohibition (1919-32) promoters never hesitated to make it available to those whose favor they were seeking (the favor of publicizing their event). Once beer and liquor were legal again, those preferences would not be ignored.

And remember the extra attraction of a "free" press box ticket? Well, a free drink, to Depression-conditioned adults, was a deeply appreciated social amenity, as well as a venerable lubricant for easy conversation (which is the lifeblood of news gathering). In an age that paid more attention to things said "in confidence" and "off the record," one could assume that things said "while we're drinking" would not be used to embarrass the speaker. But information acquired this way helped you understand what was going on, and could be used without attribution.

The rhythms of the sporting life consist of tension and release, and just as players relaxed with a beer after a game, so did writers when their work was done. They still do.

This aspect of a major league writer's life caused undisguised envy throughout the newspaper business. But there were other aspects their envious co-workers knew little about. Everything exacts a price, and the price that sportswriters had to pay was travel.

5

The Road

At first, and to all outsiders, it seemed glamorous, a most desirable perk. You traveled first class, stayed in first-class hotels, ate in fine restaurants, had your baggage looked after, and your local transportation provided or paid for. You hobnobbed with famous athletes and shared some of the special treatment they got as a matter of course. None of the cost came out of your own pocket, since you filed an expense account, and all the arrangements were made for you. At work you were provided with comfortable surroundings, food and drink, and just about any kind of assistance you asked for.

With all this, your job consisted of watching games other people paid money to see, in places the fan back home rarely if ever could get to, with access to all the inside dope your readers imagined you had. It can't take that long to knock out the couple of stories required, so there must be ample free time to visit whatever attractions a particular city has to offer, and do whatever socializing you may do there.

And all you had to do, every day, was go to a ball game that lasted a couple of hours. As an umpire once said, "You can't beat the hours."

Who wouldn't envy such an assignment?

Almost everyone did, especially at the newspaper that hired you. The nice people there considered you merely lucky. The mean-spirited ones burned with jealousy. And those who also believed (as most did) that they could do your obviously cushy job as well or better than you did, if only they were given the opportunity, didn't bother to veil their hostility.

But.

While all the goodies just mentioned were authentic enough, other things that go with them were just as authentic and inescapable.

Constant travel produces certain types of loneliness, fatigue, disorientation and family difficulties seldom considered by people with "normal" homebound lives. Today, a great many people in all sorts of businesses experience it. But back in mid-century "living on the road" was still the province of only a few professions: Traveling salesmen, entertainers and musicians, railroad and other transportation workers, the maritime and military communities, and sports teams with their entourage of writers.

Fatigue and disorientation are mental discomforts for which creature comforts don't compensate. You packed and unpacked every other day; dragged yourself and your 10-pound typewriter to ball parks and railroad stations or airports; wondered which papers or other small objects you might have lost along the way; adjusted to a different bed every couple of nights; confronted inflexible but irregular schedules about deadlines and transportation; juggled whatever outside writing you had to do (an economic necessity in that world). All that wore on you.

One, two or five trips were no problem, and actually fun. But after the 50 or 100 of them, you started to lose track of where you were, where you'd been, where you were going, and why. Each downtown started to look alike and the maze you ran—station-to-hotel-to-ballpark-to-hotel-to-airport—was as narrow as a lab rat's.

At each stop, most of your apparently "own free time" wasn't really free. If you arrived early in the morning after an overnight train ride, the rest of that day was shot if there was a day game and even more so if a night game. If you flew in very late at night (which became the normal pattern by the 1960s) you slept (if you could) 'til noon. If you worked for a morning paper, you had to file in an early-edition story that your desk wanted by 5 p.m. Eastern Time. If you went coast-to-coast, or even through two time zones, you had to deal with jet lag. (If you're the sort who functions best when you eat regular meals at regular times, and sleep at regular hours, forget it.) If you took the team bus to the ballpark or airport (by far the most practical way), you'd spend an extra half hour or so waiting in the lobby or on the bus for it to go, and probably more than that in the terminal or sitting on the plane.

If you worked for an afternoon paper, with no Sunday edition, you could skip a Saturday game if you wanted to. But could a day away from home count as a "day off"? The Newspaper Guild decided, eventually, that it shouldn't and couldn't, so you got home with a couple of accumulated days off that had to be made up. But if you were conscientious about covering "your" ball club, you didn't want to miss the Saturday game; and back home you probably went to the games anyhow on your "off" days for the same reason: To keep the continuity of your score book and information flow complete.

Suppose the first game of a road series was at night. You had to be at the ballpark at 4 or 5 p.m., so no local contact was practical that day. If you finished work close to midnight, you probably couldn't get to sleep until around 2 a.m. If the second game was also at night, you could have lunch with some friend, or take in a museum or afternoon movie or shop, but you'd have to be back at the park by late afternoon. If the third day called for a day game, you experienced the double whammy of a day-game-after-a-night-game (which disrupts all you body clocks and makes any in-between activity impossible) and "getaway day," which means have your bag in the lobby before the bus goes to the ballpark. Then it's wait-around time until you arrive at the next city many hours after the game ended (if it's a short jump) or in the early hours of the next day (if it's longer).

So in terms of social or recreational contact, you had just blown Detroit, then Chicago, then Los Angeles, then Kansas City.

(How could you tell a "good" city to visit from "bad" one? A baseball player summed it up as we were coming in for a landing in Pittsburgh one night. "This is a great town," he told the rookie sitting next to him. "My girl is flying in tomorrow.")

Today, by the way, in addition to all this, many writers are expected to make their own arrangements on road trips, since some teams don't include them on their chartered flights.

So you arrive home, after an absence of 10 days or two weeks, tired and confused.

Football, of course, is not bad at all, since it is only a two-day trip twice a month. Basketball and hockey, however, are as bad as base-ball in a different way. Although they have half as many games, with lots of off days, every stop is a one-night stand.

When you're young, single or both, you can adjust your "lifestyle" (a phrase we never knew then) to something satisfactory. But if you have a wife and children, all the normal tensions of family life are aggravated enormously. You're not there when they need you, and they can't provide the support, love and comfort that you crave.

It boils down to this: On the road, you are spending all your time with people you did not choose to be with, separated from those you care about the most—family, old friends, neighbors, even fellow workers from your own paper—in places and situations not of your choosing. Your companions are forced upon you by circumstance, whether or not you enjoy or dislike any of them, and their mix constantly changes (through change of assignment and player trades). And the schedule, in itself, becomes a tyranny that virtually eliminates voluntary activities, even when you're home for only 10 days or two weeks at a time.

It wears you down psychologically, even when it's soft physically.

Before the social revolutions of the 1960s, we took such depri-vations for granted. Through the Depression and war years, the "job"—whatever it was—came first, and anything personal had to be adapted to its needs. Keeping the job (any job) was far and away priority No. 1, and you did what you had to without questioning that you had to. Your family understood that too, no matter how much it disliked it, because that's the way the world was. You remembered, as Bob Cooke told me, "you could always be working in a bank." Cookie was my first sports editor at the *Herald Tribune*, in a career that took him straight from Yale to covering the Dodgers until his sudden elevation to the editorship just in time to make me his first hire, and that represented his idea of ultimate workplace boredom.

I agreed completely.

Today, working people have more choice, by legal right and custom, about making their private lives fit. Far fewer young people are satisfied to make traveling on a sports beat a lifelong career. They move as quickly as possible to becoming a columnist, going into radio or television, or into another kind of assignment or field. Trips are skipped, days off are observed. Absence for private needs (a family problem, a birth, a wedding, a funeral, a graduation) is accepted practice. Even so, that's why the traveling beat writer assignment, once seen as the most desirable in the sports department, is no longer prized, and a move to "higher" status eagerly sought and welcomed.

But not then, in the heyday of the press box.

Si Burick, a nationally known and highly respected writer and editor in Dayton, found himself in Columbus, sitting next to one of his well-established Cleveland colleagues at the opening game of an Ohio State football season. Moments before the kickoff, his companion looked at his watch.

"They ought to be going down the aisle just about now," he said.

"Who?" asked Si.

"My son. He's getting married."

"Married? What in the world are you doing here? Why aren't you there?"

"They knew perfectly well," was the indignant reply, freely displaying hostile feelings, "what the Ohio State football schedule was. Scheduling the wedding this way was their own decision."

First things came first.

6

Clubhouse and Bench

Players and coaches feel the clubhouse should be "their" home, an inherently private place where they should be able to talk and behave free of outsiders' observation. They resent, although they must accept, what they consider to be intrusion.

They are wrong. The clubhouse, which in other entertainment venues is called "a dressing room," belongs to the club management, which provides them with a place to get into and out of their uniforms, clean up, and get medical treatment. Access to it follows rules set by the club, not by the hired performers who use it. Since the club wants maximum publicity for the sake of selling tickets, it allows news media people to enter and mingle with the players before and after games.

So we say to the players, "it's not your 'home', it's your office—and it's *our* office too." It's a place where we transact our separate roles in the same business, the players preparing to play and we getting material to do our own job and make theirs possible by publicizing it. The club decides which players to hire, and which media members to accredit, but once it does the "right to be there" is equal for both groups. And it soon became apparent this was the most sensible arrangement for all concerned. Press and participant had to interact somehow, and this was the best time and place to do it. The alternative would be for a writer to try to track down a manager or player at home or in a restaurant or a bar or wherever, or go room to room in a hotel, which would be even worse for the players than the writers.

So protocol developed for correct clubhouse behavior, on both sides, well before 1920.

Accredited writers could be in the clubhouse up to game time and after the game was over, but only accredited writers. Players would tolerate their presence and answer legitimate questions, the degree of co-operation left to individual preference. Writers would not report or quote what they "overheard" or got by eavesdropping, but only what was being said openly "on the record." Players could rely on reasonable confidentiality being observed. Writers could share information picked up separately, according to their discretion, but within the above understandings. Players would learn who their "regular" writers were, since they were relatively few and so many of the same ones were around year after year. Veteran players would become familiar with prominent writers from other cities as well.

Some writers took more notes (on a steno pad or simply folded blank paper) than others, but "exact" quotes were not an obsession. That is, the substance and meaning of a remark was to be correct, but cleaned-up grammar, condensed wording and family-newspaper vocabulary were left to the individual writer's judgment and expected by his editors. At the same time, "making up" quotes was dishonorable and unacceptable (although it was—and is—done); but paraphrase that accurately conveyed meaning and context, and condensed versions of previous conversations, were considered legitimate.

Before the prevalence of tape recording and portable micro-phones, transcript-like exact quotes were not demanded, and the only "media" people in the clubhouse were writers. So writers didn't "interview" their subjects, except in rare formal situations. Material for stories came out of conversational exchanges, much of it simply chit-chat, with questions aimed at eliciting information and focussing on content related to whatever the writer had in mind.

When all or most baseball and football games were played in the daytime, the writing cycle was well defined and relaxed. A morning paper writer, whose story was supposed to describe the game and report any other news, had an early-edition deadline of perhaps nine o'clock. That left plenty of time to think over what you were going to write, and check out whatever you thought needed checking. An afternoon paper, if it needed a play-by-play account for its later editions, could rely on a co-operative telegrapher to keep sending it. Meanwhile the writer, concerned primarily with a "second-day angle" as a follow-up, could compose his story after a post-game clubhouse visit, or even a subsequent discussion back at the hotel or elsewhere. He had all night to file it. (If news broke during the day—an injury, a trade—the writer could file immediately.)

Night events, like basketball, hockey, fights or track meets, meant the morning paper writer might have to do some "running story" material during the game, but still had time for a complete wrap-up with post-midnight deadlines for most of his editions. The afternoon paper writer had nothing to file until the game was over.

The idea that the old-time writers "didn't have to go to the clubhouse," so often cited by younger commentators, is simply untrue. They went all the time, but they didn't write about everything they heard and they weren't collecting quotes just for the sake of quotes. They were supposed to be telling people what they—the writers—knew and observed, not simply what someone said, because their position defined them as an authority (justified or not). Morning paper writers did their game stories without post-game interrogation, on the basis of what they felt they already knew, unless something specific needed clarification. Afternoon writers got their material before and after the game—as well as after hours—but didn't consider quotes a basic necessity. "What did you think when you..." wasn't seen as a mandatory question.

Today, if it's not in quotation marks it is considered "un-sourced." Editors would rather have Barry Bonds saying "Today is Tuesday" than the most perceptive analysis by the writer himself or some less notable figure—even if today happens to be Thursday. Bonds said it, and that's enough. And anything within anyone's earshot is fair game for being reported, in or out of context, which puts everyone on guard all the time. Players must be careful about what they say, and reporters must make sure they don't miss it.

Furthermore, the presumption used to be that anything during and within the game, and matters of planned strategy and tactics, was legitimately secret. A team was not supposed to be able to know what the opponent was planning, because that could affect the outcome. But television, paying so handsomely for the privilege, broke that line of confidentiality. Once teams gave in to television's desire to put a mike on competitors or coaches, to push the camera into play diagrams being drawn during time outs, to endlessly show facial-expression reactions to whatever was happening on the field, the "privacy" of dugout, bench, sideline and clubhouse was breached, inevitably, forever.

So today's clubhouse is crowded with microphone holders and notebook users buttressed with tape recorders. Players feel besieged, and with good reason, since much of what they say winds up unused or distorted (or misunderstood) anyhow. Knowing they're "on," they don't respond naturally except to the select few a player happens to know well. At peak times, bulky television equipment adds to the discomfort, and aggravates the conflict between the print people and electronics people. (Before television, still photographers were not permitted in the clubhouse except rarely by special arrangement.) Add to the mix the buddies, family members and associates players are now allowed to invite in, and the frictions become triangular.

No wonder it's less congenial.

In baseball, a "cooling off" period of 10 minutes or so right after a game became institutionalized during the 1980s. Then writers are funneled into the manager's office first. By that time many players have disappeared into the off-limits confines of the trainer's room or their private eating lounge. The clubhouse is barred to writers (but not necessarily to agents or buddies) half an hour or more before game time, to let players get "mentally ready." In football, access to clubhouses and practice sessions has always been severely limited. Other sports vary from more relaxed to totally inaccessible (like big-time tennis) except for formal press conferences and special appointments.

Before that, the dugout and batting practice cage were as open to us as the clubhouse, right up until game time. We'd hang around the dugout, usually with the manager and regular players, until the umpires came out. It was informal and natural in a way that's no longer possible, and produced a climate of inclusion instead of today's subdued (but inescapable) antagonism. Restrictions on access are a not-so-subtle message to participants that the media are the enemy. The employer who used to demand cooperation (for the sake of publicity) now approves of indifference (to suit the million-dollar employee), and attaches more importance to player cordiality toward luxury-ticket buyers, advertisers and promotional partners.

Not surprisingly, writers resent being excluded from such new privileges (especially the in-game interviews), and participants take for granted the legitimacy of that exclusion and behave accordingly. The hostility becomes permanent even as its expression becomes routinely more subdued.

The secret of life, someone has said, is simply showing up. The secret of good reporting is simply being around. Hanging around in clubhouses, dugouts, hotel lobbies, airports and stations and on buses, trains and planes—that's how a writer learns to know what he needs, what and how to write about it, to evaluate relevance and fairness, and how to distinguish the important from the trivial. One gained knowledge more by osmosis than by prosecutorial cross-examination.

That's much harder to do than it used to be, when major league sports were less extensive, with smaller populations, dealing with much smaller stakes (in dollars) in a less pervasive spotlight. So the job is also less enjoyable, less envied, less avidly pursued and less often a lifelong career, and being in the clubhouse is more of a chore than a pleasure.

But it's still a lot better than working in a bank.

7

Country Clubs

The term "country club" had quite different connotations before 1950 than it has today. Class distinctions were much more evident then, and membership was not merely a matter of qualifying wealth. In the suburbs and towns surrounding major metropolitan centers, their hallmark was exclusivity based on social position in some appropriate ethnic context and family association. They discriminated openly against Jews, blacks and all the other not yet clearly classified minorities, and limited the activities of their own female members. They prized and enforced privacy. Some were called Golf Clubs, a smaller number Tennis Clubs, but most had facilities for both. They were primarily social not competitive, venues.

Most of the golf and tennis events that newspapers covered took place in such surroundings. Here the press box, as such, did not exist. Some room was set aside to house the reporters and telegraphers admitted to the grounds, but they were expected not to wander around. The competitors were still "amateurs," even in local, state, regional and national championships. A lot of intra-club tourneys got significant coverage in papers like *The New York Times* and *Herald Tribune*, in recognition of the social and business clout of the members, so important in terms of readership and advertising. Much of this coverage was done by permanent part-time stringers, who could service several papers (and the wire services) at once, and who were in effect the public relations arm of the country club set. They were knowledgeable, accurate and indispensable to the papers that used them and familiar to club authorities—and they weren't about to make any waves.

When staff reporters were sent to cover the more important events—a city or state championship, or higher ranking tennis and golf tournaments identified by long tradition with particular clubs—the stringers were a great help to the less informed big-paper journalists, and teachers of the proper protocol in this "upper class" setting.

Similar situations existed in horse and polo clubs, where even major international competitions took place; in boat clubs, that provided the takeoff points for crew races on big-city rivers or upstate lakes; in yacht clubs, which set up sailboat races in Long Island Sound; and in city-based athletic clubs (like the New York Athletic Club) that sponsored track and field athletes and meets, amateur boxing, basketball teams that played local colleges, fencing tournaments and so forth. And, of course, all the local college activities below major football also did without real press-box facilities.

These "non-press box" assignments went primarily to the newest reporters, but even veterans got their share. We all understood that our treasured journalistic independence and free-wheeling behavior had to be kept under wraps in these surroundings. The stories we wrote were straight enough, but our conversation was more circumspect and our awareness of being tolerated was acute. Only the biggest events—the U.S. tennis championships at Forest Hills in Queens, the track meets and horse show (one a year) that made it into Madison Square Garden, the intercollegiate rowing regatta on the Hudson River at Poughkeepsie—acquired true press box facilities.

That entire level of competition, as far as the news media are concerned, is long since gone. Professional public relations people are in charge everywhere, even in minor colleges, while the golf and tennis circuits have become thoroughly professional in players and organization, conducted by professional marketers with the "country club" merely a location. But the old system did have the benefit of teaching a reporter self-reliance, adaptability and per-spective.

In my first few years at the *Herald Tribune*, among the things I covered were the annual Coney Island to City Hall walking race; the Albany to New York outboard motorboat race; fencing, college wrestling, swimming meets, track meets, cross-country runs, boxing (in small clubs), all those minor golf and tennis events, polo, yacht races, crew races, dog shows, equestrian, soccer, lacrosse, squash and (on its last legs—or should I say wheels?) the six-day bike race.

So I learned early the two main imperatives of newspaper reporting: (1) Get the story you were sent to get, not some other story, and (2) get it into the paper on time. How to do it was *my* problem, not someone else's.

A favorite memory remains. Weekend yacht races on the Sound were covered from the committee boat, anchored at the finish line (which was also the starting line). Each class of sailboat, starting with the smallest, had to hit the starting line at a set time (with about 10 or 15 minutes between races) when a cannon shot marked the moment. Even if a particular class had no entries, the starting shot was fired at the stipulated time so that the order (which all racers knew) was preserved.

When the weather was bad, rainy or foggy, the schedule was maintained. The first race could be held up, but once the sequence began, everybody depended on it. On a bad day, some classes were empty.

This day was misty, rainy, foggy and windy. We had the smallest turnout of the season, but enough intrepid sailors to prevent cancellation. Two classes went by empty and then, just as the third cannon shot went off—with no sailboats in sight—a U. S. Navy submarine surfaced right at the starting line and went on its way. When I told Willard Mullin, the cartoonist, about it, we had a good laugh. Then he drew (and published) a cartoon showing Kon-Tiki, Thor Heyerdahl's famous reproduction of a primitive Pacific craft, crossing the starting line. I still have it somewhere.

8

League
Meetings
and Strikes

Another non-press box working area was the hotel lobby.

That's where we waited, impatient but resigned to wasted hours, during league meetings, player association meetings, labor negotiations, strike and settlement announcements, and special occasions when news was being made by someone who would have to pass through there sooner or later.

Strange as it may seem to today's generation, accustomed to upper-floor registration areas in relatively little public space, all hotels used to have ample lobbies on the ground floor, just inside the main entrance. There were armchairs and couches, with end tables next to them, lots of standing around room and columns or posts to lean against. (A post could have strategic as well as architectural value. One beat writer, on road trips, was known for coming down early to catch the club's road secretary to join him for breakfast, so that the club would wind up picking up the tab without the writer using his own meal money. In Detroit, the road secretary, Bruce Henry of the Yankees, started to come down earlier still, and hide behind a post where he could see the elevators open, and watch his frustrated hunter search in vain for his prey. But the writer, John Drebinger, eventually caught on, would beat Henry downstairs and hide behind a pillar, pouncing out just when Henry thought he was safe. This was not primarily a matter of saving a buck, on either side; it was a game they played, John liking the idea of sticking the club with another breakfast check and Bruce secretly enjoying John's company.)

Entrances to the bar, restaurant, newsstand, barbershop and drug-store-gift-shop were all in plain view, with bellhops and doormen always in evidence. Public phones were plentiful and a Western Union telegraph office was not uncommon. Today's hotels do not have lobbies suitable for loitering. In those days, lobby-sitting was considered an art.

The meetings themselves were always strictly private (including the college draft sessions in football and basketball in the 1940s and 1950s), and the meeting rooms used for business were usually on the same floor as the lobby, or only one flight of stairs away. Our working procedure had evolved into a routine: Collar anyone who came out to make a phone call or rest room visit, hoping he'd drop some hints; then file into the meeting room for formal announce-ments (with a chance to ask questions) when the meeting ended; then chase down our special sources among the participants (we all had someone) to try to get the "real" story; then rush to a phone or to our rooms to write and call in our stories.

Most meetings lasted at least several hours, and we had to be in place beforehand, to ask questions of those going in. If they would break for lunch or dinner, that would simply prolong the assign-ment. So our "work" consisted mainly of sitting around, fighting boredom, exchanging information and theories about what might be going on, and watching the clock with increasing tension as our various deadlines approached. Periodic phone calls to the office would keep our desks informed that there was no news yet and what the latest speculation was.

On these occasions, the writers were usually a small group, consisting almost entirely of experienced beat writers or columnists with sufficient background and access to key sources to make sense of whatever transpired—or at least of what was announced. They would be from various cities and we all knew each other, so it was an exceptionally good opportunity to interact, tell stories (not necessarily lies, but freely embellished), trade views and educate any newcomers. When some wanted to repair to the coffee shop or bar, someone always was willing to remain on guard duty to call the others if anything broke. Depending on the importance of the particular meeting, some local radio and television crews might show up, to be ignored or (if they acted nice) filled in.

The key individuals on these occasions were the top-grade wire service reporters, either from New York or a major regional center like Chicago or Los Angeles. For baseball (which had by far the most meetings) this meant Joe Reichler of the Associated Press and Milton Richman of the United Press (not yet called United Press International). Their bylines, virtually unknown in New York, were well recognized everywhere else. They had the most knowledge, the best contacts and the broadest view of what was the most important news nationally, and they had to live with 24-hour 60-minute deadline pressure. Writers from particular cities usually had more parochial concerns, but we all knew that our desks would be looking at the wire stories—usually before our own stories got in—and would be comparing agendas. Joe and Milt were always willing to share and guide, once their instant bulletin obligations were discharged, and we tended to follow their leads unless someone had some specific reason to contradict them.

In other sports, senior New York-based wire service perennials included the AP's Will Grimsley, Whitney Martin, Murray Rose and Mike Rathet, the UP's Norman Miller and Frank Litsky, Pat Robinson of INS (International News Service), and Harry Grayson of NEA (a features syndicate). Reichler and Richman, of course, covered all sorts of other sports too.

Club owners often met in luxurious resort hotels in places like Palm Springs, the Arizona Biltmore in Phoenix, Dearborn Village outside Detroit, Florida's Clearwater, Miami Beach and Palm Beach, and Hawaii's Maui. Most of the time, however, we found ourselves in first-class commercial hotels in major cities.

Nowadays, of course, every such meeting ends with a formal press conference, live on television, firmly controlled by the public relations department involved, at which experienced writers are spectators or unpaid extras throwing out questions. (If you had a really good question and expected a serious answer, would you ask it—and put it on the air—in front of that whole crowd? Of course not. You'd try to pursue that topic your own way once the conference broke up.) Like most news today, baseball news is more canned than ever with less and less opportunity (or need) for individual initiative on the part of the writer.

When a strike or lockout actually occurred—in 1972, 1976, 1980, 1981, 1985, 1990 and 1994 in baseball, 1970, 1974, 1982 and

1987 in football—it meant working the phones from the home office most of the time, then scrambling to get to wherever the settlement was to be announced.

The granddaddy of all meetings (Saddam Hussein would have said "mother of") took place in Chicago's O'Hare Inn, right next to the airport, on Friday, Dec. 20, 1968. It lasted 13 hours.

Baseball club owners had to elect a new Commissioner. Two weeks before, in San Francisco, they had fired the totally unqualified Gen. William D. (Spike) Eckert, the Air Force procurement expert they had hired less than four years before (for reasons never fully explained then or since). His selection then had been greeted with the cry, "They've hired the Unknown Soldier!" Their next choice would be big news.

They started at 4 p.m. and broke—without coming to any decision—at 5 a.m. having talked through the winter solstice, longest night of the year (in the northern hemisphere, anyway). Determined to choose an insider, neither league would accept the candidate from the other league. About a dozen of us made it through the whole night, without catnaps, and spent two more hours trying to sort out what had happened from our particular best contacts. Then (I was with *The Times*) I had plenty of time to write for my next edition, which went to press about 6 p.m. on Saturday as Sunday's paper.

They didn't reconvene until February 4, sensibly finding much pleasanter surroundings. They met at one of the big luxury hotels in Miami Beach, in the morning. After an hour or so of continued deadlock, they called a recess, then quickly called us together to announce that Bowie Kuhn, one of the National League's lawyers, was their unanimous choice as "Commissioner Pro Tem." He would run the office as a caretaker for a few months while they figured out a better way to vote for a "real" commissioner. So in a sense the story that started Dec. 20 took 46 days to complete. Finally, in August, in a hotel in Seattle, they made Bowie the real commissioner with a seven-year contract and a raise.

In 1974, just after *The Times* had moved me to California, the football players went on strike at the start of pre-season training in July. I hustled down to San Diego, where they were setting up their first picket line outside the Chargers' camp. It was at the foot of a hill at the entrance to the campus of the college they were using, and television crews showed up to film sign-carrying players doing their thing.

Ed Garvey, head of the players' union, knew I had covered baseball and basketball labor negotiations extensively and had a reputation for treating the player positions fairly. (That was their view; management thought I was a misguided radical but who did, at least, avoid personal invective in the influential *New York Times*.)

"How do you think we're doing?" he asked.

"I can't tell you," I said, "until I look at the films."

He loved my choice of football-speak as an answer, and repeated that anecdote for years. (It never did him any good.)

Towards noon, however, the weather had become quite hot, so it was time for me to leave.

"Ed, I want you to note," I told Garvey, "how conscientiously I discharge my responsibility to be impartial and give both sides equal time. Having spent all morning down here with you, I'm now going up the hill to be with club officials, and eat the air-conditioned lunch they serve up there."

That has been my proud boast throughout my career. In 50-plus years as a newspaperman, I have never failed to find the location of my assignment—and where they serve lunch.

9

Courtrooms

Another off-field venue that took up a lot of time was courtrooms. Especially during my years with *The New York Times* (the "The" was always supposed to be capitalized). I got more than my share of those assignments because *The Times* paid more attention to such things than other papers did. In recent years, many prominent athletes have been embroiled in criminal proceedings involving violence and drugs. But in the 1970s, personal and off-field problems of prominent athletes were still being handled routinely by city-side reporters and editors, as "general news," rather than in the sports sections. So the cases I had to deal with grew out of labor-management conflicts and antitrust issues.

Most sportswriters hated covering the court cases. They didn't enjoy writing about the business side of sports any more than people liked reading about it. The sports fans' interest was focused on games, players, results, prospects and gossip about those subjects. The business aspects—salaries, collective bargaining, franchise moves and especially lawsuits—were unavoidable, but no fun.

In covering meetings and strikes, however, we were at least talking to people we knew—club officials, players, union officials, owners—about matters we had learned something about during previous private conversations. In a court of law, we were in a different universe.

First of all, one must behave differently. Courtrooms are small. Most of the people present are involved in some way, with personal or business relationships to the people inside the bar. The press sits in the "audience" and not at a table. We are supposed to be still—even a whispered conversation can be noticed and frowned upon—and to just watch and listen. We certainly can't interrupt to ask a question. During a recess, a brief exchange with one of the attorneys is possible, but any real talk takes place out in the hallway. American court proceedings are open to the public, but only to the small portion of it that can fit into that room. Our journalistic privileges got us inclusion in that public segment, but that's all. We are guest-observers and are expected to act that way.

I learned some new rules rather quickly.

One: I must find at least one attorney on each side who will explain to me his or her side's view of what has transpired, what is planned, what were the important elements in that day's testimony, and what the next step in the procedure will be. It doesn't have to be, and usually isn't, the senior member of the team, but I have to establish enough trust with at least one subordinate willing to be patient with my often ignorant questions. Obviously, each side is telling you what it hopes to see in your story (we didn't yet use the term "spin"); but you have to hear both, and it's surprising to what extent they usually agree.

Two: I must also make contact (preferably before the trial) with one of the judge's law clerks, who can keep me straight on procedural issues and point out complications I wouldn't recognize otherwise.

Three: No matter what the judge says when he makes a ruling from the bench, in what appears to be plain English, it may not mean what I think it means. Therefore, I need the law clerk or one of the junior attorneys to explain it, even if I think I guessed right.

Four: The same goes for much of the testimony and cross-examination. I mustn't assume that I understood the true significance of what I heard. I must check with a professional.

Five: In reporting the trial while it's on, I mustn't forecast or project the eventual result on the basis of any one session's developments, but stick to describing the high points of that session in their own context.

Six: Tell the story as straight as I can. This will guarantee that my story will seem dull to anyone who is not actually interested in the case; but I owe it to the judicial.

All that sounds idealistic, but it is essentially practical. Only by following such rules can I learn what I need to know and live up to the basic ethical rule: Get it right. I'll have plenty of chances to interpret and explain the result's meaning and consequences after it's in.

In one way, however, I found my idealism to be naïve. I went out of my way (at first) not to attribute any amplified point to a particular lawyer, thinking I was preserving a degree of confidentiality. Then I discovered that the lawyers hated that. They *wanted* to see their names in the paper. They knew they were never telling me anything truly confidential, and did want their names associated with a case important enough to be covered by *The New York Times*. I was not doing them a favor; I was depriving them of attention they craved. At the same time, they were very sensitive to how accurately I reported whatever it was they gave me, and would let me know if I didn't get it right. Too much of that would cut off that source.

The fundamental difference was that this was an official, legal process going on, with real-life consequences for all concerned. A ball game, a trade, a fired coach, a second-guessed manager, a player's performance or quote or peccadillo—as serious as they may be in their own terms—are not something for which the government can send you to jail or make a financially crippling civil judgment. This was The LAW.

Anyhow, that's how it seemed to me.

Only a few sportswriters were ever put in this position. Most papers relied on the wire services, which, like the papers who did use staff people, relied on their regular courtroom reporters. They knew little about any of the subtle sports issues involved (or worse, were fans who thought they did know), but were familiar with the legal procedures, courtroom etiquette and the predilections of lawyers and judges. They were enormously helpful, but had to be filled in on sports background matters by the sportswriter. Because *The Times* actively covered so much more of the sports legal scene than other papers, I became an unintended "expert" in this area, and because of my own inclinations, enjoyed becoming educated in it. And because what I wrote appeared in *the Times* (pardon me, *The Times*), it had disproportionate importance to the legal and sports communities and for future researchers. It was, after all, "the paper of record." I was very aware of that responsibility and made a conscious effort to avoid the light, flip and irreverent tone that I felt was generally appropriate for my "fun and games" (rather than "life and death") approach to sports.

The Law was definitely not fun and games. It may not have been life and death either, but it was serious enough to be treated with care.

Still, there were exceptions. The most celebrated trial was Curt Flood's antitrust suit against baseball's reserve clause in 1970. Baseball's top officials testified that no other system was possible. Flood's chief attorney was Arthur Goldberg, who had been a U.S. Supreme Court Justice, but the actual cross-examinations were being handled by Jay Topkis, who happened to be one of my classmates back at Columbia. And all Columbians then were steeped in awareness of its great football upset victory over Stanford in the 1934 Rose Bowl, 7-0 on a 17-yard touchdown run by Al Barabas.

The witness was Bob Reynolds, an owner of the California Angels, who had been a star lineman on that Stanford team.

Topkis asked Reynolds, "Where were you when Barabas went around left end for that touchdown?"

Reynolds smiled and replied, "I was on the other side of the line and couldn't do much about it."

The exchange got a satisfactory laugh, and the cross-examination continued without any more jokes.

But as soon as I got Topkis in the lobby, I bawled him out.

"How could you give him that opening?" I cried. "You're lucky you got away with it."

"What do you mean? What opening?"

"All he had to say," I told him, "was 'I was flat on my ass, which is where baseball would be without the reserve clause', and you'd have blown your whole case."

Jay was unimpressed. "You know nothing about law," he said. "Stick to batting averages."

He was right. Two years later the Supreme Court ruled against Flood anyhow.

10

The
Halls of Congress

Meetings and strikes are a sort of free-for-all, characterized by lots of boring waiting time. Court proceedings are highly structured with an air of solemnity, in which major turning points are often under-dramatized. Both, in their very different ways, are hard work to cover.

Then there are Congressional Hearings.

They're fun.

Sports subjects come before Congress primarily in antitrust contexts. Reserve and draft systems are challenged as part of labor negotiations. Start-up leagues accuse existing leagues of monopolizing the pro player market. When teams move, the other league members who let them or tried to stop them are charged with conspiracy. Any kind of scandal, from gambling to drug use to death in the ring, also offers an opportunity for a legislator to draw attention to himself by holding a hearing on changing some law. A change is almost never made, but the limelight is almost always captured.

In sports hearings, the witnesses are not under oath and face no threats (as witnesses did in more serious congressional investigations, like Watergate or the Red-hunting forays of the 1950s). Their self-serving remarks are expected to be that, and the questioning by Committee members is just as transparently self-serving, according to the legislator's agenda and geographical loyalty, so it's unlike any real cross-examination. Only two issues are ever on the table: Somebody wants Congress to grant some kind of advantage, or to prevent it from taking away an advantage already possessed. In court, once a decision is reached, the result is binding on everyone. In a hearing, nothing is binding on anyone. It's all rhetoric to be used as ammunition in subsequent action—to pass a bill, vote it down, or kill it by never bringing it to a vote.

In the process, however, a tremendous amount of previously undisclosed information becomes public, especially about finances. Most witnesses are sports celebrities in their own right, and the characteristics of various Senators and Representatives are exhibited to a wider (and generally non-political) audience. Neither group minds the publicity.

What's more, the politicians and their principal aides are accustomed to dealing with (and trying to influence) the media, so material is plentiful, leaks are common currency, a press row is made available and the hallway outside the hearing room is choked with TV crews and people with microphones. In those days (before 1980 or so), print journalists still received more co-operation and respect than all but the most prestigious electronic representatives.

The antitrust question had a fascinating facet. Baseball had been declared exempt from federal antitrust law by the Supreme Court in 1922, on the grounds that it wasn't "interstate commerce," which is all that Congress has the right to legislate about. During the 1950s, a series of other Supreme Court decisions established that federal antitrust laws did apply to football, boxing and all other sports. But to everyone's surprise, the Court in 1953 upheld the 1922 decision concerning baseball only. Admitting this seemed illogical, the Court said it was up to Congress to change the discrepancy (which it had never contemplated in the first place) if it wanted to.

That was a godsend to lobbyists, congressional committees and commentators only too happy to publicize their points of view. Dozens of bills were written, in both the House and the Senate, either putting baseball under antitrust law or exempting others from it, according to some particular legislator's influential constituency. Most never got out of committee, or even provoked a major hearing. A very few passed one house or the other, but no comprehensive bill ever got past both to reach the president's desk for signature. The battle was fought entirely on the lobbyist level and in the media, with each legislator's eye fixed firmly on (a) his or her own voters and (b) how this vote could be (or had to be) traded for some more important (to that Senator) vote.

As I say, this was great fun when they let you in on it.

The first (and still the greatest) baseball hearing was conducted by the House Judiciary Sub-Committee on the Study of Monopoly Power, in the summer of 1951. It was headed by Emanuel Celler, Democrat from Brooklyn, and in its final report (in May 1952) put on record for the first time financial and other historical information never before publicly available in credible and coherent form. The main subject was the reserve-clause system of player control, how it could be reconciled with antitrust restrictions on conspiratorial practices if baseball were not exempt, and what other legislation might be needed to "preserve America's national pastime" if the exemptions weren't there. The topic had become hot in 1949, when an Appeals Court found the exemption unjustified (for blacklisting players who had played in a Mexican League). Baseball quickly settled that case out of court, but additional suits were in progress and by 1951 another case, involving keeping a player in the minors, was on its way to the Supreme Court.

At that time, no comprehensive history of the business had ever been published by a serious historian, so this was the first full revelation of baseball practices to be spelled out in public and on the record. Virtually every witness agreed that some form of the reserve system was essential. Even those who spelled out its evils, and described how they suffered from them, had no practical suggestion for an alternate system. Distinguished testifiers included Branch Rickey, Ford Frick (just named Commissioner), Clark Griffith, Larry MacPhail, columnist Red Smith, a host of star players and, representing the "common-people" type of player, a catcher from St. Louis named Joe Garagiola, whose glibness set the stage for his eventual television career.

The committee concluded no new laws were needed now, since the Supreme Court would soon rule. But in 1953, when the Supreme Court did, it upheld the exemption by a 7-2 margin. Then the same court found, in other cases, that boxing, football and all other sports were not exempt, and wouldn't be.

From that point on, congressional sports hearings became an almost annual affair, generating a huge amount of information. No new comprehensive law ever emerged, but many hearings led to significant negotiated changes within each sport.

In 1957, when the court found football's reserve system illegal, the National Football League found another way to quash free-agent movement (the so-called Rozelle Rule, requiring a team signing a free agent to compensate the team which lost the player; It was finally ruled illegal in 1976). When, in 1959, a third major baseball league was being organized, Sen. Estes Kefauver conducted elaborate hearings aimed at legalizing the reserve for all sports but putting them under antitrust for other purposes. This resulted in limiting a major league team's control of players to 40 rather than hundreds, and paved the way for the expansion of the existing majors as a means of avoiding an independent third league. In 1962, when the National Football League wanted permission to make a national television deal to cover all of its clubs, it got an antitrust exemption just for that. In 1965, after the Columbia Broadcasting System bought the New York Yankees, the Senate investigated the ramifications of a major television network owning a team while competing for its league's national television rights. It decided there was no problem, opening the door to countless team-television ownership partnerships now so common in many sports.

In 1966, when the young American Football League and National Football League wanted to merge (to end their upward spiraling salary war), another antitrust exemption was needed. It slipped through as an amendment to another bill with the aid of a powerful Louisiana senator, Russell Long (and—surprise!—the granting of an expansion franchise to New Orleans).

In May 1970, the National Basketball Association and American Basketball Association wanted to merge for the same reason and expected to take the same path. But the NBA players, more astute, better led and aware of the football example, quashed the attempt in Senate hearings before a Judiciary Committee headed by Sen. Sam Ervin, D-North Carolina, not yet as famous as he would become in the Watergate hearings. (In 1976, a merger finally was carried out by settlement of an antitrust suit brought by the players, to remain under a judge's scrutiny for 10 more years.)

After that, the increasingly immense conflicts shifted back to the courts and labor negotiations, ending in prolonged strikes in all four major sports. Congressional hearings became less frequent.

Since the 1980s, every sportswriter, editor and electronic

commentator has had to deal with legal, financial and labor issues as a matter of course. Few, however, have gone beyond accepting the statements of both sides at face value, repeating oversimplified explanations, taking one side or the other or condemning both, or simply rehashing the established clichés. One must have a sincere desire to do the extensive homework required, to discern the real issues, to understand the legal and legislative frameworks, to keep an open mind about persuasive arguments from various points of view. Most sportswriters, like most sports fans, don't want—and don't care—to make that kind of effort. More important, their editors, directors, producers and publishers don't demand—or care—that they do. Sports issues, like most news in the television age, are judged by their entertainment value more than by their informational content. "Tell me" has been superseded by "hold my attention."

Thus the press box, in the old sense, has been devalued even in its non-press box venues, and the importance of the newspaper story—in the eyes of the participants in a controversy—is less than the importance of a TV sound-bite's impact or talk-radio's agenda.

Time lurches on.

11

Cameras and Microphones

The physical surroundings in the press box and clubhouse are dramatically different than they used to be. The change began gradually in the late 1950s and was fully established by 1980.

Up to 1950 or so, writers were the only clubhouse visitors. They were numerous, since most large cities had at least three and up to a dozen daily papers. But a sloppily dressed man (as so many were—Oscar Madison was not entirely a figment of Neil Simon's imagination) holding a notepad wasn't terribly disruptive and easy to ignore if a player wanted to. The dressing rooms themselves were quite small in the older parks (until most were remodeled after World War II). The regulars (which most were) were known by sight, if not by name. (Babe Ruth was famous for never knowing anybody's name, addressing everyone as "hiya, kid." John Drebinger, who covered more games for *The New York Times* than anyone else between the 1920s and 1960s, was the Babe's particular pal from an early stage on. With great pride, John used to tell us, "I was the only writer the Babe ever called by his first name. He called me Joe.")

In those clubhouses, there were no agents, players' children, brothers-in-law, or radio people with tape recorders. The broadcasters were almost exclusively concerned with play-by-play during a game and brief pre-game and post-game interviews. So a certain degree of business-like calm pervaded the premises.

When television came in, it was not a clubhouse presence except at the World Series and All-Star Game, or Opening Day. Bulky cameras, a couple of technicians with each one, and a broadcaster wearing make-up got in everybody's way, but these occasions were such a small fraction of the total that the atmosphere wasn't changed. Pretty soon, however, there were radio people taping interviews, and sticking microphones in front of us to pick up the answers to our questions—and they DID get in our way. They also crowded the facilities, and a lot of conflict developed. This, in turn, annoyed the players who thought of the clubhouse as their private preserve (see Chapter 6).

Nowadays, of course, radio and television have a 24-hour cycle for some stations devoted entirely to sports, and countless featurettes on other stations. And almost all writers use tape recorders to back up their notes. After a game, a mini-mob scene takes place around that day's key figures, and most players disappear into the off-limits areas—trainer's room and player lounge—where they can't be bothered. A degree of mutual trust and familiarity, which used to evolve naturally over the course of a season, no longer develops.

These physically changed conditions aggravate the hostility that characterizes player-media relations today. The old intimacy would be gone in any case. A $3 million-a-year 26-year-old has little in common with a 40-to-60-year old writer (especially if it's a woman) living on a five-figure salary. Their lifestyles and daily life experience are too different. Established players are surrounded by a coterie of advisors and gofers, some of whom have clubhouse access. (Management isn't about to tell a $10-million star with a guaranteed five-year contract whom he can't invite in.) On the road, players have single rooms, hire limos, don't need the team bus and use room service rather than any hotel coffee shop. Most of all, as any human being would, they react to the presence of microphones and tape recorders as a signal that they're "on," consciously performing and wary of consequences, not engaging in a normal conversation. They go through it patiently enough, but real life resumes only when that's over.

The rookies, marginal players and others who don't yet make big money (although the minimum is $300,000!) are merely waiting, hoping and expecting to reach the established player's status. Rookies always did take their cues from the older players, about how to dress, talk and act as "big leaguers"; now they absorb just as easily the snub-the-media attitude, and the need to switch on the charm when a major national TV celebrity comes around.

Finally, a whole new set of workers has appeared in the press box and clubhouse, just in the last few years of the dot-com revolution. They cover games, do interviews, need space and must be serviced just as print media have always been—but they aren't working for a newspaper, radio or television station. Their stuff appears only on computer screens. They face either no deadline at all or (depending on the service) the non-stop wire service deadlines. Some are supplying statistical services, some special outlets connected with baseball itself. By and large—so far—they are newcomers and transients, seldom if ever covering road games, lacking the opportunity (so far) to acquire the background and acceptance traditional media reporters have (or had). Where this segment of the media community will be five or 10 years from now, I have no idea, and I'm not sure anyone does. We shall see.

At any rate, that's the way it is. In the rest of this book, we'll be talking again more about the way it was.

Part Three

Personal Items

12

Childhood

I was nine years old when I decided I'd like to be a sportswriter. We were living one block east of Yankee Stadium, on 157th Street in an apartment house that ran through the whole block from Gerard Avenue to Walton Avenue. This was 1933 and I was in the fourth grade. I'd been fully exposed to the Yankee magic, although baseball still ran second in my interests to college football (because New York University used Yankee Stadium as its home field, and the Army-Navy game, complete with marching cadets and midshipmen, was being played there in those years).

My father brought home three or four of New York's 12 papers, not always the same ones, every day. I devoured their sports pages and comic strips (and nothing else), and was fully aware of the Babe Ruth era, which was still on. Naturally, all the kids on the block knew all about the Yankees and I, the reader, more than most. On game days, we could hear the crowd's roar, and see people streaming in and out before and after the game. Now and then, I'd be taken to a game.

I already knew from experience, playing punch ball in the street, that I'd never be a big league ball player, and didn't even dream about it. But I did notice that an hour or so after every game, when the crowd had long since cleared, some extremely non-athletic-looking middle-aged men carrying square black boxes ambled up to the corner of River Avenue and headed for the (elevated) subway station at 161st Street. I realized that these were the baseball writers whose stories I was reading, and that they went to games *every day*.

The Depression was at its height (or depth?) in 1933. I already understood that the most important thing in life would be to have a job where you got paid every week, as my father fortunately did. As a small but literate person, I knew I'd like to make a living by writing—it involved no heavy lifting—and that the only way a writer gets paid every week is to work for a newspaper. It added up. If I were a baseball writer, the paper would pay me every week and I would go to a ball game every day.

And that's how it worked out.

I'd been born in the early hours of Sept. 15, 1923, in Moscow, at just about the time Jack Dempsey was knocking out Louis Firpo in New York (where it was still Sept. 14). My parents had grown up in Kerch, in the Crimea, and were able to get higher education in St. Petersburg because, after 1905, some of the restrictions against Jews had been relaxed. After World War I and the Russian Revolution, they settled in Moscow, where some of my mother's brothers and sisters were being well treated by the new regime because they were engineers, doctors and photographers, desperately needed by the new Soviet state. My father, who had been trained as a musician, had a different asset. His father had run a major fishing and cannery operation (soon confiscated) and had made his oldest son learn the business. The Soviets didn't need another musician, but did need someone who could sell their caviar and herring for hard currency outside their borders. The family name (Kopeliovitch) was well known to European importers, so that's the job they gave him. In 1927, they sent him to New York to Amtorg, their foreign trade office there. In 1928, they let my mother and me join him as his temporary assignment dragged on. In December of 1929, when Stalin had consolidated his power, the first purges began—as it happened, in the food ministry, to which my father was technically attached—and the family in Moscow sent word: "Don't come back, you'll be one of the first scapegoats."

So we stayed, got first papers in 1933 and were full-fledged naturalized citizens in 1938. But I was an American from 1930 on, Americanized primarily by means of my sports interests. A child in such circumstances—especially an only child—has to latch on to something permanent, continuous and simple. Spectator sports were my handle, and dovetailed nicely with my desire to write (no heavy lifting) and watch ball games.

In the spring of 1934, we moved to Manhattan to Riverside Drive and 78th Street. I felt honor-bound to root for the Giants. (In the Bronx, it had been a walk of less than a mile across the Harlem to the Polo Grounds, but we did that only a few times.) In the spring of 1935, my mother took me to Miami Beach for three weeks (while my father was on a trip to Europe). It just so happened that the Giants were training there, three blocks away in Flamingo Park. I was at their practice or game every day and learned an important lesson. Watching a pepper game from behind the bench (there was no dugout), I took a soft line drive right in the middle of my forehead. I was too stunned to cry. Sitting on the bench was Travis Jackson who said, without turning to look at me, "hang with it, kid." The lesson? Don't stand behind pepper games.

The other important facet of my life then was piano lessons. In New York, my parents had gravitated to the many musicians in the Russian refugee community (which had an enclave in Sea Gate, just off Coney Island in Brooklyn, where we lived the first year and went back each summer). My father knew many of them from his St. Petersburg days, including one of the most high-powered piano teachers of her day, Isabella Vengerova. As soon as we got a piano (in the Walton Avenue apartment when I was eight) I started taking lessons from a distant cousin by marriage and former classmate of my father's, Boris Jivoff. He brought me along so fast that they decided to bring me to Madame Vengerova, whose specialty was child prodigies. I clearly wasn't, but she was willing to take me on, once every two weeks with the regular lessons (two a week) provided by one of her young assistants, Mildred Jones. I lasted with Madame through high school, but only because of her loyalty to my father and his ability to deliver all the caviar and herring her social life required. My talent was limited and my willingness to practice four hours a day (which the prodigies did) was non-existent, and my parents never pushed. But I did enough to avoid expulsion for the following reason:

In March of 1935 we had moved into a house my father bought in Sea Gate. In the fall of 1936, I would start high school. But Abraham Lincoln, on Ocean Parkway, was already on double sessions, and I would have to go to the afternoon sessions. That would wipe out the lessons with Miss Jones, who had to come all the way from Manhattan. It was the piano or Lincoln; it couldn't be both. So they sent me to Poly Prep, out near Fort Hamilton, and I could be home in time for the pre-dinner lessons. But for me, the real deal was this: If I went to Madame's at 93rd Street and West End Avenue every other Saturday morning, I could continue on to Yankee Stadium or the Polo Grounds for the ball games. That was my true and only motivation to practice hard enough to keep Madame from throwing me out. (I'm sure the caviar was the most important part of the equation.)

Once in Sea Gate, I started to write up every game I saw after I got home, for practice. At Poly, I became sports editor of the school paper. My algebra teacher was also the baseball coach, Fred "Maje" (for Major) Bohnet, and he taught me both subjects superbly. He also started called me "Kop," being unwilling to wrestle with Koh-pell-ee-oh-vich, and friends and family have called me that ever since.

As a Brooklynite, I had to take more interest in the Dodgers and got to Ebbets Field more often than to the Stadium. But these were glory years for the Yankees (1936-39) and I wasn't about to let go of that. The Giants were also pennant winners in 1936 and 1937, and contenders in other years. The Dodgers were hopelessly, but amusingly, inept with a clown named Casey Stengel serving as their manager.

Until 1938, the three New York teams, by agreement, did not put their games on radio, believing it would hurt attendance. So our listening was focused on Earl Harper, doing the Newark Bears (who were loaded with Yankees-to-be). We could also pick up Byrum Saam from Philadelphia, doing home games of the A's and Phillies, and on a car trip into Westchester or Connecticut, Frankie Frisch when he was doing the Boston Braves. But in 1938, Larry MacPhail brought Red Barber to Brooklyn and revolutionized fan response to radio. The next year, Mel Allen was dealing with the Yankees and Giants, and our ability to hear games became universal.

World War II began in September 1939, the start of my senior year in high school. Leaving Ebbets Field after a game now forgotten, I saw the newsstand headlines blaring "Germany Invades Poland," and I understood fully what that meant. By May, when

France had been overrun, all of us knew we would certainly be in the Army and undoubtedly in the war itself sooner or later. Any life plan involving four years of college and then a career was simply unrealistic. World War I stories suddenly seemed very real. Whether or not one would still be alive whenever this war ended, and what kind of world that might be, was best pushed out of consciousness. One lived today, for today, with a time horizon of no more than several weeks.

In that frame of mind I started college at Columbia in September of 1940. (This was the final instance of piano lesson influence. The choice had come down to Yale or Columbia, and at Columbia I could continue with Miss Jones even though Madame was finally dropping me. Mildred lived on 91st Street and Columbia was on 116th; New Haven was too far.)

For becoming a baseball writer, I had acquired serious preparation. I could write, I had the background, and I'd seen a lot at the highest level, including the Yankee home games of the last four World Series. But the question had become, as the bombing of Britain began, would there be a future in which baseball—and I—would even exist? But you don't dwell on such thoughts at 17. What had me excited was that I was about to be exposed to the newspaper pros.

13

KF-79 and Columbia

Columbia, in 1940, was still a major football power. Lou Little had been brought in to coach in 1930, from Georgetown, and starting in 1931 produced four straight one-defeat seasons. The high point was a 7-0 victory over Stanford in the Rose Bowl on New Year's Day 1934, with Al Barabas scoring the touchdown on a 17-yard weak-side reverse designated in the playbook as KF-79. (That was the last year in which that was the only Bowl Game. The Sugar and Orange started in 1935, and the Cotton in 1937.) KF-79 became a magic word in Columbia (and New York) lore, symbolizing the great underdog triumph of Columbia's "thin blue line" against the powerful Stanfords. Forty years later, when *The Times* moved me to Palo Alto, I made KF79 my personalized license plate, hoping to discomfit those Stanford residents old enough to recognize it.

After 1935, Lou's teams won less often but featured a spectacular All-America, Sid Luckman, through 1938. Games against major opponents sold out the 33,000 seats in the wooden structure up at Baker Field. In New York's pecking order of football importance, Columbia and Fordham were tied for second, behind Army (because of its annual game against Notre Dame at Yankee Stadium and occasional other New York appearances). The National Football League's Giants ranked fourth. N.Y.U. and Manhattan had become lesser lights.

That meant the downtown papers sent senior reporters and

columnists to the rickety wooden press box above Baker Field's east-side stands. Staff reporters were also frequently sent to basketball and baseball games. The football games were on a local radio station, and the very first American televised sports event was a Columbia-Princeton baseball game at Baker Field in 1939 (in which Luckman played shortstop).

This was big league stuff, and Columbia needed a big-league public relations man to handle it. His name was Bob Harron. He had been a prominent sportswriter in Boston and New York before Columbia brought him in to polish Little's image the year before the Rose Bowl. He had moved into public relations with the high-powered Steve Hannegan firm. Soon his Columbia job became full-time. The position of Sports Publicity Director was in its infancy, and Harron was one of its pioneers.

He became, in my first few months on campus, the most important substitute father figure, professional guide, teacher, friend and formative influence—a true guru, no less, although we didn't use that term then—I have ever had. I've been fortunate in having several others, but he was the first and had the deepest permanent impact.

I, more than any of the other freshman sportswriter candidates on the *Columbia Spectator*, gravitated to his office on the mezzanine floor of John Jay Hall, overlooking the Van Am Quadrangle which was the center of college life. I spent as much of my free time there as I could, hanging around and doing anything they'd let me do: Stuff envelopes, fold releases, write a paragraph on a minor sport, answer the phone, add up and file statistics, take messages, run errands, whatever. I was not bashful about expressing my opinions and showing off my accumulated sports knowledge, but—hard as it is to believe now for anyone who knows me—I listened more than I talked. And I absorbed what I heard and saw.

At the first two home games, I sat in the stands trying to mark down first downs and yardage on a file card. By mid-season, I was in the press box doing whatever flunkies were needed for: Showing reporters to their seats, handing out programs, hanging coats, taking copy from writer to telegrapher, distributing statistics and notes, carrying messages, delivering sandwiches at halftime, giving maximum definition to the phrase "beck and call."

Here I was among the men whose by-lines had become so

familiar to me for almost a decade—among them Lou Effrat, Arthur Daley, Allison Danzig, Jesse Abramson, Stanley Frank, Jimmy Powers, Gene Ward, George Trevor, Joe Williams, Kenny Smith. I delighted in hearing their banter. I strove to anticipate their needs and answer any question. I learned how they behaved, what bothered them, which ones had to be catered to more than others, who made unreasonable demands (which had to be satisfied no less than the reasonable ones), who welcomed bits of information and who didn't want to be disturbed.

Then, when I had devoured every word they wrote about what I had seen myself, I learned what each, individually, had decided to stress, to ignore, to bring alive and to express cleverly, and I pondered why and how they made the choices they did. In quiet moments during the week, I'd ask Harron about such things, and he loved to share what he knew. He was deeply idealistic, yet supremely practical, a born teacher.

The last game that season was against Colgate. We had two sophomore passers, Ken Gehrmann and Paul Governali, who had been fighting to be the first-stringer since they were on the fresh-man team. Governali had taken the lead, and was starting against Colgate.

Shortly before kickoff, Harron had a new assignment for me.

"Go over to the radio booth," he said. "They need a spotter."

The radio booth was a tiny shack at the top of the opposite (western) stand. The broadcaster was a young fellow with an already familiar voice, Mel Allen. I had little experience in what could be a tough job, but Governali turned into a star that day, and since I was spotting only the Columbia team, I got by. Paul was my next-door neighbor in the dorms, so I had a pretty good fix on what was supposed to happen while he was the center of things. His performance enabled Columbia to finish the season with five victories, two ties and only two losses.

Allen and his partner, Joe O'Brien, paid me $10. It was the first money I ever earned from sports. I wouldn't earn another cent for the next 22 months.

By February, an on-campus student radio station was ready to take the air. (Well, not exactly the air. Its signal was radiated through the pipes of campus buildings, and couldn't be heard even across a street.) A junior, Bill Levinson, recruited me to join him in a

15-minute sports news show (dealing strictly with Columbia teams). It required a lot of legwork, and my insider status in Harron's office really paid off. Bill, sharper and more mature than I was, became another teacher. We learned to write faster than ever, to ad lib a lot, and to pay attention to more than the big sports. This gave us an identity throughout the college and especially with the Department of Athletics hierarchy. Between that and an increasing share of assignments on *Spectator*, I was getting priceless training and learning the advantages of access.

Dec. 7, 1941, occurred late in the first semester of my sophomore year. I was 18. Now it was only a question of time before I'd be drafted, and any idea of finishing a normal college career was gone. But my contact with newspaper pros was increasing, and I'd get a chance to write minor-sports releases. Meanwhile, George Knobbe, the professor in my sophomore composition class (a requirement), happened to be a one-time sportswriter. We had to do two 1,000-word papers a week. Would he accept sports subjects? Sure. So I wrote nothing but sports columns for him, pontificating on outside subjects I couldn't get into *Spectator*. He gave me good marks, and I have been a tireless pontificator ever since.

Harron's chief disciple, his right-hand man, was Bob Cherneff, and I gradually became his unofficial assistant. Cherneff also served as the campus sports correspondent for *The New York Times*, the plum among several such jobs other papers also had. It dealt with covering football practice, minor sports and anything else *The Times* didn't send a staff man to, and paid good money (in space rates). His class graduated in the spring of 1942. He went into the Navy and I inherited *The Times* job.

Now I was mingling with the pros on their own turf, in the office on 43rd Street. The older writers, whether they knew me from Columbia or not, were uniformly cordial to kids like me. Joe Nichols, who covered hockey and boxing primarily, was particularly avuncular.

"Always remember," he'd tell me, "not very much matters, and nothing matters very much." That seemingly cynical philosophy is actually excellent advice for (1) keeping a sense of perspective, (2) writing on deadline and (3) coping with egos, your own as well as the ones you come across.

I didn't get called up until March of 1943, so I stayed in school through the first semester of my junior year, but school work got precious little of my attention. I was immersed in *The Times* work, the radio station and *Spectator*. Harron, who had been in World War I, managed to re-enlist in the Navy (although he must have been in his late 40s) as a P.R. officer, and had to be replaced at Columbia. The new man was Irving T. Marsh, assistant sports editor of the *Herald Tribune* (under the already legendary Stanley Woodward), who served in a temporary wartime function. (In those days, it was standard practice for newspapermen to double as publicity men, with no ethical questions raised; the papers that were underpaying them were glad to have them not need raises.) For Irving, I could help the way I had under Harron (becoming, in effect, his Cherneff). Now I was also official scorer at the football, baseball and some basketball games, and rubbing elbows with the downtown writers more than ever.

In practical terms, my connection with Irving became by far the most important element in my eventual career. Harron had taught me attitude and outlook; Marsh taught me the nuts and bolts of the work I would have to do, and eventually opened the doors to the profession.

But on March 1, I was in the U.S. Army, headed for a different kind of basic training.

14

The ETO

During my 33 months in the Army, the last 30 as a private first class, I was in Kansas, Wyoming, Ohio, Missouri, North Carolina, England, France, Germany and North Carolina again—in that order. None of it is relevant here except one anecdote, coming up. By and large, the experience of other sportswriters was quite different.

Many of the big names had made their biggest impact and important money writing for mass-circulation magazines, much as today's newspaper people thrive on their radio and television identities. *The Saturday Evening Post, Collier's, Liberty, Esquire* and other slick-paper magazines were the most prestigious, but pulp—for fiction as well as fact—was not looked down upon. Some of these "stars" became war correspondents (Jimmy Cannon among them). Many more, and especially the younger ones, simply served in every conceivable role in the armed forces. My impression, totally unsubstantiated, is that a disproportionate number became fighter and bomber pilots, naval officers and other participants in the true hazards of war (as did some war correspondents). A handful wound up active in their profession, assigned to various editions of *Stars and Stripes* (the Army's newspaper) and other military publications.

Since the avowed purpose of the war was "to preserve our way of life," and since the 48 United States were physically out of range of bombs and battlefields, much effort went into keeping spectator sports going. In terms of morale, this was even more important to the millions in service than to the civilians at home, because it so strongly represented the "cultural glue" of the civilization we were defending and hoping to return to (if we survived). That the tradition of the World Series and the Army-Navy football game be kept intact seemed to matter, and Armed Forces radio brought those events to every corner of the globe.

The press box then, like the teams on the field, became populated by those deferred from military duty by age, medical condition, family circumstances or some sort of war-related civilian work. Visitors in uniform were welcome whenever they showed up, however minor their pre-war position had been. (Unlike in the war plants, women did not enter the scene of what was accepted as a male preserve, undoubtedly because the activity—unlike war plants, other essential work and the military itself—was so clearly unessential.) The machinery of news coverage and radio worked as efficiently as ever. But the glamour and self-importance of the press box was on hold.

From my personal point of view, my army time constituted an interruption of what had been, from age nine to 19, my mental preoccupation with sports. I could not maintain the continuity of following events. The pattern had been broken. In a young army conscript's mind, one thought overrides everything but the immediate task at hand: When—if I ever do—will I get out? Nevertheless, to the majority of us, awareness that the sports continuity at home was being preserved seemed somehow comforting. Sports talk was plentiful in non-combat areas. In moments of idealism, real or feigned, the Britishers might say they fought for king and country, the French for the Glory of France, the Russians for Mother Russia or sheer survival; the Americans fought just to get back to life they way it used to be.

An example of where sports fit is the anecdote I promised.

In September of 1944, after Paris had been liberated and the German armies were being pushed back towards the Rhine, my outfit—a repair and supply headquarters depot in the Ninth Air Force (fighter planes)—moved into Villacoublay, an air base between Paris and Versailles. SHAEF—Supreme Headquarters Allied Expeditionary Forces, Gen. Eisenhower's base—was set up in Paris. Here it became possible for officers to get sports equipment for the recreational use of enlisted men. Such physical exercise and combative spirit were certainly appropriate activities for rear area desk soldiers, mechanics, truck drivers and supply sergeants.

So we (the 42nd Air Depot Group Headquarters) formed a unit football team, complete with pads and uniforms. So did some nearby outfits, including SHAEF itself. By December, our team and SHAEF's were unbeaten after four or five games, and it was decided to have a "championship game" right around Christmas.

Needless to say, the SHAEF people could arrange anything they wanted. A football (soccer) stadium was commandeered, and our game was to precede a civilian soccer match scheduled to draw about 25,000. Heavy snow the day before left two or three inches on the field and prisoners of war (mostly German) were brought in to shovel it off. (The crowd, coming out early, liked that.) We had no yard stripes except the goal lines, jury-rigged goal posts, only a couple of soaking wet footballs and an unreliable 10-yard chain, but what the hell, it was wartime, right?

The SHAEF officers were sure their team would win easily. They had more personnel, the ability to assign good players to football duty, and a rooting section. But we had a kid from Philadelphia named Collins, who was a terrific running back and team leader. Before a completely mystified Parisian audience, we slogged through to a scoreless tie.

Huge amounts—in dollars, alcohol and other goodies—had been bet by the officer class. SHAEF suggested (ordered?) that we play an extra period, hitherto unheard of in football. Their suggestion was "keep going until someone scores," and who was going to resist a SHAEF suggestion?

So we had one more coin toss, lost it, and in line with football custom of the time, SHAEF chose to kick off. We started around our 35, marched down the field, and Collins plunged into the end zone from about two yards out. The gnashing of SHAEF teeth could be heard all the way to the Ardennes, where the Battle of the Bulge was just starting.

I sent a letter describing this game to Irving at the *Herald Tribune*. He gave it to Red Smith, who ran it in his column. My point, to which Red added approving comment, was to note how much Americans cared about this aspect of the "way of life" we were struggling to protect. The fact that the *Trib* printed it reflected how widely that feeling was shared.

It wouldn't be that way in later wars.

15

Columbia
Again

On Aug. 6, 1945, I arrived back in the United States, granted emergency leave because my father had been suffering from leukemia for over a year. (He would die in December.) The first newspaper headline I saw was "Atom Bomb Dropped on Japan."

As a long-time reader of science fiction with some schooling in elementary physics, I knew exactly what that meant: The war was over, I would not be shipped to the Pacific, and one could think again about a civilian future.

During the next three months, one in New York and two in Greensboro, N.C., waiting to be mustered out, I went through the mental decompression process. I pored over college catalogues from all over the country. Would I now want to be a musician, or mathematician, or physicist? Or to write for the theater, or fiction? Were all my old assumptions about a newspaper career still my true feelings? I had turned 22 and was no longer a teenager. I could go in any direction I wanted, anywhere I wanted.

A few weekends settled the matter. One was spent in New York, at a Columbia football game, being welcomed home. The rest were spent filling in on the sports desk of the Greensboro paper, handling its heavy diet of high school and college football games. One sniff of the old sports scene, plus daily exposure to sports pages again, was enough to dispel alternate dreams. It would be back to Columbia, where I needed one more semester to complete my degree (since they gave you some credit for Army time) and go on to wherever that might lead.

Irving Marsh was still in the sports publicity office part-time, with Bob Cherneff in the process of taking over. I got my *Times* job back, and quickly became a one-man bureau. I was also campus correspondent for the *Herald Tribune*, the *Daily News*, the *Journal-American*, the Associated Press, the United Press and any out-of-town papers that wanted a story when their teams came to visit Columbia. I also wrote most of the routine releases for Marsh and Cherneff, and did the scoring and statistics for home football and baseball games.

All my old contacts were renewed and widened. The whole *Times* group knew me from before: Effrat, Danzig, Daley, Joe Sheehan, Phil Burke (who was the department secretary), Roscoe McGowen (who lived cross the street from Baker Field), Joe Nichols. The *Tribune* people, through Irving, became familiar with me too: Jesse Abramson, Harold Rosenthal, Smith, Everett Morris and the rest. A younger generation of newly established hot shots was only a few years older than I was: Dick Young, Leonard Lewin, Jack Lang, Murray Janoff, Lou Miller, Norm Miller, Reichler, Richman and his brother Art (on the *Mirror*).

Columbia's football team, 8-1 in 1945, was very strong in 1946, 1947 and 1948 because ex-G.I.s—some transfers, some Columbia returnees now older and more experienced—were combined with a couple of outstanding freshman classes. Lou Little's reputation was back to its Rose Bowl peak. Baker Field had sellouts, and Columbia was the top football story in town. So the important writers from the other papers—Kremenko, Dave Eisenberg, Larry Robinson, Milt Gross, Cannon, Gene Ward, George Trevor, Ken Smith—also crossed my path as I served them.

We didn't call in "networking" then, but that's what it was.

In June I got my degree. I made a perfunctory application to the School of Journalism (only a graduate school at Columbia, enrollment about 75) but wasn't accepted, fortunately. It was fortunate because if I had gotten in and done well, I'd have been promptly placed on some paper somewhere and might or might not have ever gotten back to New York. As it was, I could branch out my stringer activities to many non-Columbia events, while keeping the connection, and piece together enough to live on by becoming a full-time part-timer on several fronts, including Columbia.

Sooner or later, I felt, a real job would open up somewhere. It did in the summer of 1948, at the *Trib*.

Harron had become the pubic relations head for the whole University, under its new president, Dwight D. Eisenhower (whom I referred to as "my old boss," but never brought up the SHAEF football game). Bob was still my guru, although our contacts were less frequent, but he had taught me the key lesson back in my sophomore year.

"You have to be sure you know what you want," he said. "If what you really care about is going to ball games, go into the ball game business somehow. If you want to be a newspaperman, it shouldn't matter whether they send you to a ballpark or anywhere else. You have to want newspapering for itself."

That was the choice I had really faced up to coming out of the Army in Greensboro. Now, at the *Tribune*, I was given another choice. I could be schoolboy sports editor, writing right away; or I could enter as a desk man (where I had some fill-in experience) and take my chances as to when another writing opening would occur.

I thought: I know how to cover high school ball games well enough; but if I'm going to be a newspaper man, I'd better learn how a newspaper works and what goes into making it come out every day. The only way to do that was to work on the desk.

When I chose that, I had made my commitment permanent.

I didn't love the ball games any less, but I wanted even more to be part of the process—as writer or anything else—that produces a good newspaper. I had been brought up to value the full meaning of the team concept: Any one role was less important than the whole. No matter how brilliantly one could write, the story did no good unless it got into the paper. Inside, I would learn what was involved in making that happen. The fun and glamour, no doubt, was in being out, as a writer. But the work took place inside. So that was the place to start.

As it turned out, I got to write soon enough, but we'll get to those details later on.

16

The Baseball Dinner

Nothing reflects the change in lifestyle, and status of the press box occupants, more vividly than the annual dinner of the New York Chapter of the Baseball Writers Association of America.

From the 1920s through the 1960s, this was the premier social occasion of the baseball world and a major event on New York's social calendar. Since the 1980s, its focus has changed to simply an award presentation dinner, and is still a big deal for the 1,400 or so who attend. But the impact that it used to have on celebrities beyond the baseball orbit no longer exists and is no longer possible. And that impact came from the full-scale musical show we put on, written and performed by the writers, poking fun at the previous year's happenings in the style the Gridiron Club uses to rib Washington's political establishment.

The "show," as we always referred to it, started in the 1920s as an off-season get-together for baseball writers, their baseball contacts and newspaper friends in the idle days of late January, just before starting south for spring training. (Only much later, stimulated by television and movie clichés, did "the show" become used as a synonym for the major leagues, shorthand for "the Big Show." Players spoke of going to "the bigs," as in Big Time or Big Leagues, or "the majors." But one never thought of the serious competitive business of baseball games as a "show," which implied a rehearsed performance. Of course, for television, *everything*—including elections and wars—is a "show," and our language has reflected our changed perceptions.)

Our show evolved as a way to brighten an evening that had no agenda but camaraderie, even though a few awards came into existence. The minstrel format, then still popular in vaudeville (in what was still a Jim Crow culture) offered a chance to write song parodies and comedy sketches, poking fun at the previous year's baseball events and personalities. The writers had plenty of talent for this kind of composition, and by performing the songs and sketches themselves, they gave the audience of insiders the satisfaction of seeing them make fools of themselves in front of people whom they so often bothered in real life.

Very quickly the "show" grew into an ever more elaborate stage production, with a 12-piece orchestra in the pit, scenery, props, costumes and the aid of professional stage manager-directors. It was intended to run an hour but usually lasted an hour and a half. When well-known and recognizable (to that audience) writers blew lines, sang off key, and generally messed up a good script, the people who were usually victims of their year-long second-guessing loved it.

Since the show followed some presentations of player awards and a distinguished guest speaker (like a senator, governor or other dignitary on the dais), the audience was well enough lubricated by the time the curtain went up to have shed its critical faculties and inhibitions, so a good time was had by all.

The Monday papers would run extensive stories quoting the best lines and lyrics, and being able to attend this sold-out affair became as desirable as admission to a World Series press box.

Chapters in other cities, notably Chicago and Boston, had their own annual dinners but not as elaborate as ours. Ford Frick, while still a writer and broadcaster, was one of the early guiding lights of the show. When he became commissioner and moved that office to New York (in 1951), he would schedule a business meeting of major league owners for the week of our dinner. That enabled a large portion of baseball's national leaders to be present, and of course the three local clubs (Yankees, Giants, Dodgers) brought lesser staff members as well. With New York's nine daily papers, a half dozen suburbans, foreign-language papers, the major press associations and radio networks and top advertising agencies also on hand, the density of "insiders" was at a maximum.

My first exposure to this was in January 1950, when Bob Cooke included me in one of the *Herald Tribune* tables. That show, directed by Edward Duryea Dowling, a prominent Broadway professional, was one of the most elaborate ever. Many of the songs were taken from *South Pacific*, then new, and the climax was a choreographed sextet waving fake and elongated left arms while singing. *There is Nothing Like Joe Page* to the tune of *There is Nothing Like a Dame*. Page had been the Yankee relief ace in that last-day pennant victory over the Red Sox and the World Series triumph over the Dodgers.

Other memorable moments were *Happy Chandler, He Go Talkie-Talk* sung by Bill Bloome in a Polynesian grass skirt. The quality of the lyrics used in such parodies is exemplified by Dick Young's classic dig at Dodger manager Burt Shotten, after the 1947 World Series, through *These Foolish Things*:

And in the last game trailing five to zero,
Why you let Banta just isn't clear-o,
Oh, how your strategy stinks!
These foolish thinks, remind me of you.

The substitution of "thinks" for "things" is sheer brilliance.

By the next year, I had my own baseball writer card and was a regular chorister. Pretty soon I was writing and submitting songs and sketches, while plunging into the grunt work of preparation—typing and mimeographing scripts, making phone calls, ordering props and costumes, going out for sandwiches, and so forth. Before long, some of my stuff was getting in and I was getting better parts.

In that decade, the venue was the grand ballroom of the Waldorf Astoria, which had a fully-equipped stage, room for 900 or so on the main floor and two tiers of balcony tables. During the month leading up to the show (usually the last Sunday in January) we had a fourth-floor suite to use for rehearsal, writing, hanging around, planning and taking all the necessary pre-production steps. Most of all, we told stories.

The most avid participants were Lou Effrat, of *The Times*, and Kenny Smith, of the *Mirror*. Effrat, who actually wrote many of our best songs and improved lots of others, complained endlessly about how many of his submissions weren't accepted ("I lead the league in rejections" was his mournful boast); but since he offered 10 times what could have been used, that was inevitable. Smitty had a high tenor voice of good quality, a passion for operettas, a good sense of theater and total inability to remember lyrics in performance that he had done flawlessly in countless rehearsals. They and Dowling became my mentors, and my own indirect theatrical background (exposed to the New York theater and its people from childhood on) made me a receptive disciple.

Two perennial stars were Roscoe McGowen, the gentleman from *The Times* who sang basso profundo and quoted Shakespeare beautifully, and Arthur Mann, who wrote some of our greatest numbers (one of which I'll quote in a moment) and also regularly portrayed Dodgers' general manager Branch Rickey, not just because he worked closely with him, but because he could make himself up to look like him.

Ben Epstein, of the *Mirror*, was a double-threat star. Recognizing early the power of Elvis Presley, he portrayed retired commissioner Happy Chandler, always making his entrance shouting "Ah *loves* baseball!" and "I heerd the call and here I is!" Even better, he played the straight man in the audience to Jerry Mitchell's Swami act, leading him through endless confusion, wrong guesses and missed hints to finally identifying the audience member picked upon.

Technically, the person in charge of the show was the current chapter chairman, serving a two-year term. But actual operations were delegated to Effrat and Smith, who worked with Dowling and the assistants he brought in. It was understood that Eddie would not suggest numbers or decide on acceptance of material (although his opinion counted), but that his authority about staging, movement, curtains and performing hints would not be challenged, because only he knew about lighting and moving scenery. (Yes, we used union stagehands.)

The key man in such an enterprise is the pianist, who must teach, coach and rehearse us, and nurse us through the actual performance. For that, we had the beloved and devoted Cliff Burwell, a jazz musician and composer of note.

At our creative and organizational sessions at the Waldorf, we kept reprising past hits as models for new ideas. Most often mentioned was the classic composed by Bill Slocum (and sung by McGowen) after Pepper Martin had stolen seven bases in the 1931 World Series, leading the St. Louis Cardinals to a seven-game upset of the great Philadelphia Athletics and their celebrated catcher, Mickey Cochrane (after whom Mickey Mantle's father would name his son). The tune was *Good Night, Sweetheart*, a universally known pop favorite. It went:

"Goodbye, Mickey, this is Pepper Martin,
I'm on first base, and soon I'll be startin',
Down to second I'll flit like a bird,
And then on my word, I think I'll steal third.
Then I'll say goodbye, Mickey, tie your glove and mask on,
If your jock strap's loose, tuck another clasp on.
The way I feel, there's nothing I won't steal,
So goodbye, Mickey, good bye."

Appropriate internal rhymes are the essence of good parody writing. This technique peaked in Arthur Mann's master opus about Bobby Thomson's playoff home run in 1951, the famous "shot heard around the world" still being commemorated on television 50 years later. The Dodgers had a 13-game lead in August, and after the Giants caught up and forced a three-game playoff, still led 4-1 in the ninth inning of the deciding game. Thomson's three-run homer off Ralph Branca for a 5-4 Giants victory remains the most dramatic single moment in baseball history.

Mann's template was *Because of You*. Branca would blame Thomson for his tragedy, Manager Charlie Dressen would blame Branca, owner Walter O'Malley would blame Dressen and George McLoughlin, head of the Brooklyn Trust bank (which had financed the Dodgers since the 1930s) would blame O'Malley. Then he realized, in rehearsal, that it would play better in reverse order. The stage scene contained five large easels, with recognizable caricatures of each person, and the singer would step out from behind his picture and sing to the next picture:

McLOUGHLIN to O'MALLEY:

Because of you, my old bank has gone bust
Because of you, we have lost Brooklyn's Trust
Because of you, old friends act strange,
*They bank their dough with Corn Exchange**
And leave us their dust and disgust.
Will someone tell how the hell you could miss
With any tailor-made ball club like this?
Fan rant and rail, they want Rickey AND MacPhail,
And ME in jail, because of you!

(*A prominent rival bank.)

O'MALLEY TO DRESSEN:

Because of you, fans are chasing O'Malley
Because of you, I sneak home through an alley
Because of you our fans last fall
Nearly tore down Borough Hall
*And threw out Joe Sharkey for Halley**
None of your lip or your lung, Charlie Dressen.
Go sell your tongue to some delicatessen
It killed our gate, and I sustained a fate —
Fate worse than DEBT, because of you.

(*Rudolf Halley unseated Sharkey as Borough president in the November 1951 election.)

DRESSEN TO BRANCA:

Because of you, writers tear me apart.
Because of you, I must eat out my heart.
Because of you I bear the shame,
You know the bullpen was to blame
*Clyde** said he was ready to start!*
I called relief for a brief interim
And got a chauffeur of gophers like him!
Each pitch I call, but I CAN'T GUIDE THAT BALL!
We lost it all because of you.

(*Clyde Sukeforth was the bullpen coach.)

I reproduce all of this as a textbook of parody writing. Among all those interior rhymes, mixed with redolent clichés, contemplate "chauffeur of gophers." A "gopher ball" was baseball slang for a pitch hit for a home run—it would "go for" four bases. If you were writing, how often would you think of that particular rhyme?

Then came the climax. From behind his picture, out stepped Ralph Branca—in person. In his fine singing voice, he sang to Thomson's portrait:

Because of you, I should never been born.
Because of you, Dodger fans are forlorn.
Because of you they yell "drop dead"
And several million want my head
To sever forever in scorn.
One lonely bird had a word for my ear.
The ONLY girl was a pearl of good cheer.
I lost the game, but wound up with the dame,

She* took my name, in spite of you.

(*Everyone knew that Ralph had just married Ann Mulvey, daughter
of one of the Brooklyn owners.)

And from behind his portrait, out stepped Bobby Thomson—in
person—to sing:

Because of you, there's a song in my heart.

Because of you, my technique is an art.

Because of you, a fast ball high

Became a dinky, Chinky* fly.

Now Leo and me-o won't part!

My fame is sure thanks to your Sunday pitch

If high or low, I don't know, which is which.

But come next Spring, keep throwing up that thing

And I will swing, because of you!

(*In those pre-politically-correct days, the short fly homers at the
Polo Grounds were known as "Chinese homers.")

This number, as you can imagine, brought down the house on
the strength of the two principals taking part. It was seen as a great
act of sportsmanship, especially by Branca, and widely regarded as
such for the next 50 years as they became a sought-after duet at one
affair after another, willing to reprise it. At the All-Star Game in
Seattle in the year 2001—the next millennium, for heaven's sake!—
they did it again, after repeating it, a capella from the dais, at the
Baseball Dinner that winter.

This musical number gives you an idea of the quality we could
achieve, but there were many, many others that reached a
comparable level. Just the titles and first lines of some of them will
give you an idea.

1926—"I wonder where my Babe Ruth is tonight…He grabbed
his hat and coat and fled from sight…I wonder where he'll be at
half past two or three…I know he's with a dame…I wonder what's
her name."

1933—"Brother, can you spare a nine…"

1943—"Will the lights go on again in Larry's saloon…," about
MacPhail's well-stocked press room after Branch Rickey took over
the Dodgers.

Of course, Branca and Thomson weren't writers—they were
"ringers." But the unannounced appearance of ringers was one of
the strongest traditions of our show.

At the very start, in the mid–1920s, George M. Cohan, no less, took part and helped direct. Besides being one of Broadway's greatest names, he was also a buddy of John McGraw at the Lambs Club. Then Rudy Vallee, as big a name in early radio as anyone, appeared. In a sketch of *Breakfast with Leo and Laraine*, when Durocher was married to actress Laraine Day, they slipped in Laraine to play herself, without telling Leo (portrayed by Effrat). By now, Dowling was our pro director and the next year he wanted another "jumbo" act to top off the night—and got Tallulah Bankhead, a big Giants fan, to threaten to replace Leo as manager.

Then a sentimental finale built on *I Believe* was sung by Eddie Fisher, at the peak of his fame, to everyone's surprise because Effrat did all the rehearsals to keep the secret.

When I inherited the writer-directorship in 1961, I was a total convert to the need for a jumbo. Laughing at our ineptness, or surprise at our good performances (by Young, Effrat, Smith and quite a few others) went only so far. There had to be a moment of high professionalism, especially since we had just moved to the brand new Americana Hotel (now the New York Sheraton) which had a larger stage and ballroom.

One of my Broadway gypsy friends was a tenor named Arthur Rubin, with a truly world-class operatic voice, who was in great demand in Broadway shows but not interested in an operatic career. In the 1962 show, the finale was Babe Ruth singing encouragement to Roger Maris to *Hello, Young Lovers*, a song from *The King and I*. I had Arthur sing it into a mike off-stage while the actor mouthed the words, and the effect was electric. (Those who realized it was an off-stage voice assumed it was Bob Teague, of *The Times*, clearly one of our best performers, but even Teague couldn't have done what Rubin did.)

From then on, I always found some way to get Rubin into a late number—often on stage, and well identified—and started writing operatic numbers for him: Pagliacci (Yogi crying all the way to the bank when fired as Yankee manager and exiled to the Mets); Figaro (Joe Pepitone complaining of how the Yankees treated him although he was "the greatest"); and the famous tenor aria from the third act of Tosca with the lyric consisting entirely of the names of all 25 players of the 1969 Miracle Mets. At times, we had to find a soprano to sing with him, and that made possible our most elaborate number, a medley built on the Student Prince and the Sextet from Lucia. It portrayed owners Dan Topping and Mrs. Joan Payson commiserating when both the Yankees and Mets were on the bottom, ending with:

Deep in the cellar, we often dream of first.
How long our ball clubs, must go on being the worst?
If we're so clever, must we be lousy forever?
Deep in the cellar, always we dream of first!

The introduction of authentic beautiful showgirls in a scene also did wonders. A director quickly learns to stop at nothing.

We now had a new pro director, Jack Effrat, Louie's older brother, who was a Broadway stage manager and top official of the Actors Fund. (Later, Dowling came back.) We also had a successor to Cliff Burwell, a living doll of a man with a Catskills background, Irv Carroll. More outgoing than Cliff, he also became our music director for the basketball writers' dinner, which did a show modeled (more modestly) on the baseball show.

Meanwhile, baseball stars began making surprise appearances after the Branca-Thomson blockbuster, with or without lines. Stan Musial posed for his statue in St. Louis (with Horace McMahon, the actor who was his good friend, as the sculptor showing him how he should hold the bat). Sandy Koufax, Whitey Ford, Yogi, Mantle, Pepitone, Jim Bouton, Phil Linz and Joe Garagiola took their turns.

The dais, through the years, was graced by Will Rogers, Mayor Jimmy Walker, Irvin S. Cobb, New York governors Herbert Lehman, Averill Harriman and Nelson Rockefeller, Senators Jacob Javits and Robert Kennedy, Vice-President Richard Nixon, Mayors Fiorello LaGuardia and William O'Dwyer, ex-president Herbert Hoover, Cardinal Spellman and more. One of the governors (Harriman, I think) referred to the baseball commissioner as "Ford Frisk," and we used that as a gag for years. But the more a guest talked, and the longer the presentation got as new awards kept getting added, the more impatient (and inebriated) the audience became for our show to start.

This made it tougher to satisfy that audience, and made us depend more on the ringers and painted signs (after Met fans began displaying them). Effrat taught me the sad truth. The cleverest lines will fall flat because they can't be grasped fast enough; but if you say, "George Weiss (or any other big name) is a louse," they'll laugh like crazy.

But he also taught me never to settle for less. I did a parody on *It Ain't Necessarily So* in which Chandler (Epstein) tells players "Whenever the owners say you're pullin' boners, it ain't necessarily so." It ends with the famous final phrase of the original lyric:

"I'm preachin' this sermon to show, it ain't nessa, ain't nessa, ain't nessa, ain't nessa, ain't necessarily so."

"What is that gibberish?" demanded Louie. "You can't just repeat silly syllables like that. They don't say anything."

"Louie, it's that way in the original *Porgy and Bess*. If it's good enough for Ira Gershwin, it's certainly good enough for me."

"I don't care if it is Gershwin, we can do better."

"Better than Ira? Are you nuts?"

"It's just repetition. We can do better."

He wouldn't let up, so we worked on it until we came up with:

"I'm preachin' this sermon to show, you cain't cast no spell when you know goddam well that it ain't necessarily so."

With all due respect, that IS better. But I doubt the listeners cared.

And the best lesson came in a song of which I'm most proud. When the Braves moved from Milwaukee to Atlanta, we dressed Dave Anderson, representing John McHale of the Braves, in a fancy Confederate Army general's uniform. *Singing You Can Buy My Ball Club With a Dixie Melody*, he finished with:

Buckle down, Milwaukee, try to show a little class
How come you-all, didn't bawl when we-e-e left Boston Mass.
A million bucks Atlanta will deliver
As soon as we go 'cross that Swanee River,
You can buy a runaway ball club with a Dixie melody.

Dave's entrance was preceded by the line, "Here comes John McHale now," and his appearance in that uniform brought down the house, setting off one of the loudest ovations we ever had before he opened his mouth. But by the time he got to my brilliant rhyme of "class" and "Boston, Mass.," they were still cheering the uniform, not the words.

But after the Giants and Dodgers moved to California, and expansion began, a smaller and smaller fraction of the attendees were important baseball people, and there were fewer points to be gained by a politician for showing up. Casey Stengel, when a guest on the dais, once cut to the heart of the subject with his usual caustic style by saying, "I see the mayor isn't here and the governor isn't here. Maybe that's why two teams have gone."

So by the 1970s, the show was struggling. Most important, the principal writers no longer had free time in January: There was football's Super Bowl and the playoffs leading to it, more and more pro and college basketball, and an entirely different set of mid-winter assignments. Then there was the lessened importance (in the eyes of baseball brass) of newspapers as compared to television, and less concentration of activity exclusively in New York. The world in which the show flourished, including the habit of late-night sitting around in Toots Shor's, Leone's and other hangouts, was disappearing. By the 1980s, the baseball dinner, still going strong, had a couple of dozen awards to hand out and a dais comedian, and no show at all. A pre-packaged television highlights routine, tied to the award winners, had taken its place. And the audience, as large and passionate as ever, consisted of more autograph-seeking fans than of baseball professionals. Times had changed.

The effect on the sports world—not just baseball's—was signifi-cant and part of the larger evolution. The dinner and show had been the result of, and a strengthener of, a professional intimacy that no longer exists and can no longer be developed. The insiders knew and respected one another to a degree no longer possible, and the dinner solidified those relationships, as much through its year-long anticipation as through its one-night occurrence.

Like the press box itself—and the clubhouse—the dinner and all other aspects of off-field social interaction have been reduced to merely working venues. The insider social whirl is now the province of television people, marketers, agents and millionaire athletes. Informal and intimate relationships no longer include (with few exceptions) what used to be called "the ink-stained wretches of the press."

All season long, the press box used to resonate with possibilities for songs and sketches whenever something interesting came up, some of which would eventually be worked up to usable form, while most went into the mounting pile of rejections.

But I haven't heard anyone suggest anything like that for the last 20 years.

17

The Broadway Show League

Jack Effrat, Louie's brother, was a professional theater man (and member of the Lambs Club) but also one with promotional instincts. He was secretary of the Actors Fund, the charity that looked after aging and needy show people and raised its money through special Sunday night benefit performances of hit shows. He also organized and produced several revues to let young and unrecognized performers display their talents, in a Broadway theater, to the community of agents and producers. And he was, naturally enough, a big baseball fan.

For many years, Broadway actors and backstage workers (stage-hands, electricians, carpenters, musicians) had been paying softball games in Central Park on an informal basis. Jack always sought a chance to advance Actors Fund interests by generating publicity. He decided to formalize what came to be called the Broadway Show League.

He declared himself commissioner, got permits for the complex of diamonds inside 62d Street (between Tavern on the Green and the zoo), and set Thursday noon as the time for games (because there were Wednesday matinees and either Sunday or Monday was a non-working day for shows). He arranged for uniforms, in the form of T-shirts with a show's name on the front and "Actors Fund" on the back, devised ground rules for limiting the use of ringers and authenticating the connection of players to that production. He worked out a season-long schedule (April to July) leading to an official champion, and came up with a trophy to present the winner at a season-ending party.

The idea was to generate publicity, for the shows and the Actors Fund, and increase the fun for the players by having a pennant race.

This was around 1955. I had just gone from the *Herald Tribune* to the *Post*, which was read by far more Broadway gypsies than the *Trib*. Jack drafted me to lay out the schedule patterns for him to fill in.

The enterprise became a roaring success. The players liked the systematized competition, which they took very seriously. The producers liked the publicity and the boost to internal show loyalty and morale. Jack liked his authority and visibility. Onlookers liked seeing some (not all that many) identifiable Broadway personalities up close and off stage. Most of the better players were backstage people rather than actors, and liked having the ringer problem under control, while actors liked (of course) the attention.

In the informal years, there were always a few girls who wanted to play—dancers, in particular, are terrific athletes—and guys would let them. But once the games began to count, no team wanted to "weaken" itself in this way. This was an age of forthright male chauvinism, not yet to be bucked.

But females do have influence, and some, at least, were unwilling to accept exclusion and relegation to roles as cheerleading spectators for their boyfriends and husbands. They wanted to play.

So a girls' league auxiliary emerged in 1958, and got serious in 1959.

I was living on 55th Street between Eight and Ninth Avenues, a block overflowing with singers, dancers, musicians, actors, comedians, other theater workers (like box office personnel) and their spouses. My social life (I was single then) was centered on this circle and its far-flung offshoots (that's how I met Arthur Rubin). In my building was a singer-dancer named Marsha Rivers, a sports-loving Brooklynite and a ringleader of the girls-league movement. My baseball-writer identity defined my place in this environment.

Marsha was in the chorus of *Gypsy*, then in Philadelphia tryouts before opening in New York, and eager to form a *Gypsy* team in the new league. I was going to Philadelphia a lot, since the Giants and Dodgers had left, to catch National League games. Her team would need a coach and, turning to me for advice, she decided it should be me.

Why not?

So when the show got to New York, I found myself in the basement of the theater (was it the Broadway?) addressing her recruits. It was a large cast, with well over a dozen women, and enough were interested to form a team.

Some had never seen a ball game. A few were avid fans. A couple of them were even newcomers to America. A session that began with questions like "what does 'outfield' mean?" progressed, within 20 minutes, to "how do you pitch this one in that situation?" These girls were quick.

I gave them one rule and two promises. The rule was we'd have a practice session at noon on Tuesdays and you'd have to attend it to stay on the team unless you had a legitimate excuse. The promises were (1) I would issue no orders, just make suggestions intended to be helpful, and (2) they'd have fun and if they didn't, they or I would quit without any fuss. (As Mimi tells Rodolfo in Act III of *La Boheme*, "senza rancor.")

It worked great. There was a little lopsided diamond at the southwest corner of the softball complex, with a very short right-field fence, that was set aside for our use. As it turned out, we became undefeated league champions—because the league acquired only one other team, Flower Drum Song, all of whose girls were (for casting reasons) rather small people of Asian heritage. We beat them every week.

On Tuesdays, I would pitch batting practice to them and give a few polite pointers on how to swing or catch or throw. On game day, I'd make out a batting order and devote all my attention to seeing that the right girl went to bat. Marsha pitched or played first, and was our best hitter. (She hit left-handed, and yearned to drive the ball over that short right-field wall by pulling it sharply, but there was no way she could do that. Her ample upper-body contours made it physically impossible. But she never stopped trying, while getting plenty of key hits to center.)

Our clean-up hitter was Faith Dane, who played the stripper whose gimmick is a bugle in the show's famous number. She was also our third baseman. The team as a whole was loaded with great looking women, unselfconsciously clad in T-shirts and shorts, so we drew plenty of spectators and photographers.

But no really good shortstop emerged, so I did what any decent coach would do: I found a ringer. I had just started dating Suzanne Silberstein, who was teaching English at Hofstra, and was a very good ball player. She was just as good-looking as the rest, but the other girls loved her for two reasons: She didn't wear make-up and didn't care about having her picture taken or getting publicity. And she could really play shortstop.

One day, Faith couldn't make it and I asked Susie to play third. She tried it a little bit in batting practice, then refused. "Too close to the hitter, the ball gets there too fast," she said, and that was that.

(Many years later, after we were married, I introduced her to Clete Boyer in Yankee spring training.

"He's one of the greatest third basemen ever," I told her.

"How are you able to do it?" she asked. "The batter's right on top of you. It's suicide."

Clete nodded and put on a solemn expression.

"I do a lot of drinking," he confided.)

But let's get back to 1959. That summer our championship team was invited to Kutscher's, in the Catskills, where basketball was a big deal. The St. Louis Hawks were being honored after three straight seasons of finishing first in the NBA's Western Division. They'd heard all the stories (from me) about our Broadway Show League adventures, and accepted a challenge to play a softball game against the *Gypsy* team. (Against showgirls? Sure. They'd have to bat left-handed or opposite-handed and walk instead of run the bases, but it sounded like fun.) We bused up, had lunch, and drew a large crowd. All the players were introduced, one by one.

The girls produced the visual effect you'd expect, but they all had neutral or catchy stage names, even the solidly Jewish ones (as Marsha was). But when the public address announcer intoned, "Suzanne Silberstein," that got the biggest hand of all. Ethnicity triumphs.

We also won the ball game, 5-3.

Meanwhile, the men's Broadway Show League thrived, and continued long after Effrat died. For many years, Fran Lewin, an inveterate first-nighter whose husband Dick was Lenny Lewin's cousin, ran it and fought the ringer battles. Producers saw the virtue of sponsoring their team. Non-show teams were also formed, and admitted, like the Associated Press. Much newspaper and magazine publicity fallout was enjoyed by all. But by the end of the century, Broadway, like sports, was a different world with much less of the informal trust and interaction it used to have. In sports, it was millionaire athletes who changed the relationship equations. On Broadway, it was the multi-million dollar cost of production that changed all sorts of equations.

One day Frank Green, one of the Jets and understudy to the lead in *West Side Story*, pitched a no-hit game. He was appropriately fussed over. As we were leaving the park with an exuberant coterie of celebrants, his wife Margot suddenly stopped.

"I don't get it," she said. "You're all talking about a no-hit game, but I remember seeing guys on base."

"It was a no-hitter because nobody got a hit," I explained. "He did walk a couple of guys, so it wasn't perfect game but still a no-hitter."

"Not perfect?" said Margot. "Huh! So what's the big deal?"

Everybody's a critic.

18

Toots
Shor's

In those days, from the middle 1930s through the 1960s, certain restaurants were hangout headquarters for various segments of society. For the upscale theater crowd, it was Sardi's, on 44th Street opposite Shubert Alley. For the less prosperous (but working) theater folk, it was Downey's, across Eight Avenue between 44th and 45th. For the Madison Square Garden regulars, it was Leone's, on 48th near Eight Avenue. On 40th Street, alongside the back door of the *Herald Tribune*, there was Bleeck's (pronounced Blake's), and the back stairs of *The New York Times* building led to Sardi's. On the East Side in the '40s, accessible to the offices of the *News, Mirror* and United Press, was the Pen and Pencil. The sports crowd also frequented Gallagher's, a steak house on 52nd Street (where it thrives unchanged), and a wide variety of Chinese restaurants.

The most celebrated, however, was Toots Shor's, because of the proprietor's personality. Its original home was at 51 West 51st Street, just east of Sixth Avenue, before the CBS headquarters building was built on the corner. When another huge office building went up on the site in 1959, Toots opened a new place at 33 West 52nd Street at just about the same distance in from Sixth Avenue, and that lasted to 1971.

His shtick was insulting celebrity customers while protecting them from intrusive fans and journalistic quote-hunters. Most of them liked it for two reasons. They could relax in that atmosphere better than in most of their appearances in public, and say whatever they wanted while trusting it wouldn't be used against them by those Toots allowed to come near. And his brash "you crumb bum" salutation was a welcome relief from the yes-man surroundings in which important people inevitably function most of the time. Those who didn't like it simply didn't come back, so the clientele became more and more in-group as time went on.

Toots also had a private banquet room in which the weekly meetings of the football writers took place during that season. (The basketball writers were at Leone's, and the baseball writers didn't need weekly meetings.) Shor's was also a favored spot for press conferences, book launchings, and special occasions of any sort. The night of the Baseball Dinner, this was the chief gathering place for post-mortems and unwinding, most of all for the cast.

This became my home away from home.

The main thing was, you could drop in any time—lunch, cocktail hour, dinner, pre-game, post-game or midnight—and be pretty sure of running into someone in your business. New Yorkers were regulars, but out-of-town athletes, executives, writers and broadcasters were almost certain to check in whenever they were in town. The bar was always surrounded by newspaper, broadcasting, publicity, advertising, theater and sports people, not to mention recognizable politicians and celebrities who happened to be sports fans. No appointments were necessary. You just dropped in and someone of interest was bound to be there.

I was an anomaly, a young reporter who didn't drink (as a matter of taste, not morals), play cards or gamble (because I hated losing more than I enjoyed winning). I liked opera and symphony concerts as much as musicals and ball games, and read serious books as often as murder mysteries, a combination of tastes by no means unique in that set, but certainly not common. Nevertheless, Toots liked me, since I was there at least six times a week and had been introduced to his in-group by people like Effrat and Young. I could hold my own in trading funny stories, and was a good listener. As my circle of sports acquaintances widened, routines became set. Lunch, in addition to writer meetings and other affairs, put me there two or three times a week. Post-game stops, virtually mandatory, alternated between Shor's and Leone's. Dinner, on my own time unrelated to sports events, especially with a date, was there as often as possible. But even if I came alone, there would certainly be someone to join. It was my club.

As I've said, the essence of covering any subject is simply hanging around. Shor's was the place to do that. I could stand at the bar, without drinking, as long as the company required it; seated, there was always someone "in the business" to talk to. And often enough, when things were slow or the evening was late, I could share a table with Toots and whoever was with him at the time. (Toots never picked up your check for food, but he did stand for drinks. Too cowardly to refuse, I learned to nurse along a scotch.) Only when "drinking together" was talk really uninhibited—and not to be improperly repeated.

On those occasions, I learned more about the way the world really works, especially in politics and business, than in any of the college courses I'd had. Toots had been a bouncer in the days when mobsters ran restaurants during Prohibition, and had graduated to managing and owning his own place afterwards. He knew all the politicians—local up through Supreme Court Justices and Presidents—all the lunch-time advertising and other operators, all the law enforcement people, and had heard their unbridled conversations. Shrewd and observant, he told stories that greatly increased my otherwise naïve and sheltered education.

His regular friends weren't necessarily friends of each other. One was George Weiss, who ran the Yankees and was widely disliked. Another was Jimmy Cannon, who labeled Weiss "Lonesome George" and ripped him in column after column in the *New York Post*. Weiss had a habit of keeping newspaper clippings in the breast pocket of his jacket, and he would pull one out to show and complain about.

"He's a friend of yours," Weiss said to Toots one day. "Why does he keep after me like that?"

Toots, the diplomat, said nothing.

"Oh, well," said Weiss, "I guess I shouldn't let it bother me. After all, who reads his lousy paper?"

"You do," said Toots.

Another time, Toots was sitting with two of my distinguished *Post* teammates—Cannon and Leonard Lyons, the Broadway gossip columnist—and a novelist named Ernest Hemingway. In the middle of some brilliant conversation, Toots started to laugh.

"What are you laughing at?" they asked him.

"I just realized," said Toots, "that I'm the only guy at this table who doesn't think he's the greatest writer in the world."

He had them dead to rights.

But he could deal with strangers, too. A customer called him over and said, in a purposely-loud voice, "Hey, Toots, back in Kansas City I can get a steak twice as big and twice as good for half the price you charge."

"Yeah," said Toots, "and when you're done eating it, you're still in Kansas City."

And he had his own ideas about running his business, based on being open to his "regulars" every night.

When times got tough, his accountant tried to persuade him to stay closed on Sundays.

"You'll save $5,000 a week," the bean counter told him.

"Why don't I close seven nights and save $35,000?" Toots replied.

It was a noble answer—but the fact was, he eventually did go broke, in the 1970s.

The world, you see, had changed. His post-game and post-theater crowd of the 1940s and 1950s had lived in Manhattan and Brooklyn. In the 1960s, they started moving to the suburbs, which meant they'd go straight home, and didn't come into the city as often. (That included sportswriters.) With more and more baseball games at night, those out-of-towners would go back to their hotel instead of to dinner at Shor's, especially with a day game the next day. As football started overtaking baseball in glamour, especially with the great Giants' teams of the 1960s, those players and coaches became Shor's insiders—but they played only once a week, for three months. At lunch-time, the commissioners—baseball's Ford Frick, football's Pete Rozelle, basketball's Walter Kennedy—remained loyal, but television was pulling more and more actors, producers and ad agency big shots to California more often.

Television. As it changed the sports and newspaper landscape, it also drove the Toots kind of hangout out of existence. Its life-blood had been conversational exchange, lubricated by booze. A population geared to watching *The Tonight Show* and late movies stopped looking to conversation as a recreational resource.

Before long, its reading habits would change too.

19

Baseball Writers' 1984
Association of America
Leonard Koppett
REPRESENTING Times Tribune
CITY Palo Alto
IS A DULY QUALIFIED MEMBER, AND IS ENTITLED TO PRESS COUR-
TESIES OF THE CLUBS OF THE NATIONAL AND AMERICAN LEAGUES
OF PROFESSIONAL BASEBALL CLUBS, SUBJECT TO THE CONDI-
TIONS SET FORTH ON THE BACK HEREOF.
SECRETARY
REP FOR San Fran-Oakland NO 21

Chairman

During the late 1950s and early 1960s—the exact years run together and I feel no inclination to sort them out—I took my turn, as a responsible citizen of the New York sportswriter community, in acting as chapter chairman of three of our "associations": The New York Chapter of the Baseball Writers Association, a national organization; and the purely local Metropolitan Basketball Writers Association and the New York Football Writers Association.

These positions were filled by vote of the members, who ganged up on someone who seemed unwilling (or insufficiently alert) to fight back when stuck with the job.

The duties were few, since all the real work was done by a secretary-treasurer who tended to hold the reins for many years at a time, until a new sucker could be found. The chairman usually served a two-year term after being vice-chairman, so there was a painless (to the others) progression that avoided internal politics. His ceremonial role was to preside at the baseball dinner and the basketball and football lunches, which involved only trying to keep straight the names of the speakers to be introduced. (At the luncheons, these were primarily local and visiting coaches.) His other main function was to listen to, deflect, and if possible try to do something about members' complaints. The main purpose of the office was to have someone to complain to, since the secretary-treasurer was busy making actual arrangements for the rooms, food, record-keeping and paying bills.

But the baseball chairman also had more serious functions. When the World Series was in New York (which was every year, then), he headed the committee that assigned press credentials and seating for the several hundred writers, from around the country and abroad, who applied. This responsibility had been assigned to the BBWAA by the commissioner back in the 1920s, and was taken seriously by each chapter. In those days, the commissioner's office and the team's publicity man really did keep hands off the decisions we were making, restricting their input to being helpful and having their staffs carry out the mechanics.

Today, of course, that whole operation is run by the professional P.R. people of the various sports, with writers reduced to "consultant" status, if any. It was always that way in pro football and basketball.

Also under the baseball chairman's purvey was the official scorer's list. In New York, with up to 10 papers and three teams, there were 40 "regular" baseball writers (one swing man for each paper). Each league had delegated the job of official scorer to the writers, also back before 1920. Our system was that a writer became qualified after he had covered at least 100 games for three years. That gave us enough to rotate three to five at each ballpark, for stretches of 20 games or so. (In one-team cities, with only two or three papers, one writer might do the whole season.) We kept that roster carefully. The scorer had to decide plays during the game (hit or error) and later file the elaborate boxscore form that became the official league record.

And the baseball chairman was, technically, in charge of the dinner and its show.

Once again (I'm repeating myself, as is my habit), this created a community of interest, a familiarity with each other, a professional networking exchange and apprentice-type mentoring that no longer exist. We were closer to the people we covered, who knew us better, than is considered desirable or possible today. Were we less "objective?" I don't think so, since indiscriminate, unsubstantiated and often misguided criticism is every bit as subjective as effusive praise to gain favor. Being willing to knock something is not "tougher" reporting unless the knock is demonstrably justified. In the closer interactions of that day, we had a better chance to know what was justified and what wasn't. We weren't "softer," just better able to be aware of what was really going on—in context—and why. We didn't pull our punches, but we didn't throw them around indiscriminately, either. We had to feel we had a good reason to "rip."

At the luncheons, coaches talking about upcoming games were expected to cry. Every opponent was described as terrific, and his own team's injuries or limitations were sadly acknowledged. So we were startled when we heard Nat Holman, venerable coach of always-underdog City College of New York, start his season-opening remarks in 1949-1950 by declaring "Gentlemen, we're loaded."

He had four sophomores, Ed Warner, Ed Roman, Floyd Lane and Al Roth, who would be terrific (and would actually end up winning both the NCAA championship and the National Invitational Tournament that season).

"And the fifth starter," he concluded, "is—uh-er—the kid with that good left-handed shot."

He meant Irwin Dambrot, a senior whom Nat had singled out two years before as "the best player I've ever coached." Now, suddenly rich in talent, he couldn't remember his name.

A year later, of course, this championship group was embroiled in the widespread game-fixing scandals that rocked college basketball.

The basketball scandals, which erupted in January of 1952 and by mid-summer spread to a dozen colleges in half a dozen states, were followed by the West Point cribbing scandal before the football season began. The football players, including coach Red Blaik's son, had been tipping off teammates to exam answers, to make sure the team stayed strong, putting football loyalty above the honor code. During the war, Army's football team had become the most successful and admired of all college teams, when the pros were still considered second-rate, and was still a power on the post-war scene. Suddenly it lost almost all its regulars and, after West Point went through a catharsis of regaining proper priorities, was never a power again.

The double blow of the basketball scandals (which we'll come back to in a later chapter) and the West Point affair marked the end of my naïve innocence. I had shrugged off the talk of fixed basketball games, which had swirled around me, as show-off cynicism, since my own background had been so sheltered and idealistic. (Michael Strauss, of *The Times*, had started telling me, gleefully, "it's all fixed—fights, races, ball games, hockey, and jai alai—everything" while I was still in college, and he never failed to repeat the theme every time we met.) But Young and Effrat and Lewin, the more experienced writers around me, knew better. They had no proof, and they weren't detectives, but they also had no illusions. I was getting better assignments at the *Trib*, especially in pro basketball, which benefited so much from the college debacle, and this eye-opening experience taught me to look harder at the real world.

No, not everything is crooked, but yes, anything *can* be. Don't assume it, or be suspicious; but don't be blind to the possibility.

20

Name Leonard Koppett

Representing N.Y. Times

City Palo Alto, Calif.

Expires July 1, 1979

Secretary-Treasurer

№ 136

California

In 1957, the major league baseball map went no further west than Kansas City. In basketball, the western-most outpost was Minneapolis, in hockey, Chicago. The National Football League had teams in Los Angeles and San Francisco, but with a week between games, the long trip could be made.

Twelve years later, there were five baseball teams and four football teams just in California, seven basketball teams in the Pacific and Mountain time zones, and a hockey team in Oakland. In the winter months, more of the expanding professional golf and tennis tournaments were taking place west of the Rockies.

The New York Times, which I had joined in 1963, had a long-standing policy—as "the paper of record"—of sending a staff man to every out-of-town game played by a New York major league team. At this point, New York had two baseball teams, two football teams, two basketball teams and a hockey team, all with cross-country treks.

As the new decade of the 1970s approached, various departments set up planning groups to discuss possible future needs. Since 1967, only three papers within the city were still alive: *The Times*, the *Post* and the *Daily News*. Clearly, the future would demand new approaches.

In the sports department's group, we suggested that, sooner or later, it would pay to plant a reporter permanently on the West Coast, to pick up New York teams whenever they went beyond the

Rockies. It was just a concept that sat on paper until 1972, but it made a lot of sense.

Then I brought it up, wrote up a detailed memo on how it would actually work, and said if the idea were acted upon, I'd like to be the one who goes. (I'll come back to this in greater detail when we talk about *The New York Times*, in Chapter 24.) The higher echelons decided to do it, and we chose June 1973 as the time to move, since that would be the end of the school year.

My motives were selfish enough. Susie and I had married in 1964, and now had a seven-year-old daughter and five-year-old son. We were living in Riverdale, an upscale section of the Bronx, but the New York City public schools at that time were not what we wanted for our children. The standard move to the suburbs had its own drawbacks. Since I had been getting more of the coast-to-coast assignments than anyone else had anyhow, I had found that New York wasn't the only possible place to live. But the only job I had, and it was a good one, was in New York. Here was a way I could both move and keep the job.

But it also made a lot of sense for the paper.

Everyone assumed I'd go to Los Angeles, but I knew I wanted Palo Alto specifically. It was dominated by Stanford University, its school system was highly regarded, and it was only a half-hour south of San Francisco, the most cosmopolitan American city outside of New York. For a dyed-in-the-wool New Yorker, almost anywhere in California would mean a massive culture shock; but Stanford and San Francisco would minimize that.

And the plan worked just the way it was supposed to. I traveled up and down the coast, into Phoenix and Las Vegas and Utah, whenever the Yankees, Mets, Giants, Jets, Knicks, Nets, Rangers and Islanders came through. Major fights and tennis specials were often in Las Vegas. The baseball Dodgers and Giants, still of residual interest in New York, were in my territory. NBA championships were being won by Los Angeles, San Francisco, Seattle and Portland. The Oakland A's were winning three straight World Series, the Super Bowl came to Los Angeles every few years. I had the best of all worlds, covering New York visitors as my "home" team and welcomed as a "visiting" writer by the California teams.

But in 1976, everything changed. *The Times*, in re-organizing itself, started having earlier deadlines. Now a West Coast final game story couldn't make even the last edition. And the staff-all-New York-teams policy was finally being abandoned in favor of stringers in the middle of the country, so why not out west? Game stories gave way to features.

There was still plenty for me to do, but now it involved more traveling than ever, to special events for special stories. Once the accountants found out that travel from San Francisco to Houston, Dallas, Kansas City and Minnesota cost no more than from New York, they became part of my "territory" too.

By 1978, the children were moving towards high school, and I simply wasn't home enough. I'd been on the road constantly for 30 years. Enough was enough. In August, I simply quit. Amicably ("*senza rancor*"), with decent severance, with no need to be replaced under the new conditions. I figured that as a free-lance writer, working at home, using all the unproductive hours I'd been spending on planes, in airports, in hotels, sitting through three-hour games to write 30-minute stories, I'd get by.

Meanwhile, the Tribune Company of Chicago, in 1978, purchased the *Palo Alto Times* and *Redwood City Tribune*, two fine local papers in adjacent but totally different communities. The idea was to combine them into a "metropolitan suburban daily" on the model of Long Island's *Newsday*. In April 1979, they became the *Peninsula Times Tribune*.

David Burgin, a fiery and brilliant newspaperman, had been brought in by Chicago to carry out, as editor, the merging of the papers. His background was Dayton, Ohio, the *New York Herald Tribune* and the *Washington Star*, and the *Times Tribune* contained the best talent of both staffs and a lot of outstanding newcomers. Dave was a terrific talent scout, as he would prove again and again on half a dozen papers.

We had never met, but he knew I'd left *The Times* and was in Palo Alto, with that imposing "*New York Times*" credential attached to my name. He wanted to hire me as sports editor/columnist. I wasn't interested. To start with, I had no experience being an editor or managing anything. But I couldn't even imagine working in sports without traveling all the time, and that was the reason I'd quit.

"How about writing a column once a week?" he asked.

I'd been doing that for *The Sporting News* for the last 15 years or so, and still was. "Sure," I said. "That's easy enough." And that was the deal.

For a few years, I had been moonlighting as a guest lecturer at Stanford, in the Communication Department. (*The Times* imprimatur opens all sorts of doors.) From one of these "Sports and Society" courses, I had derived a book that turned out to be *Sports Illusion, Sports Reality*. In July 1979, I had to go to New York to meet with the publisher. I noticed that the 49ers and Raiders were scheduled to play in New York on adjacent weekends. Well-trained in free-loading opportunities, I thought, "If Burgin would let me cover just those two games, I'd have that week in New York with no plane fare." But of course, I could only do that if the regulars covering the two teams were willing to forego that trip. I'd have to ask them first.

So I asked Burgin, "Whose covering the 49ers for you?"

He said, "Nobody yet. You want to do it?"

"You mean all season?" I said.

"Yes, but you'd have to join the staff."

Wheels started spinning. The Niners play only 16 games, once a week, with only eight one-night trips. They practice mornings or early afternoon in Redwood City, a 10-minute drive from my house (near Stanford). Joining the staff would mean picking up all the medical benefits I had abandoned when leaving *The Times*.

"Just the season? Then what?"

"We'll decide then."

I was back in the newspaper business.

When it was time to make a permanent arrangement, I asked: "What now?"

"You be executive sports editor, but all you have to do is write. I've got a young city editor I want to make the real sports editor, and you can give him some advice now and then. And your name is good for us if you just circulate and be visible."

The young editor was Bill Harke, from Redwood City. Whatever help he needed from me he absorbed in two weeks. Then he proceeded, on his own, to turn out award-winning sports sections for the next two years. Burgin's talent-spotting touch was amazing.

I had a ball. The 49ers had just been taken over by Bill Walsh, whom I'd covered occasionally for *The Times* in his two successful years at Stanford. The Niners had a 2-14 season in 1978 and the same record under Walsh in 1979. Having covered the Original

Mets, as well as Columbia football, I was well prepared for this circumstance. In 1980, the Niners moved up to 6-10, with a mid-season streak of last-minute losses. In 1981, I switched to the Raiders while the 49ers suddenly went 13-3 and went on to win the Super Bowl.

The Tribune Company owned a larger paper in Los Angeles and a smaller one in Escondido (near San Diego), so the chain of command ran through Los Angeles. Once the 49ers made the play-offs, we decided to put out an instant paperback book using our whole sports staff and recycled in-season material, just in case they won. Seeing that project through was my job, which brought me into closer contact with the Los Angeles executives and our publisher, Bill Rowe. *49er Fever* wasn't out fast enough to make any money, but it was an artistic success and the prestige was a plus.

At that point, right after the Super Bowl, Chicago decided to move Burgin up the ladder. Their paper in Orlando was a cash cow but a low-quality product. He was the man to improve it.

Choosing a successor put Bill Rowe in a tough spot.

Both the Palo Alto and Redwood City communities resented Burgin, as poor a diplomat as he was a good talent scout, as an "outsider" foisted on their local scene by absentee landlords in Chicago. And the two staffs had never really meshed. Bringing in another "outsider" was out of the question, but promoting from within created a dilemma. A Redwood City veteran would cause a rebellion of the Palo Alto crowd, and a Palo Alto choice would cause a rebellion of the Redwood City group.

Burgin urged Rowe to try me.

Me? *Moi?*, as Miss Piggy would say. Why me?

Well, I'd become a recognizable Palo Altan for seven years, with that *New York Times* label that nobody resented. But I'd never been on the old *Palo Alto Times*, and I certainly had nothing to do with Redwood City, so I was a neutral but not an outsider. Also, approaching 60, I was no threat to anyone else's ambitions. Maybe that was a way out.

I thought they were crazy. And I knew I was unqualified.

But by now, my book, *Sports Illusion, Sports Reality* had been published. In it I had a major section on how journalism works. If I was smart enough to outline all the facets of the newspaper business, shouldn't I be willing to try?

"If you've got the guts," I told Rowe, "I've got the guts."

So I became editor of the whole darn paper.

I had one demand. Harke would have to be my managing editor, because he knew how to get the paper out every day and I didn't.

Thus began the two most educational years of my life.

I learned that (1) an editor doesn't edit anything but is "management," obsessed with budgets, hiring and firing, putting out personnel fires and engaged in inter-departmental wars; (2) in the incessant planning meetings, we were trying to look good to each other, and trying to guess what would look good to Chicago, rather than identifying real problems; (3) what fantastically intricate teamwork it takes to get out a paper every day, and how this is accomplished, despite numerous failures and hitches all along the line, by individuals whose dedication is amazing.

When I had been just in sports, and looked up to because of my *Times* identity, I used to tell a lot of the younger people, who felt inferior working for a small local paper: "Take my word for it. You do what you're trying to do, with your resources, better than *The New York Times* does what it's trying to do with its resources." They didn't believe that, or understand what I meant. But now, day by day, I found out how right I was. The quality of the work done "under" me—in the context that Burgin had set up—was remarkable.

And I did preside over one major accomplishment. We had always been a six-day afternoon paper. But we would have to add a Sunday edition if we were to stay alive, and that had to be a morning paper. Only then could we have enough weekly advertising to make it go. Because a Saturday afternoon-Sunday morning turnover would be too hard to handle, we had to make the Saturday paper a morning edition also.

Figuring out how and when to make the transition, with what changes in format and content, was a fascinating enterprise. We had to put out roughly 20 percent more pages each week with 15 percent less editorial personnel, because the pressure to cut staff never let up.

We did it by the middle of 1983, and it worked the way it was supposed to. But we had missed the boat. The right way to go about it would have been to keep the local papers separate and start a combined Sunday paper right away and only after that had been established for a couple of years, roll over the daily papers into a combined daily. Then we wouldn't have been seen as "robbing" the two communities of their distinct local identities.

By now I had been in California for 10 years and somewhat—not completely, by any means—acclimated to an entirely different civilization. Back east, *The Times* and *Washington Post*, *Chicago Tribune* and some others were considered "serious" papers (and considered themselves that), while the *Daily News* was the prototype of the brash, common-man, mass circulation, breezier tabloid that nevertheless maintained all the serious journalistic virtues. In California, "serious" was not considered a virtue at all, just one of the countless peculiarities anyone was entitled to have. The dominant San Francisco paper, the *Chronicle*, was sneered at everywhere else for its triviality and unreliability, but in its own area it was more perfectly in tune with the local culture than any paper anywhere else. It had the best collection of columnists—starting with Herb Caen and Arthur Hoppe and George McCabe and Stan Delaplane—anyone could want and the whole paper reflected exactly what its readership felt and wanted. You simply didn't judge it—or anything else in California—by back-east standards. "When in Rome, do as the Romans" was a sound principle, and a reasonable one applied to life on a different planet called California.

Television, by 1980, had done a phenomenal amount of homogenizing American culture and attitudes—but not completely.

Shortly after I arrived, still working for *The New York Times*, there was a conference of newspaper people called "A Western View of the Eastern Press." Naturally, I was invited to attend. After the panel had been talking for about two hours, a woman sitting in the first row appeared more and more puzzled and restless. Finally she raised her hand.

"Isn't this supposed to be a western view of the eastern press?" she asked.

Yes it was, she was assured.

"But I haven't yet heard a single word about China!" she cried out.

And a substantial number of others in the audience nodded agreement.

It makes a big difference when the ocean is to the left (facing north) than to the right.

21

Editor
Emeritus

Despite my obvious deficiencies, I loved being editor. The daily challenge was exhilarating, the education I was getting was a revelation, my status in the community was gratifying, the people I was working with were talented and easy to get along with, and I was succeeding in maintaining what Burgin had built.

But in September I had turned 60. The main characteristic of my job was that it occupied my mind every waking moment and some of my dreams. We didn't yet have the phrase 24-7, but that's what it was. And much as I enjoyed it, too much else in life was getting shoved aside. My energy level, naturally, was lower than it had been 20 years before. Too much of what I also loved—concerts, theater, reading, playing the piano (badly but just for myself), ball games, socializing, writing that *Sporting News* column, teaching at Stanford and (important) just plain loafing—had disappeared or been severely rationed. All I thought about, all the time, was how will this or that affect the paper and what do I have to do about it tomorrow. That was fine in itself, but too narrow a focus at that stage of life.

And I didn't know how long I could keep that up.

One of the first things I'd done as editor is give myself a weekly column on the op-ed page, allowing me to pontificate on general topics, not sports. (*The Times* had invented the op-ed page for opinion columns, and the "op" did not stand for "opinion" but for "opposite the editorial page.")

So my plan was: Why don't I step down as editor and become a full-time columnist? They can find plenty of people who can run the paper as well as or better than I can; they can't afford to hire a general columnist of my range, quality and accumulated reputation. My public relations value, as a speaker and circulating in the community, could be increased. I could help out with the editorial page, do whatever internal teaching was needed, contribute appropriately to the sports section, work on various special projects as they arose. The best things I had to offer the paper would still be there; what I was giving up would be easy to replace.

I asked Rowe about it in December. He went for it, and started looking for a new editor. We scheduled the changeover for April.

To indicate to the readership that we were not going through another upheaval or retreating from any policies, or bringing in another "outsider"—a complaint that my appointment had success-fully defused—I would take the title of "Editor Emeritus." It had no real meaning but had a nice sound in the academic environs of Stanford, and indicated that I wasn't being fired and the paper wasn't dissatisfied with its course.

Getting *The New York Times* to move me to California had been the great coup of my career, envied by many of my dazzled contemporaries. Editor Emeritus was right up there with that.

Writing three general columns a week, I could touch on every-thing: Politics, science, jokes, international affairs, music, theater, literature, taxes, journalism, local controversies, far-out ideas, history, economics, cultural issues. And, of course, I could also do as much as we needed in the sports section. For a writer, this was the best of all possible worlds. I could choose any topic I wanted, when I wanted, and I never had to deal with any topic I didn't feel like dealing with—and I never had to travel anywhere unless I wanted to. And I could, and did, spend more time in my old milieu, the press box—without even having to turn out a daily story.

In the course of the next nine years, Chicago replaced our publisher three times and we changed editors three times.

But the original misconception of the Tribune Company's purchase came home to roost. The idea of a "metropolitan suburban daily" assumed that the 15 Peninsula towns were "suburbs" of San Francisco. They weren't. They were completely distinct, independent and varied communities, proud of their differences, habitually uncooperative when not actually hostile. Each resented seeing a dateline from one of the others. To serve them, a single paper had to be "zoned" four or five ways daily, and that became prohibitively expensive. They (and advertisers) had San Francisco to the north and San Jose to the south for established "metropolitan" papers. They did need local news, which the big papers couldn't provide, and Chicago accepted the idea that we had to "go local" by the middle 1980s. But it also insisted on cutting costs—which in this people-intensive business means cutting editorial and advertising staffs—and that was a fatal contradiction. You need *more* people to cover local news and to sell local advertising, not fewer.

Burgin, in turning the paper over to me in 1982, had just cut the editorial staff from 105 to 93, so that I wouldn't have to start out by doing it. When we went from six days to seven, we had about 85. By 1993, we were down to 39—all of them so good and each so willing to do the work of three that the quality of the content remained high. But starvation can be survived only so long. In 1993, as we commemorated the 100th anniversary of the *Palo Alto Times* with a special edition, there was talk of the paper being sold. In March, abruptly, the Tribune Company simply shut it down.

I was a freelancer again.

Part Four

Professional Items

22

The New York Herald Tibune

In the 1940s, the *New York Herald Tribune* was the best newspaper I have ever seen. Within the profession, its prestige was at least the equal of *The New York Times* and its circulation was similar. It was avowedly Republican on the editorial page, even all through the Franklin D. Roosevelt years, which was not a popular identification in the New York of that time. Nevertheless, it was better written, showed better news judgment, had better columnists and simply did its job better than *The Times* or anyone else. The *Daily News* was the king of the tabloids, the *Post* was the most blatantly liberal, the *Journal-American* was Hearst, but the *Trib* was both mainline and lively.

Its foreign correspondents were second to none. Its chief pundit was the revered Walter Lippman, and its Washington bureau was first-rate. Its music, theater and movie critics were outstanding and recognized as such within their spheres. Its typographical make-up was much more interesting than the "gray lady" *Times*, without crossing the line into flip or silly. And its sports section, under the editorship of Stanley Woodward, put *The Times* to shame and gave the *News* no quarter.

It managed to be, simultaneously, reliable, thorough and a pleasure to read.

Its sports staff included Jesse Abramson, considered the best all-around sports reporter in town. His voluminous memory in the boxing and track-and-field world earned him the nickname of

"The Book," as in record book. He was inherently and unabashedly argumentative—and almost always right. Best of all, he could produce uniformly brilliant accounts of a fight, a football game or Olympic events under deadline pressure, amid any distraction, including every significant facet of the event. He rarely did baseball or basketball, and rarely wrote opinion columns, but no one doubted he could, and his perceptive analyses were imbedded in his news stories.

Al Laney, the most literate and fastidious of men, would deal with tennis, boxing, baseball and anything else with equal aplomb. The acerbic columnist W.O. McGeehan, a giant of the Golden Age, was followed by Richard Vidmer until Woodward brought in Red Smith (in 1944) and freed him from the daily baseball coverage that had limited the scope of his talent (but never his enthusiasm) in Philadelphia. Rud Rennie was the senior baseball writer with Bob Cooke, fresh out of Yale in 1936, giving an expert light touch to coverage of the Dodgers. Everett B. Morris was a basketball and yachting maven, Harold Rosenthal an incredibly versatile jack of all trades. Woodward, in addition to running this operation and making sure he had an astute copy desk, wrote a good deal as a columnist and football writer.

Stanley's right-hand man was Irving T. Marsh, the assistant sports editor, a City College product from the 1920s who was also one of the earliest big-time basketball writers. Most of his work, however, was inside, scheduling assignments and supervising both writers and desk. When the war took Bob Harron away from Columbia, Irving was able to also moonlight as the sports publicity man there. In those days, this was a perfectly acceptable outside job for newspaper people, and his objectivity was never questioned—nor could it be because he was so scrupulous about maintaining it.

When I became campus sports correspondent for *The Times* in the fall of 1943, Irving was just taking over the Columbia office. The *Trib* correspondent was my buddy, Paul Sherman, and we shared our coverage of football practices as best we could. Irving's neutrality never wavered.

When I came back to the campus in 1946, Irving was still there, in the process of turning it over to the returned Bob Cherneff (with Harron over in the Journalism Building handling university public relations). Now I took both *The Times* and the *Trib* jobs (and a bunch of others) and no one considered any of it a conflict of interest. The ethical point, which I strictly observed, was to write a different piece for each client, never simply a carbon copy, making sure I used the correct score in each. With Irving back at the *Trib*, he started giving me non-Columbia stringer assignments (of which there were plenty in those days), and eventually fill-in clerkship time on the desk. I could process racing agate, take scores over the phone, and do piece work on *Trib* promotions, like the charity games between the New York football Giants and the just-graduated Eastern College All-Stars.

One night in 1948, I think it was in July, one of the deskmen died. Cooke had just replaced Woodward as editor (after Woodward had one fight too many with the paper's owner, Mrs. Helen Reid), and depended on Irving even more than Woodward had. They were getting ready to offer me the open desk job.

All these years I had been waiting for on opportunity at *The Times*, where I was still doing Columbia work. I went two blocks north to get the attention of Ray Kelly, the sports editor.

"Mr. Kelly," I said, "a regular job has opened up at the *Trib*, but I'd rather work here. I could wait for an opportunity here if you think I should."

His answer, without looking up from what he was reading, was: "Um."

So I went back two blocks south and took Cookie's offer, gratefully.

A year later, another opening allowed them to move me off the desk to reporting. That was great. But from then on, whenever illness or anything else created a temporary shortage on the desk, I was always the one being pulled back inside, because that was my original classification. Up to a point, I benefited greatly from this experience, as Irving eventually put me in charge of putting out all the inner pages of the fat Sunday edition. But now I was the base-ball swing man (it took four to cover three teams because of days off) and No. 2 behind Irving on the basketball beat, which had grown in importance with the creation of the Knicks. The desk was less and less palatable.

Everett Morris, who was a reserve naval officer, had gone back into service during the Korean War. That's why Irving had to do more basketball and I was No. 2. Towards the end of 1953, Morris returned and I was bounced back to the desk, presumably indefinitely.

The paper most interested in basketball was the *Post*. Ike Gellis, the sports editor, and Paul Sann, the managing editor, knew me from nights at the Garden and Knick road trips. They had asked me, in 1952, if I wanted to join them, but I'd said no, I was perfectly happy where I was. Now, suddenly, I wasn't. Were they still interested in me, I asked? They said yes.

So in the first week of March 1954, I resigned (with Irving's blessing) and became a member of the *Post* with a guarantee that I would be strictly a writer with no inside responsibilities.

By that time, the *Trib* was on a downward slope. In 1946, it had been the equal of *The Times*. But *The Times* had had excellent management at the top, while the *Trib* had the Reid family, Mrs. Reid and her sons, Whitelaw and Ogden (known as Whitey and Brownie) who had neither foresight nor good judgment. They also had fewer financial resources and lost the ability, over time, to hang onto some of their best people (like Woodward).

The crucial bad decision came in 1950. The tabloid *News* and *Mirror* made a lot of money by having an early edition that hit the newsstands about 7 p.m., containing horse race results, final stock market prices and sports scores (when most games were played in the daytime). People would line up at corner newsstands to wait for the trucks that would drop off this head start on figuring out tomorrow's bets.

The *Trib* decided to challenge them in that market, and to get a jump on *The Times*.

They called it the Early Bird edition. The regular first edition used to go to press around 10 o'clock, catch midtown theater goers as they came out, and get distributed to distant points. The main edition would go in about midnight, with later catch-ups as necessary. But the Early Bird not only needed a six o'clock deadline, but a jazzier make-up and mix of stories. This wasn't the "regular" *Tribune*, but a hybrid. Both the mechanical requirements and the philosophical shift began to undermine all the virtues the "real" *Trib* had built up.

The Early Bird failed to increase circulation, compounded costs, hurt morale and blurred the paper's focus just when *The Times*, better managed, was starting to pull far ahead in circulation. By

1957, the Reids had to sell the *Tribune* to Jock Whitney, and there was a flurry of "new journalism" glory at first. But the true character of the paper and its relationship to its traditional readers had unraveled, and its economic situation was beyond repair. In 1966 it joined two other sinking ships, the Scripps-Howard *World Telegram* and *Sun* and the Hearst *Journal-American* to form a single *World Journal Tribune*, which sank for good in 1967.

I had grown up in a New York that had at least 12 papers. Now, only three were left. And 35 years later, that's still all there are.

23

The New York Post

Alexander Hamilton founded the *New York Post* in 1801, so it was the oldest paper in New York. It was a Federalist paper, although his ties with the Federalist Party were frayed because he had thrown his support to Thomas Jefferson instead of Aaron Burr when the 1800 presidential election produced an electoral vote tie which had to be settled by Congress. A few years later Burr killed Hamilton in a dual, but the paper never stopped publishing.

At some point in the 1930s, when it was long known as a conservative morning paper focused on financial affairs, it suddenly became an afternoon tabloid of openly liberal leanings. Along with this total change of political affiliation, it became lively in style throughout, with a new emphasis on sports.

Hamilton was an alumnus of Columbia, then called Kings College, as a member of the class of 1778 although he, like me, left school before becoming a senior to go to war (as an officer under General Washington). And the current editor of the *Post*, James Wechsler, was also a Columbia man, Class of 1935 (I think) and as passionate about sports as his right-hand man, managing editor Paul Sann, who was the buddy of Ike Gellis, the sports editor.

Columbia had been founded in 1754, so it was exactly 200 years later—in March—that I left the *Herald Tribune*, run by the Yale-affiliated Reid family, for the Columbia-associated confines of the *Post*. The *Trib* was the voice of New York's Republicans. The *Post*, now owned by Dorothy Schiff, had become the standard bearer of

Roosevelt liberalism so welcome to most of New York's huge Jewish population. That readership was intensely interested in basketball as its favorite game and in Jackie Robinson as a symbol of breaking down the still widely accepted forms of social discrimination.

Sann and Gellis were basketball nuts, always at the Garden and often on Knick road trips, so we became good friends. Wechsler concentrated on Columbia football, which was going downhill, sitting alone at the top of the west (visitors') stands, in the rain when necessary, suffering through the increasing number of defeats but never giving up.

I think I won Gellis over for good because of the following incident: In 1953, the Knicks had reached the championship round of the playoffs for the third year in a row. The best-of-seven series was opening in Minneapolis. The only way Gellis had been able to justify going on that trip was to write sidebar stories. But most of the activity on the road (as well as before games at the Garden) consisted of card playing, including coaches and players as well as regular writers. I was the only one who had always stayed out of the card games, because (1) I'm lousy at cards and (2) I could see that once I got involved, all my free time would be consumed (as theirs was). So I was just hanging around the press room the night before the first game, killing time while others were playing.

Ike was supposed to file a routine advance on tomorrow's game. He had gotten as far as this:

By Ike Gellis
MINNEAPOLIS, April 3—John Kundla, the Laker coach,......

At that point, he got involved in a game of klabiash (a Hungarian variety of pinochle in vogue with this group). It was getting late, with deadline time approaching. I'd done my own stuff long before.

Ike looked over his shoulder, saw me standing around, and said:
"You wouldn't want to finish up my story, would you?"
He was just kidding, but I had nothing else to do.
"Sure," I said. "How long does it have to be?"
"About two pages," he said, surprised. "Would you really do it?"
"Sure, why not? I'd be glad to."
It was a common act of sheer professional courtesy. Writers had done this kind of thing for one another thousands of times for

many years. Ike wasn't even drunk (the usual reason for helping out), just eager to stay in a card game he was losing.

What I did next is what got him. I didn't put in a fresh sheet of paper. I simply picked up at his empty comma, the "John Kundla, the Laker coach," sentence he had begun, and ran out the routine advance from there, since I'd already written mine. It took about 15 minutes. After all, my stringer days had trained me in doing many versions of the same story.

He was so delighted that I had left his own words intact, because he knew (as I did) that he had no idea what he was going write next. Ike was no writer and never had been. His great asset as a boss was that he let good writers, of whom his staff had a lot, do whatever they wanted as long as they got it right. He considered me to be a good writer. That I didn't junk his opening, but just built on it, left him thrilled.

He first offered me a job on the *Post* on the way home, but I'd had no reason to think of leaving the *Trib*. Ten months later I had a good one—being pushed back to the desk—and I went.

It was the best move I ever made.

The *Post* sports department was terrific. Jimmy Cannon was the lead columnist. Milton Gross, as good a digger if not Cannon's equal as a stylist, was No. 2. Jerry Mitchell, Arch Murray and Sid Friedlander were the baseball writers. Mitchell was one of the funniest and most imaginative writers in the business, Murray was a character of irrepressible enthusiasm, and Friedlander the prototype of a great newspaperman. (It was because Sid, who had also been covering the Knicks, wanted to get off his 12-months-of-travel merry-go-round, that there was an opening for me.) Al Buck, known to all viewers of televised fights by the cigarette that always dangled from his mouth at ringside, also covered the football Giants. Leonard Cohen, who had been sports editor before Gellis, seemed happy enough being a man of all trades with excellent contacts everywhere.

Then there was Leonard Shecter, a brilliant writer who had been stuck on the desk, and had every reason to expect promotion to the job I was hired for (Knicks and baseball). He resented my arrival (as he would have anyone else's), and I certainly understood why: I had just escaped the same trap. Eventually, however, other changes enabled him to get out, and we wound up sharing the baseball beat after the Dodgers and Giants left town. He did great work, and became a charter member of the "chipmunks," the younger writers who pursued their own angles and had no use for The Establishment, and wrote wonderful stuff. *Newsday* had a bunch of them, including Stan Isaacs, George Vecsey and Steve Jacobson, and Shecter wound up writing *Ball Four* with Jim Bouton.

At the *Post*, we all took turns writing columns frequently, in addition to the daily output of Cannon and Gross, and they never hesitated to also do straight coverage at major events along with their columns. We had total "artistic" freedom, encouraged to be amusing, allowed to be opinionated, endlessly second-guessed and made to justify any non-obvious statement, and expected to be able to cover anything. Sann and Wechsler looked over everything we did all the time, arguing and criticizing us constantly without squelching our independence or making us worry about reprisals. Ike was certainly not illiterate, but as UN-literate as anyone in his position could be, with no pretensions otherwise. He certainly wasn't "educated," and if he'd ever finished high school, I didn't know. But he appreciated good and lively writing, knew the subject, chewed you out when you got it wrong, and never objected at something that worked even when he, himself, didn't understand what in the world his highly literate writers were talking about. He trusted his writers. And anything he missed, Sann and Wechsler, who were as literate as all hell, didn't.

This was heaven for a writer. We could do anything we wanted, any way we wanted, as long as it was amusing or informative for the reader, and therefore fun for us to do. I had been bred in the old school, as a stringer and at *The Times*, in making sure that who-what-where-when-why and how got into the lead paragraph, if not lead sentence. At the *Trib*, we were much more flexible but still grounded in those principles. Now the wraps were off. I could practice writing dialogue in playlets, utilize jokes, make up fantasies about historical figures, zero in on anything funny that happened or was said, as long as I made my point.

To Wechsler, I was his pipeline to Columbia football. Each week he sought desperately for reason to hope and each week I had none to offer. Why he did he keep torturing himself?

"I'm hooked," he confessed. As a flaming liberal, who had gone to the mat with Senator Joe McCarthy, he was dedicated to rooting for underdogs, and Columbia was not only a perpetual underdog but *his* underdog. "But surely we've got to get better sometime."

I knew that at Columbia in the 1930s, he was one of a radical group of undergraduates who had attacked the legitimacy of Lou Little's success in recruiting teams that lost only once a season.

"Jimmy," I told him, "maybe if you'd kept your mouth shut when you were in school, we'd still be getting better players. It's your own fault."

"Yes," he acknowledged, "but how long must I go on paying for a youthful mistake?"

As it turned out, until he died.

The chipmunks, in the late 1950s and 1960s, were changing the way sports were being written. (Cannon had pinned that name on them because they were chattering all the time, like chipmunks, while he was trying to write.) They were dedicated to finding the off-beat, personal, quotable and second-guessable material, very good at writing about it, disdainful of traditionally "straight" approaches. They were a bit younger than the Cannon-Smith-Dick Young generation, who were also much looser than their elders but still wedded to "relevance" and the internal importance of the events they covered. The chipmunks saw themselves as qualified psychoanalysts and sociologists rather than the sports "experts" whose expertise (they felt) was a sham and not necessary anyhow. To them, the sports scene was not only fun and games—rather than life and death as romanticized by the older generation—but primarily grist for their clever-writing mill. So much of what they did was so good that their influence prevailed through the cultural revolutions of the 1960s. What mattered to them was not what happened, but what they could say about it. Today's dominant style—on television and radio as well as in print—owes its origins to them.

Since I was the youngest of the Young-Effrat-Lewin group and, on the *Post*, going off on all kinds of tangents of my own, the chipmunks started out considering me one of them until they found out how basically orthodox I really was. But we always had at least partial rapport and none of the inter-generational hostility that later developed.

As time went on, and the next generation of sportswriters followed them, the "probing" impulse became primary. Looking back,

I'm astounded at the sheer arrogance and effrontery it represents. Undeniably, to get into a person's psyche and describe his whole human being is more interesting than an account of his on-field actions. But to believe that one can do this on the basis of a few minutes of clubhouse contact daily, and even an occasional private conversation, is self-deception—and self-aggrandizement—of the worst amateur psychoanalysis stripe. A Jimmy Cannon or Red Smith, after years of contact with their subjects, could do it now and then, and a Jim Murray could make jokes that related to what was happening, but it was their special talent that made them so special. The idea that any reporter, regardless of experience, working in an atmosphere of active and accumulated hostility amid a public relations machine training its players to conceal their true thoughts, could deliver this any day in any circumstances, seems to me ridiculous.

Re-reading Holtzman's *No Cheering in the Press Box* in the press box now, I'm struck by my reaction. He wrote in 1973, having tape-recorded his interviews over several years. Many of them speak proudly of being still vigorous and active in their 70s (and some in the 80s), and tell stories about their activities 30 years before that, and they all complain about the direction "modern" sportswriters— the ones of the 1970s—have taken. Specifically, they dislike the disrespect being shown for the events and people being covered, and the abandonment of telling the story straight in the first place. They were talking about the chipmunks and their then-recent influence.

Now, almost 30 years later, I'm 79 and I find myself saying the same things and feeling exactly the same way about today's journalistic norms.

That's just plain old-man curmudgeonarianism (how's that for making up words?) on one level—but also the reason the press box had its fall.

But back to the *Post*. In my nine years there, two principals prevailed. We were on duty all the time, and we would work for minimum salaries. We took that for granted and didn't let it become an issue. Ike's regular phrase, often tossed at me in midday, was "you don't happen to have a column in your pocket, do you?" meaning something had come up where the scheduled extra column (not Cannon or Gross) hadn't panned out. My answer was always "yes," since I needed only an hour or so to produce one. One of the by-products of being on duty 24 hours was that you always had plenty in your head that could be made into an instant column.

All basketball season I traveled with the Knicks, wherever they went. (The Garden was paying the travel costs for the *Post*, but that didn't matter to me; I simply turned in to the *Post* my own expense accounts for my own meals, taxis and whatever flights that I had to take myself.) All baseball season, after spring training (which basketball precluded) I traveled baseball and after the World Series caught up with basketball. I also inherited, at some point, the Thursday Pigskin Prophet column predicting that week's college scores.

I couldn't take this seriously—I had no idea who would win, let alone guess at point margins, and had always known this. Ike, who was a regular bettor on all sorts of sports, knew it as well as I did. But I remembered that when John Kieran was writing the "Sports of The Times" column, on football Saturdays, he would forecast several games under the heading of "Stuffing the Ballot Box" with an irrelevant (and irreverent) paragraph on some esoteric point ending with "one vote for Yale." I thought I could use the same device, but with one-line jokes for about 25 games, using Shakesperean quotes, play and movie titles, clichés, names of players, anything. If you read the comments down, ignoring the scores, you got a fairly related set of gags. If you looked at the scores, you had only yourself to blame.

Ike went for it and, predictably enough, my blind-shot predictions averaged not much worse than all the serious ones.

I did it for about four years, and two unforeseen things happened.

First, some readers became convinced that the jokes contained a code that they could interpret, indicating what the "real" bets should be. They wrote letters thanking me, and they were welcome. I never found out what the codes were, since they wanted to keep their secrets secret.

Then, one evening, I walked in to Shor's and Sam, the chief maitre d', greeted me.

"There was a big admirer of yours in here last night," he said. "He had your pigskin picks column clipped out and was showing it around."

"Yes?" I said. "Who was it?"

"Frank Costello."

"You mean *the* Frank Costello?"

"Yep."

Wow. One of the most famous underworld figures showing my football picks around.

I was terrified. I *knew* how unreliable my picks were.

I spent the next three days (Saturday, Sunday, Monday) slinking around. Not long before one of the biggest mob figures had been gunned down in the hotel barber shop just three blocks from where I lived. Every time I saw a big black car I flinched and tried to hide in a doorway. This was not the way I wanted my career—and my life—to end.

Then I came to my senses. I had nothing to worry about. Costello represented the bookie end of the betting business, the end that profited no matter which side won. Of course he liked my column—I was *misleading* all the bettors whose vigorish the bookies lived off. I was free advertising. And I was safe.

In 1959, I attained the apex of my work schedule, filing baseball, football, basketball and hockey stories the same day.

It was Wednesday, October 7, during the World Series. We had just returned to Chicago from Los Angeles, where the Dodgers had taken a 3-2 lead in games, and this was the off day before the sixth game.

So I wrote my World Series stuff (two stories), and my Pigskin Prophet (football) and an installment of my pre-season pro basketball series, which was winding up.

And since the New York Rangers were opening the hockey season in Chicago that night, I went over and covered them, too.

What's more, I did all this under extreme psychological pressure. Back in August, at the annual baseball writers' outing at Bear Mountain, I had won a door prize: A free week in Bermuda. My plane was to leave New York on Friday, so it was essential the Dodgers not lose Game Six on Thursday. If they lost, my rare vacation was gone.

They won. I went. A week after that, I was back with the Knicks, starting another 12-month cycle of in-and-out traveling.

I loved it. But eventually, in 1962, economic reality and my 39th birthday caught up with me. I could no longer afford to keep working just for the fun of it, as much fun as it was. I'd have to go out and begin working for a living.

24

The New York Times

When I started on the desk at the *Herald Tribune*, the Guild minimum was $90 a week to start and $110 after two years of experience. In every new labor contract, every couple of years, the minimums went up automatically. When I went to the *Post* it was $175, and I was given a $10 merit raise to $185. I was still making that in 1962. With few exceptions, the minimums in each category tended to become maximums.

Cannon, Mitchell, Murray and Friedlander were gone from the *Post*. Shecter and I were now the most senior writers behind Gross, sharing two or three columns a week in addition to our beats. But if either of us were to be promoted to featured columnist, with an appropriate raise, the other wouldn't accept the situation and one way or another the paper would lose a significant asset. As for giving us (or anyone) a raise substantial enough to make a difference while we remained as beat writers, that simply wasn't going to be done.

If I were ever to get married and start a family—and I'd begun thinking along those lines—I'd need a lot more money and a lot less traveling, and soon.

Right after the 1962 World Series, which lasted until Oct. 16 because of three days of rain in San Francisco, I spelled it out to Gellis and Sann, and they agreed that Shecter and I could never fit through the narrow economic doorway shoulder to shoulder. So I told them I'd start looking for something outside the newspaper business—P.R. probably, but whatever else I might find—and stay with them as long as it took. No hard feelings anywhere. It was simply time to grow up. They understood.

By December 8, I'd had a few leads but nothing solid, but I wasn't in any particular hurry. My usual *Post* routines were fine. It was the long-range future that was involved.

But that day, all the New York papers were closed down by a strike. It would last 114 days.

The immediate need became finding a way to survive without any income at all. A bunch of us formed a unit that could do a nightly sports report show on radio station WOR, sharing equally whatever money they gave us. We'd give ourselves assignments, cover what we could, write our own scripts, and fill a part of the news vacuum. Our group included Effrat from *The Times*, Young from the *News*, Lewin from the *Mirror*, me from the *Post* and Dave Anderson from the *Journal-American* as regulars, with Frankie Blauschild, of the *Mirror*, acting as our director and producer.

It took all our time, every day, and all our other activities came to a halt. But it kept us alive, and my future plans were on hold.

One day in February, with no end of the strike in sight, Effrat told me that Bob Teague was leaving *The Times*. Bob was the most prominent black sportswriter in New York, if not the only one with major assignments, and a star performer in our baseball show. NBC had been after him for some time to join their television news department, but he had always rejected the idea. Now he was fed up with the newspaper situation and was accepting the television job.

"So there's an opening," said Louie. "Why don't you ask about it?"

The thought of going to another paper had never occurred to me. People seldom changed papers in those days, at least in sports, and my move to the *Post* had been an exception. But I suddenly realized there were only two papers in town who didn't consider minimums to be maximums: the *News*, and *The Times*. They would actually pay more to a writer they valued. If a paper would actually give me more money, maybe I could stay in the business I knew, and hated to leave.

We were having one of our free dinners at Joe Marsh's steak house on 47th Street. It was his way of helping out the writers he knew from Madison Square Garden, the destination of so much of his clientele.

I knew that Gellis was at Leone's, in the next block, at some affair. I ran over there. I had told him I'd be leaving the business, but we had never considered the possibility of going to a rival paper. That would be betrayal. Wouldn't it?

I found Ike at the bar, and told him Effrat's news.

"What do you think?"

"Go for it," he said instantly. "Don't be silly. It's a great chance."

Sann was at the same affair, and joined us. He had the same reaction. "If they want a recommendation, they've got it."

How can you leave a relationship like that? But reality remained.

The sports editor of *The Times* was Jim Roach, who had succeeded Ray Kelly. Roach's beat had been horse racing, he'd been a long-time friend of Bob Harron, and had known me since my Columbia days. I called the next day and went up to see him. I laid out the whole situation.

"Obviously, you'd fit in well over here. You have to go through all the personnel department procedures, but it should be O.K. How much money would you want?"

I blurted out the first number that came to mind. "$225."

"That's fair enough to start. And let me tell you something. If you come over here, you can't help but prosper."

Boy, was he right. So I was going from the best boss in the world to a new one who would be just as good to me.

Within a week it was official, but the strike was still on.

On March 7, the *Post* broke ranks, settled, and resumed publication. But I was already a *Times* man. The strike finally ended April 1.

One reason Roach wanted me was that John Drebinger, their No. 1 baseball writer since 1926, had decided to retire at the end of 1963. Half a dozen of their staff members had been sharing the rest of the baseball assignments now that the Mets had become a second home team, but they also had their own established slots. I could fill Drebinger's place.

One of the reasons the higher *Times* brass so easily accepted Roach's decision was that they knew me as the current director of the baseball show, of which they were big fans. *Times* members like Effrat, Joe Nichols, Bill Briordy, Roscoe McGowen and his son

Dean, and others had often been prominent contributors to the show, and the high executives (Turner Catledge, Clifton Daniel) liked the idea of having their people associated with this glamorous social event of New York's winter calendar.

The inside people on the desk knew me too, because I and my recent Broadway show business gypsy friends often ate dinner in *The Times'* cafeteria, along with some of the guys from the *Tribune*. We all mingled. And Phil Burke, the sports department secretary who really ran the office, knew me because his son had become the sports publicity man at Columbia.

Roach's remark about fitting in was right on target. I'd had intensive morning-paper training at the *Trib*, followed by the far-out freedom of the *Post*. It was no trouble for me to slip back into morning-paper deadlines and traditional story construction, and follow stodgy *Times* rules. But the stimulated imagination the *Post* had given me enabled me to liven up stories in a way that long-time *Times* writers didn't, because they had been beaten down so often for so long by unimaginative copy editors.

In its obsession with fact-checking, old-textbook grammar and formal language, *Times* style leached out whatever originality of expression a writer found. All the writers were frustrated, and none of the readers knew what brightness they may have missed. But I, as a rare outsider with credentials, visibly backed by Roach, enjoyed more leeway than was ever given to Effrat or Joe Sheehan or anyone since John Kieran, who had left in 1942.

And I was only the beginning of a flood of new faces.

The Mirror folded that fall. Lewin, who had covered the Knicks as much as I had, was gobbled up by the *Post* to fill the role I had. Blauschild became a publicity man for the Knicks.

Three other papers were struggling, and closed in the spring of 1967. Now we had Anderson from the *Journal*, Frank Litsky from the United Press, Murray Chass from the Associated Press, Bill Wallace and Sam Goldaper from the *Tribune*, and, eventually, George Vecsey from *Newsday* and Red Smith himself. Then, when Drebby did retire, Joe Durso, who had been a high-ranking night editor on the city side, came over to start a baseball writing career in which he flourished.

The desk could not keep such a collection under wraps, even though it tried for a while, and the section became much livelier. A home-grown talent like Bob Lipsyte (out of Columbia in the mid-1950s) also blossomed in a less restrictive atmosphere, and turned out to be the best pure writer of us all.

What were some of those rules? You couldn't say "Third baseman Clete Boyer." It had to be "Clete Boyer, the third baseman." You couldn't use the phrase "back-to-back homers" because someone thought it was sexually suggestive. You couldn't refer to a player by his first name alone, no matter how often you had already used his last name. You could not use "win" as a noun; it was strictly a verb. No player could have a "lifetime" batting average or other statistic, unless he was already dead, because as long as he was alive he might add to it (at age 80?). Therefore, there were no "lifetime records." They had to be a "career records." And no situation could offer several alternatives; there could be only one alternative (singular) to a given path: An "alternate" path. If there were more than one, they would be "choices," not alternatives.

Anything considered "slang" was out. Topical references were suspect. And if you succeeded in avoiding or simply missing a chance for a cliché, you could count on the desk to write it in.

They used to drive Effrat crazy. There had been a house ad, identifying Louis as "the man with a twist," boasting about his originality—but the desk would excise any bright twist he produced. And they would change his copy for no other reason than to make a change. (I guess they thought it justified their existence.)

"If I say defeated, they change it to vanquished," he'd moan, "and if I say vanquished, they change it to defeated."

But their impulse wasn't totally wrong. This was "the paper of record." Whatever it printed would be the raw material, forever congealed, for researchers using its microfilm. I learned to take this responsibility seriously. We weren't writing only for tomorrow morning, but for posterity. That was no reason to tighten up and be dull, but it made you aware of having justification for what you were saying. All newspaper stories, by their nature, are to some degree incomplete, not quite accurate, subject to later elaboration, and subsequent corrections never catch up with a story's immediate impression.

The desk's pickiness, although often silly and congealed in tradition, had a positive side. It forced a sort of discipline on the writer concerning grammar and the true meaning of words. You had to think about what you were saying and whether you were really saying what you meant.

If you didn't let it kill your imagination, it would sharpen your powers of being interesting *and* accurate. Those who succumbed to the routine, as many who worked there long enough did, or lacked imagination in the first place, produced a duller product that nevertheless did the job the "paper of record" had set for itself: To tell the reader clearly what the story had to report. As in all the arts, being original and creative involves breaking all sorts of "rules"— but to be good at originality and creativity, you have to know the rules and learn how to break them constructively. Discipline is always necessary. When it's too rigid, it's stifling; but without it, "bright" ideas too often become merely chaotic.

That sort of discipline is totally absent in today's journalistic world, and in a context where "anything" is accepted as a right of self-expression, the skills of better self-expression are neither demanded nor developed.

So Roach preached the religion of "explain, explain, explain." His repeated example was, "If you mention a fetlock"—referring to part of a horse's leg—"make sure you tell me what a fetlock is." Why? Because *The Times* had institutionalized a thought once uttered by Joe DiMaggio.

He had been asked why he hustled so much on every play long after his reputation as a Hall of Famer was established and his aging body hurt so often.

"I always think," said Joe, "there may be somebody in the stands seeing me for the first time. I want them to see me at my best."

The attitude of *The Times* was that every day someone might be unfamiliar with the subject we were describing, and we shouldn't assume that "everyone" knew what we knew. It didn't go as far as having to explain what a strikeout was, but if the infield fly rule was called, you'd better spell it out.

Once, during my second or third year there, Roach told me that managing editor Clifton Daniel had commented on my Knick story in that day's paper. At the Garden, the Knicks had beaten the St. Louis Hawks in overtime. I thought I'd managed to weave together the details of the eventful final minutes, the clash of two ex-Knicks as rival coaches, the effect on the standings, and so forth.

"What did he say?" I asked.

"He noted," said Roach, "that nowhere in the story does it say this was a National Basketball Association game."

I was flabbergasted. This is what the top brass picked out of a story? But after I thought about it, I understood that he was right. Not everyone all over the world (which *The Times* considered its audience) might know, automatically, that the eight-column head-line, the Garden, and the names of the teams were sufficient to identify an NBA event. Why leave anyone in doubt? What harm would be done to my deathless prose if I included so prosaic a reference?

So I made sure I did, for a while at least, from then on.

The sense of historical continuity overrode headlong pursuit of originality. Large bound volumes of the previous two years of editions were kept in a set of cabinets near the copy desk. Every morning, one of Phil Burke's first tasks was to get one out and lay it open it to the same date a year ago. That was the starting point for that day's plans.

But this was the 1960s. By the middle 1970s, after *The Times* changed its typography and modernized its outlook, such accumulated stodginess was disintegrating as the internal power base was shifting from the desk to the writers and editors. In my opinion, its sports section of the late 1990s and early 2000s is the best it has ever been: Better written and presented, without loss of seriousness and with better news judgment, than when it was looked upon as a necessary but trivial inclusion in a paper with higher concerns.

My move to California had been authorized by Abe Rosenthal, who had taken over as editor after our 1967 project for an after-noon paper had not materialized. In 1974, during my first year on the West Coast, Abe came out on a regular "inspect the troops" visit to the San Francisco Bureau (to which I was not attached; I was still in the sports department, just with a Palo Alto address). He hosted a dinner and started it by asking me, "When are you coming back to New York?"

My wife started to laugh.

"You don't get it, Abe," I grinned. "I'm not coming back."

The agreement had been we'd try it for at least three years. But I already knew that one way or another, my move would be permanent.

Nine years later, when I was editor of the *Peninsula Times Tribune*, I dropped in at *The Times* on a visit to New York. Abe invited me to sit in on the daily editorial meeting, at which department heads report what they have. Some knew me, some didn't. So he introduced me, to explain my presence, with a good-natured joke.

"Koppett's visiting from California and he might want to ask me for a job."

"No, Abe," I replied. "Now that I've been an editor, I don't think I could handle a real job."

I don't know how Abe liked that answer, but the rest of the room loved it.

Fifteen years at *The Times* gave me unparalleled prestige and access to sources; a chance to mature and broaden my outlook as a writer; enough money to marry Susie; and a label that never ceased opening doors. Only the traveling finally wore me down.

Lefty Gomez, Hall-of-Fame Yankee pitcher (always explain and identify, right?) observed: "I'd rather be lucky than good." That's my credo too. You have to be good enough to be able to take advantage of good luck, of course; but first of all you have to be lucky.

My first great stroke of luck was coming to America. The second was landing on *The New York Times* when I did.

25

Newspapers on Strike

One reason I was equipped to understand what was involved in the labor-management wars that erupted in sports in the 1970s (and have gone on ever since) is that I lived through five newspaper strikes in New York. We had them in 1946, 1953, 1958, 1962-63 and 1965—and when I resigned from *The New York Times* in 1978 another was about to start.

As an employee, I learned the following lessons about collective bargaining.

Employees never WANT to go on strike. Only when they begin to believe that the unresolved issue is a threat to some vital interest (in their eyes) are they willing to take the step.

Once a strike starts, whatever the issues, the strikers *must* stick together and ride it out, whether they like it or not. Otherwise their union (if they want one) is dead. Benjamin Franklin's warning reigns supreme: "If we do not hang together, we will all hang separately." The oft-repeated observation, "nobody wins in a strike," is false. The immediate conflict hurts everyone—strikers, the business, the public. But more often that not, one side or the other gains a great deal.

The key issues in most strikes are never dollars as such, but control. Management believes (sincerely) that some union activity interferes with its right to run its own business its own way, and must be checked. The union's only reason for existence is to gain or retain control over matters affecting its members by succeeding collectively where separate individuals could not.

In any dispute serious enough to produce a strike possibility, resolution is *not possible* until the deadline hour approaches. Only at that point can each side be sure that the "final offer" really is "final." It can then be accepted or rejected, but only then can the adversarial jockeying process be concluded.

In that process, the competitive instincts of the negotiators get more intense, making compromise harder to reach than it would have been at the beginning. The chief negotiators, on each side, are always the ones most dedicated to their positions.

Whose ultimate influence counts most, for a settlement before or after a strike actually occurs, is seldom obvious. Usually it comes from someone, or some factors, outside the formal bargaining.

Only the two parties can come to an agreement. Public sentiment, the interests of outsiders (customers, dependant workers in other fields, an inconvenienced public) and extraneous issues don't count. The only exception occurs when a government takes an active role and imposes a settlement.

No matter how brilliant, perceptive, logical, factual and objectively reasoned my analysis—or any other outsider's—of the situation may be, it won't forecast or affect the real-life result. Only the participants can and will decide what that will be.

A strike is a war. Just as when you're drafted into the army, your loyalty to it has been committed for the duration. You may privately disagree with your own side's actions, and even wonder why the conflict wasn't averted. But once the battle is engaged, achieving survival is the first imperative. And that applies to *both* sides.

In New York in those days, there were 10 or 11 unions involved in producing a paper, and they usually dealt with a publisher's group that represented all the papers. So any one union's dispute with any one paper had the potential of causing a city-wide shutdown, since most unions would respect another's picket line, and since the publishers would also stick together and close down if only one or two were struck.

This happened in 1946, 1953, 1958, 1962 and 1965, with a different union setting off the war each time, at various papers. Early in 1946, a post-war wave of strikes hit every part of American industry, including the subways in New York and the railroads nationwide. In 1953, it was the engravers for 19 days; in 1958, the deliverers for 18; in 1962, the printers for 114; and in 1965, the editorial and business employees for 23.

By far the largest, and least influential, union was the Newspaper Guild, which contained writers, editors, advertising salesmen and all other non-technical workers (including janitors). Among other things, these people's tasks were most easily replaced by management and outsiders if a paper wanted to keep publishing, unlike the services of printers, pressmen, engravers or truck drivers. Also, the Guild's membership lacked the kind of single-minded common interest issues the mechanical unions had.

In general, the Guild (which had established itself in the 1930s) rode piggy-back on periodic wage increase patterns won by the others, and paid for it by supporting strikes in which its own issues and goals wouldn't have been strike issues in themselves.

So by 1966, I had learned a bunch of more specific lessons.

Any union's elected leaders are always concerned with remaining in power, so they listen most carefully to its most radical members.

The most vocal and active members of any union tend to be workers who devote more time and attention to labor matters than to their particular job requirements, since those wrapped up in their work have less time and inclination to do that. So the concerns of the less capable, less dedicated, more routine workers become dominant issues—and properly so, because they are the one who feel most dependent on union protection.

Writers in general, and sportswriters especially, tend to be followers in union affairs. They have less daily contact with fellow employees (since they're always out covering things), they don't have the time or inclination to attend union meetings, and many issues that labor contracts address don't involve them. So deskmen are more deeply involved.

Strike strategy is dictated by the calendar. A strike can be effective only when shutting down will hurt management most. In the newspaper business, the period between Labor Day and Christmas produces almost half the year's advertising income, so those strikes took place in the fall.

Those 13 points were part of my equipment when I had to start dealing with the labor problems that major league sports began confronting in the mid-1960s. I understood why the NBA players established their union's power by threatening to strike the 1965 playoffs, and why the baseball players finally turned to Marvin Miller, a steelworkers union economist, to turn their "Players Association" into a true (and formal) labor union in 1966. I could grasp the motives and methods being used by both sides in the sports strikes that followed, accepting the legitimacy of each side's view of itself. I saw why football strikes in pre-season or early-season failed, and baseball strikes in mid-season or later succeeded, following the "strike-the-papers-before-Christmas" strategy. And I knew whatever either side or anyone else told me during the battle, it could be settled only by the combatants themselves and only at the last minute. Only then could we start to sort out who won what.

On a personal level, each newspaper strike meant something to me indirectly.

In 1946, I picked up extra out-of-town stringer assignments.

In 1953, the musical *Kismet* opened just when the papers went out in December. Conventional wisdom was that critics would pan it and kill it, but since there were no reviews, it was able stay open long enough to find an appreciative audience that made it a success. Its cast contained three dancers from California, who then stayed in New York and, when I met them later, became the core of "my" group of Broadway gypsies who became lifelong friends.

In 1958, Jimmy Cannon left the *Post* (to go to the *Journal-American*), opening up the *Post*'s second column for me and Shecter to share.

In 1962-63, it produced the opening for me at *The Times*.

And in 1965, it started in September and lasted into the World Series, when it might end at any moment. So the New York Chapter of the BBWAA paid for the regular beat writers to go Minneapolis and Los Angeles, just in case. It ended in time for me to cover the seventh game in Minneapolis. And that series-time mingling helped get me a weekly column in *The Sporting News* when one opened up the next year.

26

The
Sporting News

A one-paper writer, even on *The New York Times*, achieves some local celebrity, but only syndicated columnists have national impact. *The Sporting News*, in the 1960s, was still "the baseball bible," devoured weekly by everyone in that field, while also paying increasing attention to other sports. Lee Allen, who had been doing a history-based column (with wonderful anecdotes), had died. I was given that slot to fill any way I wanted to, resting on the reputation I had acquired as an "analyst."

For me, this became the ultimate soap box.

I could comment, analyze, explain, fantasize, pontificate, harangue, make jokes and float any idea that came to mind, without the daily newspaper's 24-hour cycle of timeliness and restriction to a particular assignment. C.C. Johnson Spink, who had succeeded his father as editor and publisher, and Lowell Reidenbaugh, his right-hand man, gave me as much freedom and support as Gellis had at the *Post*. No living writer can get closer to paradise than working in such a context.

Over the next 15 years, whatever national recognition I attained was due to *The Sporting News* rather than *The Times*.

Among other things, this was an outlet for my reliance on statistics. This was before hand-held calculators and computer-produced encyclopedias, and the use of sports statistics was pretty rudimentary. I had been brought in on the ground floor by Harron and Cherneff at Columbia because Harron was one of the earliest

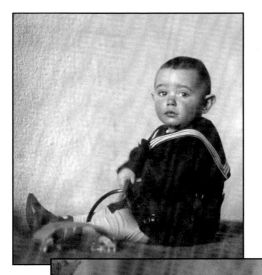

EARLY DAYS...
The two portraits
above were taken
before the Koppett
family emigrated
from Moscow
when Leonard was
five. At left, Leonard
in New York.

IN UNIFORM…
1943–45.

HAMMING IT UP… with friend Edward
Castikyan, 1942.

THE DINNER TABLE…With parents, David & Marya Kopeliovitch.

ON THE JOB… at *The New York Times*.

HOUK ON HOT SEAT…Yankees manager Ralph Houk faces a panel of, left to right, Dick Young, Koppett, Joe Reichler and Howard Cosell.

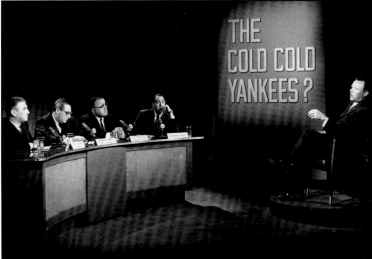

HANDS-ON JOURNALISM... Learning to scull, above, and absorbing the finer points of harness racing in 1950 for a *New York Herald Tribune* piece.

AT PLAY... Leonard, far right, wrote, directed and performed in skits staged at the annual dinner of the Baseball Writers Association of America.

STAGE HANDS... Ike Gellis at the plate, with Leonard catching and Milton Gross as the umpire.

IN ELITE COMPANY... From left, Willie Mays, Casey Stengel, Sandy
Koufax, Leonard Koppett and Louis Effrat in 1964.

ALL-STAR WRITERS... George Will and Leonard Koppett in 1991.

HALL OF FAMER...
Leonard was honored at
Candlestick Park in
1993 after his induction
into the Baseball Hall of
Fame.

IN HIS ELEMENT...
Buried in papers in his
home office at Palo
Alto. He used his
manual typewriter
until 2000.

(Renee Fadiman)

Leonard Koppett, 1923–2003

publicity men to realize that a weekly football statistics story about his team would be given space (because it wasn't being used routinely by others), and set up "records" to be approached and broken. Homer Cooke, the father of NCAA statistics releases starting in the late 1930s, had moved from the University of Washington to New York, and eventually was writing releases for him.

I was pretty good at elementary math (up to algebra but not beyond) and comfortable with numbers. I never fell into the trap of thinking statistics "proved" or "predicted probabilities"; they merely recorded whatever it was you decided to count after it happened (like a boxscore). But their psychological power was immense. They seemed "scientific" and irrefutable, convincing and quotable. Whatever point you wanted to make, finding an appropriate statistic nailed it down; and if some pattern struck you out of a bunch of numbers, it could trigger a thought to be followed up.

By the time I had gone to the *Post*, I had established my skill at this sort of manipulation, and carried my score book, a small record book and my own computations in a red attaché case.

"What have you got in there?" Cannon used to tease me. "Decimal points?"

Now, in the mid-1960s, I still had the same satchel.

"I see you're still carrying those decimal points," said Cannon.

"No, Jimmy," I replied. "Now that I'm on *The Times* it's full of colons and semi-colons."

And *The Sporting News* also let me write the too-long sentences that came so naturally.

Seriously, and more to the point, it became possible to deal with large and complicated subjects by spreading them over two or three successive columns. One could explore many of the ramifications of something—the designated hitter, expansion, a commissioner's actions—in a way no single column could. I was able to try to carry out a wise maxim of Albert Einstein's (although I came across it only later): "Everything should be a simple as possible—but not simpler."

Whether I succeeded or not, it made possible discussions that never fit in a daily newspaper.

As a baseball paper, in its day, *The Sporting News* had no peer. It carried the boxscores of not only all major league games but also Triple A, and notes on the lower minors. It staff, after 1940, also produced the annual baseball guides (which had been a Spalding product up to then), and other record books, eventually branching out into football and basketball.

Most of its stories were written by beat writers and columnists from the major league cities, so they were not only well-informed but able to summarize all the significant items concerning that city that week. As a result, one got a complete and well-balanced picture of the whole baseball scene, not just the home-city emphasis that existed in even the most sophisticated local sports pages.

When *The Sporting News* started paying more attention to football, basketball and hockey, the same pattern was followed. But its prime dedication, in those days, was to baseball, and everyone in the baseball business—players, managers, coaches, executives, scouts—as well as the truly involved fans, read it religiously, the way show business people read *Variety*. There was no better way to stay current on what was happening in their business.

A by-product of this system had an important effect on the sports writing of that time. We regulars—columnists and beat writers—read our opposite numbers from other cities regularly, staying in touch with the big picture. But each team's or city's correspondent had to follow up whatever local story was significant, even if it wasn't his own, for the sake of a weekly summarization. That meant he had to share with, and get from, his local colleagues all sorts of information and angles.

The result was a widespread intensification of what I call "collegiality." We got to know other writers, at home and from other cities, more often and more intimately than is now the case. Of course, it was easier before expansion began. There were only 16 team in 10 cities, and every team visited every other team four times during the season, so we came across each set on eight occasions. But we could also call one another anytime something of significance to us involved one or more other teams. We bounced viewpoint, speculations, rumors and reliable inside information, not—as is the custom now through the internet—by simply reading what they had written, but by actually talking to each other and pursuing lines of thought suggested by the exchange.

The Sporting News, in other words, was the "networking" mechanism of that day. When it changed, that degree of internal communication disappeared.

In 1977, the Times Mirror Company of Los Angeles bought *The Sporting News*, which had been run by the Spink family in St. Louis for 90 years. It tried to make it more of a fan-oriented publication than the trade paper it had been, abandoning the detailed baseball news for the sake of broader appeal. It became, in stages, what it is now: A magazine rather than a weekly newspaper. Magazines are fine products in their own right, like *Sports Illustrated* or *ESPN Magazine* or *Baseball Digest* and others, but they perform a different function in a different sort of presentation. A weekly newspaper deals primarily in news, with material updated within the last 24 hours before publication. A magazine deals primarily in features and pictures, requiring much longer lead times for most of its contents.

Today's weekly baseball papers are *Baseball America* and *USA Today's* weekly sports issue. They're valuable, but they haven't attained the monopolistic universality *The Sporting News* used to have, and don't create the "collegiality" I referred to.

I know times change, but I think this has been baseball's loss.

27

Official Scoring

TONIGHTS OFFICIAL SCORER - LEN KOPPETT NEW YORK TIMES

In order to have official statistics, every sports organization needs official scorers to create the raw material for them. (This is an application of a universal truth I first learned from *Horsefeathers*, the Marx Brothers movie, when I was about 11. Zeppo, playing the student body leader to Groucho's president of the college, tells him, "You can't have a good football team without good football players." It is The Law of Necessary Ingredients.)

Sportswriters, then, are heavily dependent on official scorers, appointed by the appropriate promoter: College, league, racing association, ruling body, whatever. But only in major league baseball were the writers themselves given that responsibility, from around 1920 to about 1980. In that period, that task was assigned exclusively to members of the Base Ball Writers Association of America, administered by them, by the two leagues and the commissioner's office. It's no longer done that way, although some individual writers still serve in some places.

Official scoring in baseball, in that era, was a privilege, an honor and a chore we took very seriously. The league president would accept a list of assignments from each chapter chairman, making each game's scorer a representative of the league analogous to an umpire's status. The scorer made on-the-spot decisions about hit or error, followed the rules about determining a winning pitcher, sorted out complicated plays and—the most important part—filled out an official extended boxscore and filed it with the league. He could have no influence on anything that could affect the outcome of any play—only umpires did that—but what he recorded became official history.

Why? Because baseball promoters had learned, by the early years of the century, that statistics lacked credibility if compiled by anyone connected with either team or league officials. Statistics had become so integral a part of baseball interest that any perception of hometown bias, deserved or not, undermined their value. When a game had, at most, two umpires, they couldn't also do that job. The only other "neutrals" at every game, with ostensibly some expertise, were the regular writers (before radio). They might have their prejudices, but writers from the visiting team were always on hand to monitor objectivity, able and willing to speak up to uphold it.

Each chapter had its own rules, but was intent on credibility. In a one-team city with only two or three papers, one or two experienced writers might work the whole season year after year. In two-team cities with up to 10 papers, some version of the New York rule existed. We, with three teams and up to 40 "regular" writers, used these: (1) You had to have covered at least 100 games for three consecutive years to qualify for the list; (2) then you took your turn, for about 20 games or so, in rotation, as long as you remained assigned by your paper to one or the other of the local teams.

The league paid a fee—$15 to $25 in my time—essentially for the chore of filing the report, not for making the decisions.

But deciding hit or error was of key importance. After all, it determined what was a no-hit game, baseball's most dramatic event; and it affected every player's batting, fielding and pitching record. Much conflict developed, as you can imagine. Hitters want their hits, pitchers want their unearned runs, fielders dispute errors. All stories, as well as records, are frozen by whatever the scorer decides.

The saving grace is that the scorer is allowed to make changes after the game, after consulting with others and especially the players involved. The obligation is to get it right, and a scorer could often make a corrected judgment after consultation. If colleagues lost faith in a particular scorer's competence or impartiality, he would be dropped from the list. The pressure to do your honest best—and not yield to self-serving complaints, even from the manager—was very strong.

When television came in, a prompt replay on the press box screen was a great help. The reason that scoring was not extended to broadcasters (who were certainly as qualified as the writers) was the original one. Almost all worked for the club, or a station or sponsor paying for the rights, and could not have a cachet of being "objective" no matter how much they might be personally.

Then came Watergate, and helped break the system down.

Large newspapers, embarking on a frenzy of ethical self-examination to justify the high moral tone of their editorials, decided that acting as scorer was a conflict of interest. It made the reporter a "participant" in the event. It also put him in a compromising situation with the players and manager he was supposed to interview every day, since he had to retain their good will. So they forbade their reporters to take scoring assignments. (*The New York Times* went so far as to bar its drama critics from voting for annual theater awards.)

This was silly theoretically and practically. Did the newspaper brass think their editorial endorsements, front-page news play decisions, crime reporting and drama and music reviews weren't "participating" in elections, shows and everything else dependent on public reaction? Was their baseball writer going to call a hit an error to get a better story about a no-hitter? And would a writer who wasn't a scorer be any less subject to want to maintain favorable relations with his sources? If you didn't trust your own writer's honesty and objectivity, in his area of expertise, why were you relying on him to give an honest and objective report?

At the same time, this gave the league presidents (that is, their club owners) an excuse to take back control from the writers. For 60 years, they feared "alienating" the powerful group (the BBWAA) so essential to their daily publicity by "taking away" their scoring fees. Now that radio-television was giving so much paid-for exposure, newspapers were relatively less important—especially since there were fewer and fewer papers. That had enabled them to stop subsidizing road coverage. They certainly didn't mind being allowed to chose their own scorers.

So now scoring is done by retired writers, local coaches, or anyone else the league (now the commissioner's office, since league presidents no longer exist) wants. The fee is up in the $50 range.

And the filled-in boxscore is no longer so important because the league statisticians check everything against the computerized play-by-play that also exists.

All the writers depended on the scorer to "bring me up" whenever they had missed a few plays, because he *had* to be watching all the time. Many writers stuck with doing early or running stories (for a morning paper) were often writing during a game. They were trained to look up whenever they heard the sound of ball hitting bat or glove. What they would miss most often was a soundless walk or strikeout.

Kenny Smith of the *Mirror* had an idea.

"The scorer ought to ring a ball or blow a whistle every time there's a walk or a strikeout," he said. "Then we'd all know."

It was my turn to score at the Polo Grounds. So I bought a cowbell and a whistle and carried out Kenny's excellent suggestion.

It worked for about four games, until it proved inadequate.

I'd forget to blow the whistle or ring the bell, and there was no one to remind me until too late.

My favorite incident, which I've told many times but is too good not to tell again, involves the second no-hitter of Virgil Trucks.

It was 1952, and Yankee Stadium. Only twice before had a pitcher produced two no-hit games in the same season, Johnny Vander Meer in 1938 (in succession) and Allie Reynolds in 1951. Trucks had already pitched one in 1952.

In the fourth inning, Phil Rizzuto hit a two-hopper to short. Johnny Pesky bobbled it briefly, took his time, threw to first, and Phil beat it out.

John Drebinger, the official scorer, had his head down, writing, and looked up helplessly.

"Come on, John, call it. It's an error," said all us young punks surrounding him.

But John, in his 60s, didn't trust the new breed. Dan Daniel of the *New York World Telegram*, his contemporary and the most prolific baseball writer of all, sat by himself at the extreme right end of the box, next to the broadcasting both. John looked to Dan. Dan held up a forefinger, the time-honored sign for a hit.

"Base hit," ruled Drebby.

We screamed. "How can you call that a hit?"

Daniel had an explanation. "Ball stuck in the man's glove," he growled. "By tradition, that's a hit."

What tradition? One he just made up?

John decided to stick with Dan.

By now the Tigers were at bat. The hit was on the scoreboard and the crowd (a small one) had booed.

"Come on, Drebby, at least call down to the bench."

So he did. He got Pesky.

"No question it's a error," said Pesky. "I just blew it."

Now, any player might say that to protect his pitcher's no-hitter, but Pesky was an honorable man, and Drebby knew it, as we all did.

So he changed it, and the hit came off the board.

Trucks went on to complete the no-hitter.

The next day, in the *World Telegram*, Daniel had his story extolling the historic feat Trucks had performed, with appropriate praise.

And in it, he said something like "originally, *for some strange reason*, the official scorer called it a hit." My italics.

28

The Basketball
Scandals

Many people have dated the end of innocence in many ways. Some see it as the beginning of World War I in 1914. Others ascribe it to the market crash of 1929 which set off the Great Depression. I referred to it as 1941, the year of Pearl Harbor. But for the sports world I know, it was 1951, the year of the great basketball fix scandals.

It belongs in my book because it set in motion fundamental changes in the way sports were perceived, written about and conducted, at precisely the time television was laying the groundwork for also changing all those things (and more). It began the erosion of what had been a major, if tacit, element of the press box mystique: An idealistic view of sports, sportsmanship and our role in reporting it.

It is now universally accepted that the destruction of New York's twin towers on 9/11/01 "changed our lives forever." In a similar way, although in a smaller and far less significant context and more gradually, the scandals of 1951 had that effect on our sports scene. The change is much more a matter of mood and psyche than material conditions of our "way of life." But it is no less a dividing line.

Up to the end of World War II, attitudes toward sports, among participants, followers and in reportage, stressed certain virtues.

These included sportsmanship, which entails graciousness and modesty in winning, not needing to make excuses when losing, concern for "fairness," the concept of a "moral victory" when doing well against long odds, and recognition that "It's only a game."

A romanticized view of competition and athletes was not "sugar-coating" but an honestly held belief. It was what separated "sports" from "entertainment." In the formative stages of sports in the 19th century the healthful aspect of becoming "physically fit"—especially in games that could be played outdoors in fresh air—was constantly emphasized and still embedded in the spectators' minds through the first half of the 20th.

Readers and writers shared this outlook, and what was said and written consistently re-enforced it. That's one reason the "amateur ideal"—compete for the "love of the game" rather than for hope of reward—acquired and retained such power.

Of course, there were plenty of cynics expressing contrary views, openly or privately. And no one could deny that behavior in practice often fell far short of sportsmanship's ideals. In popular literature, which introduced children to sports, the standard plot in fiction had evil-doers trying to "fix" outcomes for gambling or other nefarious purposes, and upright heroes thwarting them. Happy endings were always the triumph of the honest. More than glory, goodness was its own reward.

Fixed games, for the sake of gamblers or to create excitement for bigger gates or for personal agendas, plagued all sports from the very beginning. Cheating in recruiting college athletes, and under-the-table payments to amateurs, were well developed by 1900 and perfected in the 1920s. But these were accepted as "exceptions." The aura of "pure sports" prevailed in the public imagination.

The world is not perfect, but what was largely unquestioned was the validity of the virtues as virtues.

Baseball had lived through fixes of the 1919 World Series; football had nipped a plot in the bud in the 1946 National Football League championship game. That many fights were fixed was taken for granted. People bet on horses but not on track meets, because "horses couldn't talk" and were presumably harder to bribe than runners. And basketball was always suspect because the nature of the game made manipulation so hard to distinguish from honest mistakes. But any fix—that is, guaranteeing to lose—required some degree of conspiracy to arrange and concerted effort to avoid detection.

Then, after World War II, two things changed.

The explosion of spectator sports (including college), the vast increase in audience and dollars generated, the immediate dissemination of results through radio, stimulated the betting interests of a much larger population.

And the point-spread became universal.

Betting had always been based on odds: 2 to 1, 7 to 5, 100 to 1. This was supposed to reflect the probability of an outcome, reflecting the opinion that one contestant was more likely to win. At 3 to 1, a bettor was risking a dollar to win three (that is, in addition to getting back the one put at risk). Betting against the odds, you risked three to win one. Who set the odds? The middleman booking the bet, the "bookie." He kept, say, 10 percent of each bet (the "vigorish") as his fee, so if he balanced his book he didn't care who won. It was the loser who paid off the winners. (So winners settled for 90 cents of the dollar, which was good enough.) An "even money" bet meant you risked one to win one.

Since the result was either-or, it was difficult to fine-tune the proper odds (which would move up or down as money came in for a forthcoming event). The difference between a 3-to-1 shot and a 4-to-1 shot put the bookie in some jeopardy if too much came in on one side, and setting odds like 3.229 to 4.003 wasn't practical.

But basketball, after the middle 1930s, had become higher scoring, with each team often reaching 50 points or more, and football scores which used to be 13-7 were starting to average 21-20.

Suppose you made the bet depend not simply on win or lose, but win or lose by what margin. A six-point favorite would have to win by more than six points to win the bet, while the underdog bettor would win his bet if his team lost but by less than six. And since exactly six would be a "push," meaning no bet, setting the price at 6-1/2 would eliminate all pushes.

A 3-to-1 favorite, theoretically, was likely to win three out of four times. But a 5-1/2-point favorite, if forecast accurately enough, would produced a balanced book almost every time, getting as many underdog supporters as favorites. And if it didn't, shifting the price to 6-1/2 or 4-1/2 was easy enough to do.

The points were an added attraction to the bettors, too. The satisfaction in betting rests on being able to "pick" the winner (I've out-smarted the universe). There's not much motive (except greed) to pick a 4-to-1 underdog, but that underdog may well lose by less than the predicted six (or 20!) points.

So point-spread betting spread like a virus throughout the world, and the epidemic has never slowed down. It didn't work well for lower-scoring games like baseball, hockey and soccer, but in basketball and football it took over completely.

But the consequence to a participant became entirely different.

Now, you didn't have to risk victory to "throw the game." You just had to win the game—your legitimate goal—by fewer points. Manipulating the final score had always been accepted. A coach would not "run up the score" against an inferior opponent or one soundly beaten; this was, in fact, considered "good sportsmanship." In baseball, a team leading 5-1 in the ninth inning gladly let a runner score from third while getting an out elsewhere, as a matter of elementary good sense. In hockey, a trailing team actually took out its goalie in the final minute, indifferent to the possibility of an open-net goal against it. The final score didn't matter.

So what crises of conscience or ethics would arise in letting a 12-point margin shrink to eight while you won another game? Especially in the mind of a 19-year-old who had been bribed out of high school to wear the uniform he now had on?

You didn't need all five of the basketball players to join the agreement. Two or three could handle it nicely—without detection. Just let a safely beaten loser score a bit more.

By 1939, the center of the basketball world was Madison Square Garden, with more than 20 double-headers a year. In 1938, the National Invitation Tournament, set up by the New York writers, produced a first credible national champion. (It was successful and so profitable that the embarrassed writers promptly turned running it over to the Garden and local college authorities.) The NCAA started its own championship the following year and soon had its final round being played at the Garden.

The proportion of betting interest was clearly visible and audible. A 10-point favorite might be leading by 11 with less than a minute to play, and the crowd would be going crazy. There was no doubt which team would win. But both sets of bettors had everything on the line to the final shot. For them, it was exciting entertainment divorced from victory.

The problem, of course, was that best-laid plans aren't *that* controllable. A team intending only to keep a score close might have a bad time and actually lose "the whole game."

And that started to happen.

Brooklyn College, a very minor member of the New York scene dominated by LIU, St. John's, NYU and CCNY, was caught fixing a game in 1945, but little attention was paid. It was seldom mentioned among us and we weren't even sure of the date.

So that canary had died but no one left the mine.

From 1949 on, however, the rumors intensified, and many of the more experienced writers became convinced "business was being done." Most, however, were like me: We shrugged it off as show-off cynicism and didn't want to contemplate something so foreign (and destructive) to our ingrained beliefs about romanticized sports. And the college and Garden officials wallowing in the glory, money and national reputations that were growing so fast had their heads in the sand even deeper that we did.

But no one was in a position to blow the whistle. You could believe crookedness was going on, and cite circumstantial evidence for suspicion, but you couldn't accuse. To write it would be libel, to say it slander.

Then, in January 1951, one Manhattan College player, Junius Kellogg, blew it open. Approached to shave points, he went to the authorities. Two of his more prominent teammates confessed.

The New York District Attorney set up an investigation and a grand jury, and by the time it was through—more than a year later—we learned that games had been fixed in 23 cities in 17 states with firm evidence against 32 players from seven colleges.

These included the double-champion City College team, which had won both NIT and NCAA tournaments in 1950, and the Bradley University team it had defeated in both finals; the Kentucky team that had been NCAA champion in 1949 and a major part of the U.S. Olympic team in 1948; and the Garden "host" teams of LIU and NYU.

On the record, of the 90 fixes discussed over a five-year period, 49 games were actually rigged.

No one doubted that this single investigation merely scratched the visible surface of a very large iceberg.

Since then, basketball scandals of lesser scope and impact have surfaced every few years. With hundreds of games every month in countless non-metropolitan locations on which point-betting lines were being widely circulated, the opportunity for undetected manipulation was endless. That 99 percent of the games are honest is true enough, but that one percent still means (1) a substantial number and (2) no way to tell which they are.

Life, of course, went on, but our psyches changed forever.

Suspicion was no longer mere cynicism. We could, and should, assume honest effort, but not be absolutely certain of it. Two great protections emerged. The bookies (including the legal ones in Nevada) were a first line of defense. Any major fix would involve enough money to unbalance the carefully calibrated point-difference price, and the game could be "taken off the boards" (no bets accepted), alerting everyone who cared. More to the point, as the money increased astronomically—in professional salaries, in gate, television and other receipts, in promoters' profit and invest-ment—players had less motivation for smaller fixes and more to lose if caught. And the rest of the sports establishment devoted more money, time, staff, attention and expertise to monitoring the integrity of their product.

For the sportswriter and the fan, and especially children, the climate gradually changed. Awareness that crookedness was possible had to be (and was) put aside consciously. In my own case, I went through the following phase:

Obviously, after the college scandals broke, there were constant rumors about the pros, whom I was covering on a daily basis. We used to keep our own play-by-play record, and were very aware of point spreads. Whenever I saw a favorite playing badly and trailing early, I'd make a note about a possible fix. When it turned out, over a period of several years, that the vast majority of these "suspicious" games wound up with the favorite beating the point spread any-how, I convinced myself that one couldn't distinguish honest from dishonest effort just by watching the action on the floor. (That's the problem coaches of the crooked teams had.) That didn't prove there was no funny business going on, but it proved that you couldn't tell—and shouldn't suspect—unless you had some external indication: Knowledge of money changing hands or conspiracy. Rumors of those were worth checking out, but assumptions weren't enough to question everything all the time.

So the transition began, over the span of a generation, to the frame of mind we have today and television's influence solidifies.

We thought of sports primarily as competition.

Now we see it as entertainment, and it calls itself that.

We experienced games as a special event to be seen or heard.

Now it's just another TV show.

We perceived stars as heroes for what they did.

Now we make stars celebrities just on name recognition.

Sports used to be a small business.

Now sports is a very large, conglomerate business.

We cared mainly about what took place on the field.

Now we're inundated with what happens off the field.

As kids, we played games by ourselves and chose up side.

Now kids are imprisoned in adult-run Little Leagues.

We had a strong sense of historical continuity.

Now only today counts, and last year is ancient history.

We wanted to win, but didn't consider losing a disgrace.

Now only No. 1 counts, and even No. 2 is demeaned.

We got knowledge actively, from reading and talking.

Now we get information, passively, from non-stop TV.

These aren't value judgments, just descriptions. It's a different time, a different world, a different culture, a different society, a different set of perceptions. Those were the norms then. These are the norms now.

And the Press Box has its own, but very small, place in the Now.

29

The Book Business

Before television, the medium of communication was the printed word, and radio was only the printed word made audible. Newspapers, pamphlets, signs, magazines and books were merely different ways of presenting the printed word, each with its own necessities.

Radio is immediate. Newspapers have several editions a day. Magazines are weekly or monthly. But every book, even if part of a series, is complete in itself, becomes available only months after it has been completely written, and is updated seldom and with difficulty, if at all.

Sports books are a genre. Histories and biographies differ from others in that field only by having sports subject matter. But "personality" books are built around a sports celebrity; the name on the cover sells it. And recreations or a recent event (the story of last year's World Series winner, or review of any season) have a notoriously short shelf life. With very few exceptions (like Roger Kahn's *Boys of Summer* and Jim Bouton's *Ball Four*) the only sports books that make real money have a big-name star as "author" (ghost-written usually) or an "as told to" format promising (if not always delivering) scandal.

Sports fiction, until after World War II, was almost exclusively aimed at young readers, influencing millions of imaginations but not taken seriously as literature. Since then, many serious novelists have used sports in adult contexts, with larger non-sports themes tied in. Success varies with the status of the novelist.

In the old days, few sportswriters could live off what newspapers paid them. They were prolific magazine writers for the many general magazines as well as for sports publications. A few wrote books. Bob Considine, one of the most prominent newspaper columnists of his time, told me once in the 1950s, "Don't ever write a book. Too much typing." Any real supplementary income depended on magazine articles and fiction.

Starting in the 1980s, the book publishing business began to change. Most publishers had been independent firms, with key decisions about what to publish made by their editors and owners. They carved out their own markets. Then, as more and more mergers took place, publishing houses became pieces of larger industrial conglomerates with all sorts of other business interests, and decision-making passed into committees of marketing executives and accountants.

Most sports books have always been what the publishing world calls "mid-list." Few have huge sale possibilities. As independent bookstores became fewer and larger chains became dominant, sales began to depend more and more on the distribution system, which involves wholesalers. The mid-list has been taking a beating on all subjects, especially books intended to have a longer shelf life than some hot and time-bound topic.

So sportswriters still produce books, but it's no way to make a living.

At the same time, the quality and quantity of serious sports literature, especially historical material, is at an all-time high. But books as a whole have less of an impact on the sports-reading public than they used to. As always, television overrides everything.

For myself, experience with a dozen different publishers enabled me to figure something out. My publisher has a vested interest in *not* selling my book.

Let's say a publisher chooses to put out 100 books in a year. He or she (or a committee) identifies 20 that could become "big sellers," involving movie rights, retail tie-ins and so forth. They can be pretty sure that 10 of the 20 will hit it big, even if they can't be sure which 10. So all promotional effort and money will be allocated to those 20, for whom large advances have been laid out to the celebrity author or subject.

The other 80 books, acquired for very small advances, are needed to keep the organization functioning (so that it can handle the hot 20). If they can come anywhere near breaking even on those 80, they'll have served their purpose. Each of those will then have a small first printing (based on the estimate of what it will sell without any promotional effort or advertising).

Now, in promoting the Big 20, the publisher, among other things, "buys" shelf space in the big chain stores, the way cereals buy shelf space in supermarkets.

Therefore, my mid-list book, already identified as capable of only a limited sale, is actually as much in competition with my publisher's Big 20 as any other publisher's books. Once the publisher has decided to give me whatever (modest) advance he does, he has no motive to try to sell more than his originally calculated return. The advance becomes the author's total return, whether or not the publisher recoups it.

So the Snoopy cartoon Charles Schulz produced really hit home. Snoopy has finally submitted his famous novel, starting "It was a dark and stormy night...." to a publisher and gets an acceptance letter. It says:

"We have decided to publish your book. We will print one copy. If we sell it, we will print more."

Then comes the follow-up.

"We printed one copy. It did not sell. Your book is now out of print."

On the other hand, writing a book, on sports or anything else, is highly satisfying in other respects, and most sportswriters try.

In a book, the author has total control of the words that appear. An editor can, and should, make suggestions, and a good one is of incalculable value. But you have the ultimate authority: They can't change anything without your agreement. To those of us who spend our lives having copy desks alter our copy (as they have the right to do) and magazine editors make our product fit their preconceived ideas, this is our chance to say what we want, the way we want, when we want, in our own voice. It's gratifying.

Then there is the special feeling one gets when the physical book can be held and looked through. You've done something that has a permanence your work for newspapers, magazines or even radio and television appearances can never have. It's yours alone.

Paul Muni, a great actor, complained that actors have nothing to show for their artistic effort. The stage performance—movies didn't count for him—however brilliant, ceased to exist as soon as it was over. But a painter, sculptor, composer or writer could always look at what he or she had produced, and display it to others. He envied that.

Books are the closest sportswriters come to creating an "artistic" product. And it's worth the effort, whatever the money.

But if you want real money, forget books. Get a TV show. Or a comic strip.

30

The Tribune Company

When I went to work for the *Peninsula Times Tribune*, it had just become part of an empire the *Chicago Tribune* was still expanding. It had television station WGN, a Chicago power and one of the first "superstations" to spread nationwide through cable. It owned the *New York Daily News*, the largest tabloid in the country. Its California newspaper branch consisted of the *Los Angeles News*, a much smaller paper in Escondido (San Diego area) and the new Peninsula property combining Palo Alto, Redwood City and half a dozen adjacent communities.

Back in New York, we had considered the *Chicago Tribune* a flag-ship of anti-Roosevelt reactionary preaching, but it had long since become a middle-of-the-road, less doctrinaire media conglomerate, concerned more with the rising price of its stock than with political affiliations.

In Palo Alto, however, it was seen as the great outsider, carpet-bagger, foreign invader and usurper of home rule, which had robbed us of our hometown *Palo Alto Times* and was trying to impose non-local views on our indigenous culture.

Redwood City felt the same way.

It was a bad rap, and silly on its face. The Tribune Company, in the 1970s, was not interested in micro-managing its far-flung elements, only in making them profitable. That David Burgin, the imported editor, was highly visible in town and no diplomat, stirred up more alienation. The paper he produced actually contained more local news than the *Palo Alto Times* and *Redwood City Tribune* had been providing, and also paid more attention to neighboring East Palo Alto, Mountain View, Sunnyvale and Los Altos. It had more and better features as well as some outstanding new talent. And nothing—I mean nothing—was being dictated from Chicago. Almost all the line editors, under Burgin, were still in place and giving their input every day.

But the resentment was there, and never fully overcome. After I was editor for two years, as Burgin's successor, I began to understand what the real problems were, and to see how they reflected changes in the newspaper business from coast to coast. These involved:

The cost of newsprint (the paper itself).

Advertising.

Delivery.

Technology.

Conflicting motivations in setting a business's mission.

Sports coverage, and the press box milieu, was impacted directly by the response to each of these altered equations.

Newsprint used to cost $50 a ton (in the 1960s or thereabouts, I think). By the 1980s it was $500 a ton.

At the lower price, it was not a make-or-break element in deciding how many pages and how many copies to produce. The benefits of more space and greater circulation made up for the incremental extra cost.

At 10 times that amount, it became a major determinant of all other basic decisions. If space itself is that costly, you quickly reach a point where more editorial material, and even some advertising, can't pay for itself. So as content becomes smaller and more selective, the need to guess right about what to exclude becomes harder, and the consequences of guessing wrong (fewer satisfied readers) become more serious.

Example: When I was editor of the *Peninsula Times Tribune*, we found we could save $150,000 a year by trimming one-eighth of an inch off the margin of each page, totally unnoticeable to anyone and without affecting any of the type. We couldn't trim more than a eighth because that's all the flexibility our presses had.

In sports, less space—in metropolitan papers—means less (or no) coverage of the second-level activities: High schools, local colleges, club sports, local golf and tennis tournaments, and features related to them. At the same time, the major sports, college and professional, have expanded enormously in quantity and generated more attention through television. The result is over-emphasis on the majors, a multiplicity of columnists over straight news, greater use of wire copy from out of town, and the loss of readers whose concern goes beyond the majors to their local activities.

That, in turn, changes the nature of the staff: More chiefs (columnists and editors), fewer Indians (plain reporters), as our then politically-incorrect metaphor used to put it.

Advertising is, and always has been, the backbone of newspaper finances. You can't cover the cost of production by the price you charge the reader—two or three cents in the 1930s, then five, 10 and 25—any more than an opera house or concert hall or museum can live off just admission prices, however high, without additional contributors and subsidizers. Whatever money a book brings in depends on the public's reaction to its content, but newspapers and magazines rely primarily on advertising revenue, and radio and television even more so.

The key to newspaper advertising was that it was cheap, relative to its targeted audience, from classified through display ads. When radio and television began competing for the larger regional and national accounts, newspapers were hit hard. When the cost of newsprint (and other expenses) went skyward, all the old equations went out the window.

If space for non-paying editorial matter and profitable advertising is split 50-50, the content-oriented minds—publisher and top editors—are in control. When it becomes 40-60, as was considered proper in the 1980s, the accountants and salesmen have a bigger say, but the "wall" between editorial decisions and business decisions stays intact. But by the 1990s, that wall had been breached if not totally torn down. Content favorable to, or at least interesting to, key advertisers got more consideration, unfavorable content less.

Stories that used to be chosen by editors' judgment—wise or foolish—now must also pass tests of their effect on key advertisers, reader taste as defined by professional marketers using polls and focus groups, imitation of agendas set by television, new delivery problems.

Circulation (in print) and ratings (in radio-television) determine how much can be charged for the ads. But circulation depends on ability to deliver the paper, while airwave transmission requires only a receiver in the hands of the consumer. When newsprint and gasoline (for trucks) prices reach a certain level, more circulation can mean less profit, while more receivers add zero to the cost of airwave or cable transmission.

Newspapers can be delivered to a home or office, or to newsstands, and only at certain times of day. Morning papers have to be on the doorstep or newsstand well before 8 a.m., afternoon paper editions no later than the time offices let out. Trucks take them from the printing plant to rail terminals (for outer areas), newsstands and central points for home delivery distribution.

Starting in the 1960s, conditions in large cities changed. Middle-class moves to the suburbs cut into home delivery. Traffic made it impossible to service enough corner newsstands with afternoon editions. And corner newsstands themselves began disappearing as new office buildings placed their newsstands inside the lobby, inaccessible to dropped-off bundles.

Traffic alone was the death knell for afternoon papers in large cities, cutting in half (or more) the number of papers in those locations. That fewer daytime sports results and a later close of the stock market killed the main attraction of final-edition afternoon papers aggravated the problem. A nationwide pattern emerged of only morning papers in the cities, mostly afternoon papers (with local emphasis) in the suburbs.

And, of course, late afternoon and early evening radio-television delivered up-to-the-minute news anyhow. Advertising dollars moved there.

New technology also had unforeseen and unintended consequence for newspaper content. Replacing paper, typewriters, lead type and photo-engraving with computer terminals, photo-offset paste-up pages and modernized presses meant large-scale, long-run capital investments which further altered financial equations distorted by newsprint and gasoline prices. Reporters, ad salesmen, linotype operators and other backroom activities of putting out a daily paper are people-intensive. The whole point of using the new technology is to shift person-tasks to machines.

One consequence is less redundancy. The story that used to go from reporter-writer to rewrite man or telegrapher, to copyreader, to head of desk, to typesetter, to proof-reader before actually getting on the press to reach a reader, was now going from writer to one copy-editor to page paste-up, period. All along the line, that's less scrutiny to catch mistakes.

Another was the character of personnel. People have different talents and abilities. Many writers are careless copy-readers, and it's difficult for any writer to notice his own mistakes, even on re-reading, because his mind knows what he intended. Many of the best copy-readers are pedestrian writers. Some excellent reporters, who can dig up facts and information, are so-so writers whose stuff is refined by rewrite and desk. The qualities that make a fine reporter, a fine writer, a meticulous copy-editor, a fast processor of handling a story are not often found in the same individual.

In content-oriented journalism, you seek out the reportorial and writing talents, the editorial talents and the efficient processing talents separately and assign them accordingly. In efficient, production-oriented journalism, you settle on those most comfortable with manipulating computer keyboards and commands, rather than on more brilliant writers and reporters who are slower and clumsier in handling the technology.

A major editorial function—think it through before you publish—is adulterated, if not completely lost. Fewer people doing more tasks faster don't improve a product based on the credibility of its accuracy. Eventually, your editorial staff has a mix of people more attuned to production needs than content quality—not on purpose, but because that's how it works out.

All this I learned as an editor—who never "edits," but "manages" full-time. What I learned in weekly (or almost daily) "planning meetings" was this: The Tribune Company's underlying motives were not concerned with "putting out the best paper we can while making a decent profit," but with the profit that could be generated by the Tribune Company as a whole and especially its publicly-traded stock. What stock analysts thought and recommended, quarter by quarter, was more important than what any segment of readers or listeners actually told us—or what we thought ourselves.

The top brass in Chicago was absolutely right. That was properly their top concern and obligation. A tiny appendage like the *Peninsula Times Tribune* made no sense, even if it were consistently in the black (which it could never be without more employees and new presses). At maximum profitability it could never make a significant contribution to the Tribune Company's bottom line. By its mere existence as an expense, it's seen as a negative by the analysts (as the much larger *New York Daily News* was, and sold off). In Palo Alto, the land itself was worth more that the whole enterprise. Closing it down was correct. That no local buyer appeared to take it over was another question, but not Chicago's.

The lesson is this: In sports (baseball is the best example), using a team as a means of promoting other products of the parent company is bad for the team if good for the corporation. (See Cubs, Dodgers.) And it is bad for newspapers when they become appendages of larger agendas. And when the sports section becomes only an appendage of that appendage, the nature of sports writing—and the press box—are changed forever.

31

Spring Training

No civilization that created baseball spring training—I once wrote in *The Sporting News*—can be all bad.

It is a peculiar institution, not matched by any other sport's training regime. And it is the reward a beat baseball writer gets for the seven months of travel (remember Chapter 4?).

It takes place in Florida and Arizona, in communities dedicated to winter-time resorts, replete with beaches, swimming pools, sunshine and recreation facilities—while back home winter is still going full blast. For the participant, it's all rehearsal with nothing at stake going into the record. For observers, mostly tourists drawn to it, the practice games have all the trappings of the baseball they love, without the tension that comes with "losing." And almost all of it, half a century after this became uncommon during the regular season, takes place in the daytime, leaving evenings free for "real life" according to one's taste.

In baseball, Florida is, as I also wrote, not a geographical location but a state of mind. Arizona too.

Look through the dozens of excellent biographies, team histories and other baseball books published in the last 70 years, laden with anecdotes, and you'll find a disproportionate number of the best funny stories devoted to spring training incidents. For veteran players (and umpires), the atmosphere is relaxed. For youngsters and others not secure about the positions they're trying to gain, competitive pressure exists, but isn't as intense as in the games that count. For all the auxiliaries—club personnel, media people, various officials—there's a high degree of personal interaction, established familiarity and tension-free socializing. Many bring their families for what amounts to a six-week semi-vacation, a longer stretch of togetherness than they'll ever have during the season.

My first taste of his baseball Eden was as an outsider. In 1935, when I was 11, my mother and I spent three weeks in Miami Beach while my father was on a trip to Europe. We stayed in a boarding house three blocks from Flamingo Park, where the Giants were training, and I was there every day. In 1939, when I was 15, we did the same at St. Petersburg, where both the Yankees and the Cardinals trained. Every morning I could walk over to Huggins Field, where the Yankees practiced; every afternoon, I could walk in the opposite direction to the ballpark both teams used, alternately, for their exhibition games. A highlight I remember is a day the Cardinals entertained the Dodgers, who brought in a non-roster rookie named Pete Reiser, of whom we'd never heard. He hit a home run over the left-field fence right-handed, and then another over the right-field fence left-handed. When he reached Brooklyn the next year, everyone found out who he was, but I was in on the ground floor.

At the *Herald Tribune*, as the baseball swing man, I never went to spring training; the three "regular" writers did that. At the *Post*, my baseball and basketball beat assignments overlapped, and while the World Series ended before the NBA season began, the NBA playoffs kept me north until spring training ended.

In 1962, however, my turn came up. Since 1958, when the Dodgers and Giants went to California, Lenny Shecter and I had shared the Yankee beat, with him taking spring training. But now the Mets had come into being, and two training camps had to be covered. He went to St. Petersburg, where the Mets had taken over Huggins Field (eventually renamed Stengel-Huggins Field), while the Yankees moved across Florida to Fort Lauderdale, where a new ball park had been built for them. With the Knicks finishing last for the fifth time in six years and the NBA finals not coming up until April, I could be sent down to them.

The Yankees' headquarters was a beach-front hotel called the Yankee Clipper, shaped roughly like an old sailing ship. It had an auxiliary motel across the street where overflow was housed. I checked in around midnight, and the next morning found its street-side swimming pool being used by some other writers and mostly younger players. Around 10 a.m. we were lolling about in the pool, since exhibitions hadn't begun and the workout would be in the afternoon.

Now a Cadillac convertible pulls up alongside the pool, containing Whitey Ford and Roger Maris. Maris, of course, has broken Babe Ruth's record by hitting 61 homers in 1961, and the hot item is his holdout. He wants a 100 percent raise to $75,000. Leaning over the fence, with them in the car, we get the word from Roger. Agreement has been reached and he'll sign his contract today.

At 10 a.m., the *Post* still has two or three editions to go during the afternoon. I run back to my room, call in this big news story, which has been dropped in my lap without my going after it. In effect, my day's work is done, and the *Post* has the story sooner (by minutes, anyhow) than any other New York paper.

After giving the rewrite man what I have, Ike Gellis, my boss, gets on the phone, saying how pleased he is.

"One more thing, Ike," I tell him. "You can take basketball and shove it."

I didn't miss any spring trainings from then on.

Fort Lauderdale was to St. Petersburg like Paris or London would be to some venerable health spa in Bavaria. Only an hour north of Miami Beach, Fort Lauderdale had nightlife, a couple of accessible race tracks, a beach favored by college students from all over the country for spring break shenanigans, a sufficient collection of bars and restaurants, and marinas for countless yachts. It was the territory of Dan Topping, the Yankee owner who had been described for 20 years as a "man about town" and "millionaire sportsman." St. Pete was like an extended retirement home, lovely and with its own enthusiasms, where 80-year-olds played softball as Kids and Kats, not "swinging" in any sense. Most of its transplanted residents and tourists came from the Midwest rather than from New York or the Boston-Washington corridor.

So when the newborn Mets came over to play the lordly Yankees, we decided to rub it in. Fort Lauderdale hospitality knew no bounds for the famous World Champions. The new ballpark was the most modern and impressive in Florida, with a roomy press box, catered every day by a local restaurant that laid out gourmet fare and plenty of liquid refreshment. Word of our unprecedented sumptuousness had been fed our Met colleagues, who felt we must have been exaggerating.

But we weren't, and Bob Fishel, the Yankee publicity man, made sure the day they visited would be extra lavish. The catering included half a dozen showgirl-caliber waitresses dressed in hula skirts, hovering over your seat and refilling your glass with Mai Tai cocktails every inning. The buffet at the back of the box was even more gourmet quality than usual. Both the physical facilities and social atmosphere were something baseball writers had never been exposed to before.

A week later, we went over to St. Pete, where the old Al Lang Field press box was a couple of segregated rows at the top of the stands along first base. For about two innings, everything was normally modest.

Then the hostesses showed up: Three pleasant ladies in their 60s, dressed in Mother Hubbards, dispensing peanuts, hot dogs and soft drinks, and urging us to "eat, eat."

We had to admit the Mets won that exchange. One-upmanship can take many forms.

So spring training is a sort of paradise.

Other teams had their own adventures. Wally Moon, when he was a rookie with the Cardinals (in St. Pete), roomed with Jackie Brandt, a fellow rookie outfielder. One night, about 11 p.m., a restless Brandt said:

"Lets go out and get some Howard Johnson ice cream."

Howard Johnson's was famous for offering 28 flavors.

"We can get ice cream downstairs," said Wally.

"No, it's got to be Howard Johnson's," insisted Brandt.

"There's none around here."

"We'll find one. Let's go."

So they got a car and started driving around, got lost, cruised for over an hour (breaking whatever curfew may have existed). Finally they found a Howard Johnson's somewhere far inland in an unidentified town, long after midnight, not sure how they would find their way back. But at least it had Howard Johnson's unique menu.

"What'll you have?" asked the waitress, while Moon was trying to decide which of the 28 exotic flavors to choose.

"Vanilla," said Brandt.

Wally was ready to kill him.

But during spring training, almost anything can be forgiven.

It's different today, still marvelous, but more complicated. Every camp has new ballparks, and they sell out most games in a more affluent age geared to tourism. The informal contact with players isn't as easy for non-privileged fans, who have to order tickets far in advance. The relationship between players and writers is not easy, period. Players don't get salaries during spring training, but with average salaries of $2 million, live as they like. Stars don't stay at a headquarters hotel, and access to them in the ballpark isn't as automatic as it was. And, of course, the TV people get priority.

Nevertheless, spring training is baseball's special delight. Football, basketball and hockey pre-season training have the aura of a Marine boot camp. Baseball's is a sojourn on the Riviera. Which would you choose?

Part Five

People

32

Bettors

Of all the people who read sports pages regularly, none do so more thoroughly than those who bet. Bettors have also always been the prime customers for tickets, and the spectator sports industry would never have developed without their special interest.

But bettors come in many varieties. Gambling can be a serious, obsessive sickness, much like alcoholism, with devastating consequences. But just as not everyone who drinks (even a lot) becomes an alcoholic, not everyone who bets becomes addicted. What can be called "casual bettors" greatly outnumber the "problem" gamblers. They use their bets—whose size reflects their resources—to establish a rooting interest for each particular event. The tradition of betting on election results, horse races, contests of any sort and, of course, stocks and bonds, was fully developed in American culture well before the 1800s, and was the fertile soil in which spectator sports could grow.

All this was before state lotteries, casinos (which once were legal everywhere) beyond Nevada and Atlantic City, church bingo games and internet communication. Gambling on every level is now not merely acceptable but officially sanctioned. Sports are no longer as unique an outlet for it as they once were.

The lowest level of this activity is the person-to-person private bet. For more systematized activities, bookmakers (stock brokers) are needed. Someone has to "hold" the wager and pay off the winner with the loser's money. In lotteries, it's the state.

So sports news, however transmitted, must include full awareness that most of its readers want to know the betting odds of the event they're interested in, both before and after it takes place. No matter how high a moral ground any publication wants to take, in practice competition and betting can not be separated and the combination cannot be ignored.

Do many sportswriters bet? Sure, in about the same proportion as the total sports-following population. After all, the whole psychic attraction of non-lottery betting is *not* hope of profit. It's the feeling that you've out-guessed the universe because you're smart enough to have figured something out. To do that, you have to gather information about the contestants, and that's what the sports section provides.

As it happens, I never did bet on sports; not because of any principle but because I dislike losing much more than I enjoy winning (which is why I don't play cards). But at a racetrack, where betting is the whole point, I enjoy it as much as anyone does.

Does it affect a reporter's "objectivity?" Sometimes, on a case-by-case basis, but generally no. Just as we assume (rightly or not) that the drama critic is giving his honest opinion whether or not he likes the producer, we can assume that the writer or broadcaster is telling us what actually happened whether or not he wanted one side to win.

In our crowd, the most notorious consistent loser was Louis Effrat, of *The New York Times*. It's not that he bet that much more (or more often) than many others, but that he lost so often, and in unusual ways.

Once a horse he bet on dropped dead in the home stretch after leading.

"Did you have him to win, place or show?" Louie was asked.

"I bet him to *live*," cried Louie.

His apparently pre-ordained misfortunes were known to all. At Roosevelt Raceway, Dick Young met him in the passageway to the press box just as the trotters were following the lead car to the starting line.

"Whatcha got?" asked Dick.

"No. 5," said Louie.

Dick looked at his own tickets, which were also on No. 5.

"Well," said Dick, "that beats me"—and tore up his tickets right there, before the racers even crossed the starting line.

He was right.

It got to the point that whenever the Knicks had a big lead starting the fourth quarter, and Louie, at courtside, started writing his story to get a jump on his deadline, we yelled at him to stop. Sure enough, the Knicks would blow the lead and the game would wind up in overtime or with a Knicks loss.

My favorite Effrat story zeroes in on the confirmed bettor's passion for figuring out who the winner *ought* to be, entirely apart from the money involved. I got it from Sid Gray, Louie's buddy since childhood.

Louie's father, a union official, was an inveterate horse player, which is how Louie got the bug, and Louie was his favorite child. When Louie was about 15, he once lost 20 dollars betting on a horse. In the 1920s, that was a lot of money.

Shame-faced, he had to confess.

For the first and only time his father actually slapped him.

"How could you do that?" his father shouted. "Don't you have any sense? You'll be a bum. You'll wreck your life. How could you be that stupid?"

"But Pop,"—Louie started.

"I don't want to hear any excuses."

"But Pop"—

"No explanations, no excuses! You'll be a bum!"

"But Pop"—

"All right, all right. What is it?"

"Pop, you had to have seen this horse. He was coming down in class, he had won three in a row, he had the best jockey and the best trainer on the track, he had beaten all the other horses before, and he was going off at 10 to 1! He just couldn't lose!"

His father was outraged.

"You find a horse like that," he yelled, "and you don't tell *your own father*?"

33

Readers

Newspaper readers, before television, meant everyone. Unlike radio, television and movies, which try to capture the largest possible audience for the particular product on the air or screen at any given moment, papers have a different aim. A paper tries to be all things to all people by presenting a thousand different items of varying degrees of interest (including none) to as many readers as possible, each of whom chooses which item to read. Radio, television and the movies serve you the only dish they have, one at a time; newspapers spread before you the largest buffet they can put together.

I was taught that my obligation to the reader was not to "catch" his or her attention, but to deliver the information the reader had already decided to want. The headline did the "catching," but my story had to "satisfy." Otherwise, the reader would go on to something else, even faster and easier than a clicker changes channels.

The advertiser, therefore, counted on readers turning pages where the ad might "catch" someone's eye. In radio and television, the ad was imprisoned in the specific program, and leaving (or ignoring) the program reduced the ad's value to zero.

Therefore, the readers of any newspaper story contained a larger segment of those who knew a great deal about the subject. Many might be simply curious, but those who had a prior interest in that event would go out of their way to find the story—and recognize inadequacies.

This was truer in sports than in any other section, which is why the paper had sections, to make it easier to find. So the prime directive—get it right—was tested most thoroughly.

When giving talks to journalism groups, I always tweaked the city-side people by saying sportswriters had to be *more* accurate than "serious" reporters because their readers were so knowledgeable.

"If you cover a fire," I'd say, "and you get the homeowner's name wrong—John instead of Joe—only his immediate acquaintances will notice, and it won't change the sense of the story anyhow. But if you get one digit of Joe DiMaggio's batting average wrong, the letter writers will descend on you and your editor. For instance, if I write that Steve Garvey is a right-handed hitter when actually he's a left-handed hitter, every baseball fan will know I'm wrong."

Sure enough, someone in the audience will take the bait and call out, "but Garvey *is* a right-handed hitter!"

So I can smile and say. "That's what I mean."

Our training was, tell what happened and get it right.

Tell it attractively if you can, judge correctly the most significant aspect of it, explain what has to be explained, but tell what happened.

Today the orientation of your editor is different. Your story must "entertain," catch and keep the interest of the casual rather than the involved reader, and do so using "quotes." (The theory is that the "involved" reader is a captive audience anyhow.) Readers, naturally, become conditioned to expect that. It's a self-fulfilling circular process, in which "what happened" is merely grist for the entertainment mill. That, of course, is the television approach, which follows the laws of drama, and newspapers have bought into it.

Is that inevitable in a television age? Yes. Bosses as well as workers watch television more than they read, and have since childhood. Is it good for newspapers? Evidently not, since so many newspapers have died. But for surviving papers with local monopolies, it produces greater profits and becomes part of the "news media" homogenization.

In such a world, the press box neither needs, nor can have, the glamour it once possessed.

Reader attitudes are different too. Allowing for all sorts of tastes and prejudices, newspapers used to be considered more credible (justifiably or not). If it was "in the papers" it was probably so. (When Will Rogers used to say, "all I know is what I read in the papers," he was calling attention to a limitation everyone could identify with.) Readers chose among many papers the ones that fit their preferences, but accepted its "news" as valid.

Now, after decades of high-powered public relations "spin" and advertiser-dominated airwaves, readers are more partisan. As editor in the 1980s, I was inundated with two general complaints. One was the result of our aging population. Readers would insist, despite all denials and tangible proofs, that we were making the type smaller.

But the other was a serious cultural change. Readers would object to news stories—not columns or editorials, but news stories—that didn't reflect their own partisan views, or presented (to them) objectionable ones. Their concern was what "others" might conclude from the story, not what they themselves thought. They saw the paper as an "opinion maker" for what they approved of or disapproved of, not a "source" for their own opinion. The paper, to them, was merely a megaphone. They didn't want it to shout, or even hint at, what they opposed. They wanted it to be a cheerleader for their side.

In case after case, what they object to isn't actually in the story, explicitly or even indirectly. They read into it their own implications and don't want "others" to be misled in this way. They want their own views reinforced. If objectivity was ever a virtue, it has become outmoded.

34

Editors

The sports editor today is a mid-level executive of a special section very much under the thumb of higher-ranking editors, marketers and the "human resources" department. In the heyday of the press box, he (always a he) was a more important figure.

He had a freer hand in hiring and firing.

He made assignments with less concern for personal preferences of the assignee.

He had a greater say in exactly how the section was to look, what its content priorities would be, its style of writing and presentation, and what had to be included and excluded.

He was a much more visible personage on the sports and social scene, often a columnist himself, a prime concern of every promoter and his public relations machinery.

And he was, above all, a ticket broker.

Press credentials and complimentary tickets—"comps"—were the currency of exchange, a trading of access for space. Reception and distribution of these were the sports editor's sole province.

Remember what we pointed out about the power of a free drink or a free ticket in less universally prosperous times, when such favors were not considered an ethical issue? Well, tickets were the medium through which such power was exercised, and for big events, became the sports editor's biggest headache.

The comps were used routinely for in-house rewards—to key printers, pressmen, deskmen and so forth. Higher newspaper brass, of course, got preference. Then there were the demands of family, friends and privileged acquaintances (like your butcher, apartment house superintendent or car dealer), not only of the editor himself but of his main columnists, beat writers and closest inside assistants. (Your byline on major events made you a target for such requests, and your editor understood that.)

From the promoter's point of view, comps cost nothing because he rarely sold all his seats anyhow, extra bodies were welcome, and recipients of freebies spent money at the concession stands and tended to become ticket buyers at other times.

But when it came to the World Series, a championship fight, a big college football game or Madison Square Garden basketball and hockey, the sports editor was faced with endless pressure. Whom to accommodate? Who was a must? Who could be safely denied? How could he get some more?

Credentials, of course, were pretty much self-defined by the assignments, but there was always a gray area of favoritism, too. But comps were a matter of total discretion, and the demand never let up.

Today's sports editor still has that problem, but to a much smaller degree. There aren't as many comps circulated (because paid attendance is bigger) and there are ethical issues raised, especially by non-recipients.

And the sports editor has less command of his writing staff, just as the manager or coach has less command of his players. Stars (in any field) make more money than their bosses and have their own pipelines to higher brass. Radio and television exposure, when a writer gets it, provides much more independence and leverage than even star writers used to have. The paper puts a premium on celebrity, to which television appearances raise a mere writer, just as we now cater to celebrity for celebrity's sake in all aspects of our culture.

Editors, once the shapers of a paper's sports news, are now just functionaries in a larger enterprise—hard-working, proficient, essential and honorable, but only functionaries nevertheless.

35

Coaches and Managers

Like editors, today's major league managers and head coaches are only department heads, not a top boss.

When professional baseball was starting up in the 19th century, the team's head was called the "manager" because he actually managed all "club" activities: Making schedules, keeping books, presiding over the dinners, organizing the team. The smaller-scale tactical and strategic in-game decisions were left to the "captain," a player he appointed.

Once club owners took control—the great innovation of 1876—the playing portion of the business became the full-time concern of the manager, with the owner taking responsibility for schedule and finances. But the manager remained the chief force in finding, hiring, evaluating, training and commanding the players, absorbing the "captain" role.

In other team sports, the term "head coach," originating in college football, was applied to exactly the same function, while the school administration (or a semi-independent "athletic association") arranged schedules and paid bills. Colleges hired or appointed a "business manager" who evolved into an "athletic director," while professional teams acquired a "general manager" for front office duties, reporting directly to the owner. Procurement of players through trades, purchase, minor league development or recruitment became his province.

As late as the 1960s in baseball, the "field manager"—head

coach—often had a great deal of autonomy, and influence over a player's salary. By the 1970s, in all four major sports, the line between general manager and coach was clearly drawn. In big-time college football and basketball, the charismatic head coach remains more powerful than the athletic director, but their specialized duties are distinct.

Therefore, in the old glory-of-the-press-box days, a writer needed no higher contact in the club hierarchy for reliable information. With daily contact in a less formal and less crowded milieu, the mutual understanding and even trust (to a degree) between manager-coach and the experienced beat man or columnist was considerable, and even sports editors were often in evidence. In a more relaxed atmosphere, the manager or head coach knew that his "press" contacts were essential to his public relations function. The press knew its questions about squad make-up, salary squabbles, judgment about players and future plans were within the capacity of the manager and coach to answer as fully as he chose.

Informality was the key. Right up to game time, you could seek out the manager in his office or the dugout, or around the batting cage, for one-on-one conversation, or with only a couple of other people (media or players). Immediately after a game, you entered the clubhouse and went to anyone you wanted to see, not (automatically) the manager. Afterwards, as often as not, he'd stop by the press room for a drink. On the road, traveling with the club, everyone was equally accessible and most managers had a rule: The bar in the hotel was their territory, for relaxing and entertaining, and players were expected to go elsewhere. Writers weren't, and a lot of talking got done in the hotel bar.

Football coaches were less available and less forthcoming, except to a few favored insiders, but you didn't see them as much anyhow. But basketball and hockey coaches, in the pros, were even more intimate with traveling writers than in baseball, since the groups were so much smaller and the social status of the sport much less.

Some random examples:

Houston, 1965. The Mets are playing their first game in the Astrodome, and blow a 2-1 lead in the bottom of the ninth. Casey Stengel has started the inning by putting Billy Cowens in center to strengthen the defense—and he breaks the wrong way to allow a lead-off double. Eventually a reliever walks in the tying run and

Eddie Kasko, with two out and the bases loaded, lifts a high fly to left. Joe Christophers circles around it and it falls behind him, well short of the fence. Game over.

It's after midnight and I'm late returning the hotel. The lobby is on the second floor. As the escalator brings me into view, Stengel is on a couch, facing it, in an otherwise empty lobby. As I approach, hoping to nod good night with no wish to prolong any unhappy thoughts, he speaks to me.

"Ask me why I didn't change the left fielder," he says. And he goes on for about 15 minutes discussing the pros and cons. He simply needed to vent his frustration to somebody.

Yankee Stadium press room, 1967. The famous Yankees have gone down the tubes, last in 1966 after 13 pennants in 15 years through 1964. Ralph Houk has returned to managing, and the team is doing no better. On an off-day in late May, I write a story about the low batting averages of several key players over the last year and a half, raising the question: When does it stop being a "slump" and become their (unfortunately) normal form?

Houk, whose religion is sticking up for his players, is seething, but we've been on great terms for too many years for him to complain. Weeks go by. Now Mantle hits an important home run—maybe his 522nd, passing Ted Williams, or something like that—in the first game of a double-header. We're not allowed in the clubhouse between games, but everyone has to get something from Mantle. There's a shouting match at the door, and I (as chapter chairman) insist, "Get Houk to let Mantle come out here and talk to us." That's done.

After the second game, Houk and the coaches and some of us are relaxing in the press room, having a spirited discussion about the necessity for between-games access to players. It's heating up.

Finally, Houk turns on me.

"And you and your lousy statistics," he yells. "You helped ruin my players' confidence!"

That story had been bugging him for months.

Fort Wayne, Ind., circa 1956. Joe Lapchick, as Knick coach, is by far the most distinguished member and public relations asset of the 10-year-old National Basketball Association, struggling for recognition. The general manager of the Fort Wayne Pistons tells him they'll have a big testimonial dinner for him on our first trip there in December. Details to come later.

It is now December and details have not been made clear, but we're all looking forward to this event on an otherwise unexciting Sunday evening in Fort Wayne. We're hanging around Lapchick's room, four or five writers and broadcaster Marty Glickman, awaiting instructions.

Finally, the GM shows up, all smiles. He has a bottle of whiskey and pours a drink for everyone. He tells Lapchick how important he is, how honored Fort Wayne is to have him there, empties the bottle with another round—and leaves.

That was it. That was the "testimonial dinner."

I can't visualize any of those things happening today. We're chased off the field and out of the clubhouse 45 minutes before game time, kept out for 10 minutes after the game, funneled through the manager's office en masse, and have a private conversation only by appointment. It's a different climate in a different world.

Dealing with general managers was also important, but not as frequent or as intimate, and unfettered access to ownership was rare.

As club bureaucracies grew, internal balances changed. The general manager became the owner's chief point of daily contact, standing between the field manager and the owner. A farm director, the whole scouting system, and the greatly expanded public relations, marketing and ticket departments all had their own turf to protect, and they reported to the general manager. Each department saw the field manager more as a resource to be used for their concerns than as a boss to be blindly obeyed. He couldn't be alienated and he had to be catered to, but he wasn't the one giving them their ultimate orders.

The manager and general manager had an authentic conflict of interest. The field manager's job was to win games, today, this month, this year. The general manager's was the long-range development of roster strength within his owner's budgetary boundaries. Their "needs," in term of player evaluation, often diverged.

At the same time, specialization increased. A baseball manager used to have four coaches, all chosen by him. A head football coach had perhaps three or four assistants before unlimited substitution separated offense from defense, and maybe six or seven after that. But in the 21st century, assistant coaches, computer specialists, assistant trainers, strength and conditioning experts are part of the field manager's support system, and the front-office force has 100 or more people instead of a dozen. Internal politics blossom.

Both the baseball manager and the head coach must delegate to assistants many of their responsibilities, and they don't get to choose all the assistants. They must devote much more time and effort to the public relations aspect of their jobs, and less to actual instruction and leadership of their players in pre-game preparation. They remain fully in charge, in the old sense, only once the game starts. Before and after, they face the expanded demands of the media (each television program needs its own exclusive access), and of interacting with luxury box and advertising people for promotional purposes. They study far more videotape and statistical printouts than were ever before available. Their opportunities to relax and to simply contemplate are much fewer than they used to be.

And, like the sports editors, they have to deal with ticket requests from family, friends and business associates. When seats were far more plentiful than customers, as was the case in the old days except for rare occasions, this was easy. Since sellouts (at high prices) became common, satisfying demand for comps becomes tricky and time-consuming.

All this has changed the relationship between coaches and press box regulars.

For the writer or broadcaster, good relations with the field manager or head coach remain a must. He must rely on your honest reporting, and you have to rely on him steering you straight. In the old days, the publicity man was the beat writer's colleague and facilitator, but not the "gatekeeper" of access to the manager; the press credential assured that. (Originally, publicity was a side duty of the road secretary; after World War II, P.R. became professionalized but was vested in one man, one assistant and a secretary.)

Today's P.R. departments have many functions; servicing the press box is only one and not the most important. Whoever heads it doesn't have the time or opportunity to be a buddy of the writers they way it used to be the in the 1950s and 1960s, and the specialized duties of his several (always underpaid) assistants bury them under other tasks. At the same time, the operation of the press, control of credentials and access by appointment is entirely under P.R. control. All this is understandable and reasonable in view of the larger number of media and other people involved, and security concerns. But it has also added to a drastically different relationship between media and players. Players see media people as hunters, with themselves the prey. Writers and those broadcasters who are not rights holders see the players as hostile and evasive, and not eager to have teammates think they are too accommodating to "the enemy."

And so, in an odd form of reversal, managers tend to be kinder to the media than many of their players.

Every manager or coach, of course, is different, true to his own personality. To younger writers, they have a teacher–pupil relationship; to writers of their own generation, they develop differing degrees of trust, antagonism, respect or contempt, depending on their mutual experiences. And they perfect their own tricks.

Casey Stengel's impenetrable monologues were a purposeful morass in which nuggets of wisdom were buried, but he didn't worry too much about people's feelings. "You're full of shit and I'll tell you why," as one of his standard rejoinders.

Herman Franks, devoted to presenting a gruff exterior to those he didn't know well, started every post-game conference with "What the hell kind of a question is *that*?," no matter how mild the question was (like who's tomorrow's pitcher?). He just wanted to set the tone.

Birdie Tebbetts, who managed in Cincinnati, Milwaukee and Cleveland, liked to tell a story he insisted really happened. Succeeding a previous manager, he found three envelopes in the desk. The first was to be opened the first time things went bad. The note said: "Blame it on me. Next time open the second envelope." The second said, "Blame it on the players." The third was for the third crisis. It said, "Prepare three envelopes." Charlie Dressen, who managed four different teams, used the same story.

Wes Westrum's reaction to every close game involving his Mets, win or lose, with a sigh or a smile, was: "Well, another cliff-dweller."

Today's managers, no matter how many strong and honest relationships they establish with some media people they have come to trust, are too aware and well-trained to risk saying the wrong thing in front of a group, never sure of who's in it or how an even innocent remark may be taken. So the pressure of discomfort is greater than ever for managers and writers alike.

36

Players

World-class athletes are *not* ordinary people. If they were, they wouldn't be what they are, able to generate the attention that makes ordinary people spend billions of dollars to watch and wonder at what they are able to do.

Physically, they are (to use a repugnant but accurate phrase) "freaks of nature," in the sense of "exceptions to the norm." A 300-pound football player who can run; a 6-foot-8 basketball player with agility and stamina; a person of any size with reflexes that let him hit or throw a 90-mile-an-hour fastball; anyone who can run a marathon in a little over two hours (which means running 26 consecutive five-minute miles); a 100-pound jockey who can manage a 1,200-pound horse; or a boxer who can tolerate and inflict the punishment involved in the prize ring—these and all others able to operate at that level are not "average" human beings. They are at the extreme end of the scale of human variation in some respect.

Even more important, they aren't "ordinary" psychologically and emotionally. They must have exceptional ability to tolerate pain, achieve intensive concentration, master intricate techniques and maintain competitive desire on a day-to-day basis for many years, to a degree the rest of us confront only rarely. They are under enormous pressure to perform, against opposition, difficult feats with every failure publicly and unambiguously revealed and the consequences inescapable. In the process, they regularly reach "highs" we seldom experience, and need recuperative periods of comparable frequency.

Even most of those who have the exceptional physical gifts don't have the mental and emotional make-up to function at major league or world-class levels. And those with even the most perfect mind-set and competitive fire can't make it without appropriate physical gifts.

Unless a writer understands that, his relationships with such people are not likely to be comfortable.

In addition to their intrinsic qualities, these athletes and most coaches (who have had exposure to this level of playing) have had a different life experience. They have been praised and treated as "special" from teen-age on (and often as children). They've been immersed in a world where a successful result justifies everything, and pursuing it overrides all other considerations. They know the effort and sacrifices they've made are not "ordinary," and how fragile their status is if injury or just plain bad luck intervenes. If their rewards, in terms of money and records and adulation, are so much greater than what "ordinary" people achieve, they begin to take for granted their special status.

In the glory days of the press box, an easier relationship between player and writer existed for three reasons:

The tangible rewards in money and lifestyles weren't so large.

The spotlight, however bright, remained focused on the competition itself and its meaning, turning to private life only occasionally and less judgmentally.

Newspapers were still the only medium that really counted, with radio devoted mostly to play-by-play rather than interview and commentary. Television was not yet pervasive.

On the one hand, players and writers had more contact, since there were smaller numbers of each, encountering each other more often and traveling together. More of them could get to know one another better. On the other hand, the spotlight was turned off most of the time, not shining relentlessly through all 24 hours. Writers, their editors and their readers were concerned primarily with what happened on the field and whatever directly affected it, so that private life stayed private. Players did not have to fear that any remark, anytime, anywhere, might make trouble for them. Writers did not have to worry they were missing something they were expected to have if not on permanent alert. Plenty of friction arose between the inherently conflicting needs of a player (for privacy and avoidance of criticism) and a writer (for not missing a story and reporting negative events), but it stayed within reasonable bounds. It was not part of a prevailing climate.

Two topics in particular were subject to a version of the "mutually assured destruction" policy that the Cold War had made a common thought: Drinking and sex. One can image how the family back home would react to seeing in the papers that their player was drinking too much and/or chasing skirts. Unless it became necessary through an arrest or visible effect on performance, it didn't have to be reported. But since the population of writers also included its share of drinkers and carousers, they were equally vulnerable to having their families hear of their transgressions from a sufficiently provoked player or club official.

When most "regulars"—players and writers—knew each other at least by sight, and were less often confronted by strangers in the workplace, this standoff made life easier. The "drinking" silence extended to drug use and abuse, if known or suspected; the "sex" silence extended to marital difficulties of any type, included domestic violence, if known or suspected.

Then big money and television changed all equations.

Millionaire players are in the spotlight 24 hours a day, targeted by strangers (to them) who feed off scandal and sensationalism for the insatiable news cycle. At the same time, a much larger proportion of those asking even legitimate questions with microphones and cameras on hand have insufficient knowledge to make valid critical judgments. They simply echo the most provocative aspect of what they (or their bosses) heard someone say.

The player develops two defense systems, and uses them. One is to perfect trite answers or lie. The other is to surround himself or herself with an entourage of agents, gofers and "spokesmen" to make himself or herself unavailable when away from the arena, and to institute limitations on accessibility inside the arena. Clubs investing millions of dollars in the player are only too willing to go along with locker-room restrictions which, they once thought, interfere with their free publicity. In the television age, that's no longer important to them, at least not to the same degree, and the old "special status" of the occupants of the press box continues to evaporate.

There are plenty of exceptions, of course. Many players, even the biggest stars, develop cordial and mutually respectful relationships with particular writers, and vice versa. But the air in the clubhouse is chilly, guarded, suspicious and visibly uncomfortable. Media people stand around talking mainly to each other or cluster around one designated target, while most players seek refuge in the off-limits areas.

Sic transit gloria Presspassorum.

In former times, card playing was a great unifier. Poker games required group arrangements, bridge needed a foursome, but gin, pinochle and related games could be one on one. Barney Kremenko, a tireless gin player, had Durocher and Alvin Dark as regular partners on flights and train trips with the Giants. There were other pairings. In Cleveland in 1965, a bunch of us were "front-running," chasing the "other contender" in September while our regular beat men were with the Yankees. One evening Joe Reichler was trying desperately to round up enough hands for poker. He was button-holing people in the lobby, including Effrat, Kremenko and Sid Gray, who had known each other all their lives. I was there, as a newcomer to this routine in my second year on the *Post*, but just a bystander.

Effrat said something that offended Kremenko, Gray chimed in, and we all laughed. Barney, furious, declared he wouldn't play. They cajoled him into relenting, saving the game, and he finally blurted out what had got to him.

"I'm used to Effrat and you other guys making fun of me," he said, "but that Koppett, what right has he got to laugh?"

I wasn't yet the insider I eventually became, and I never had a better friend than Barney, (whom the players called "Gromyko" because that was the only other Russian-sounding name they knew.)

My best relationships with players grew through talking, not cards. And I learned a lot. With the Giants, Dark preached to me about the virtue and necessity of hitting the ball to the opposite field. With the Yankees, I liked Joe Collins, the left-handed first baseman who hit some homers but was often under .250 and rarely that day's star. Stengel was always telling him not to try to pull everything, so I chimed in with my Dark-implanted theories. "Just go the other way a few times," I'd tell Joe. "It'll really help."

At that time, I was playing frequently in pick-up softball games with the Broadway Show League folks in Central Park. I was a very poor hitter, but I started to apply Dark's system. I tried (right-handed) to simply poke the ball through to right field.

It worked, and I gloated about it to Collins. For about two weeks, I was hitting something like .600, thanks to grounders through the right side. Now, feeling confident and stronger, I thought I'd hit the ball harder.

First time up, a hard liner down the line, possible double. But the first baseman reached up, caught it, stepped on first, double play. Next time I hit it harder and further, but the right fielder made a spectacular running catch. Next time, furious, all discipline forgotten, I'm back to swinging from my heels and striking out. I had experienced the power of even a little frustration to overcome good sense. The next time I saw Collins, I apologized. "Now I get it," I said.

Fast-forward to 1962. The Mets have been created, and our annual (hardball) game between what used to be the Brooklyn and New York writers is under way at our Bear Mountain picnic. I am a thorough Dark convert, and three times in a row hit a ground single to right. But Pete Davis, one of the minority owners of the Mets (from the Davis Cup family), has been watching the game and gone in to play right field. I hit my fourth grounder through the hole, but he's playing way in and throws to first, beating me by two or three steps. But his throw is wide and Jim Ogle, in order to catch it, has to come off the bag and falls down, several feet away from the base, which I finally cross.

Stengel is the umpire at first, arms folded, not ruling anything.

"Come on, Case, what is it?"

He says: "I got to admit he's off the bag, but they made such a splendid play I'm going to call you out anyhow."

I got up one more time, one out, men on first and second, and swung as hard as I could, and connected. One bounce to the pitcher, double play. As I crossed first base, Stengel was shaking his head.

"You're just like all the rest of them," he said. "When you were doing it right you couldn't stand it."

In short, we all recognized that were all human, just like the players. I'm not sure how many of today's players would be willing to admit that writers are.

37

Veteran's Committee

Leonard
Koppett

Commissioners

This is the smallest, but most high-powered, subgroup writers have had to deal with, and it has also changed the most.

Before 1920, when Judge Landis assumed his position as "czar" of baseball, the highest rank in the sports hierarchy belonged to league presidents. Ban Johnson had created the American League and ran it with an iron fist. In the older National, presidents had less power while a few key owners and the unofficial backroom influence of sporting goods giant Al Spalding made the key decisions, but legally they were in charge, and exercised the important power of hiring and managing umpires. In 1903, when the leagues agreed to form Organized Baseball, a three-man commission was created to handle inter-league disputes. It consisted of the two presidents and Garry Hermann, an owner of the Cincinnati Reds, as chairman. But Johnson (the driving force behind the leagues' merger) was far and away the dominant voice.

Landis, whose judicious frame of mind lay somewhere between Genghis Khan and Atilla the Hun, was also a genius at public relations and self-promotion. He created the czarist myth—to baseball's great benefit when it had to counteract the loss of credibility the Black Sox scandal of 1919 had created. He portrayed himself as a "neutral" looking after the "best interests" of players and fans along with baseball as a whole. His first goal was to cut Johnson down to size, which took several years. His second was to show "zero tolerance" to gambling, including patronizing legal racetracks. This was accepted by the public, although some owners owned race horses and some actually had business dealings with gamblers. Then, since he was against the idea of the farm systems, he would "free" minor league players who were being "covered up," scoring points with both players and public (but not owners).

He catered to the important writers, and enjoyed a positive press. His baseball fandom was authentic. His office—the Commisionership—consisted of himself and one assistant (Leslie O'Connor), so internal communication was no problem.

And the magic word "commissioner" implied non-partisan power that "president" did not.

All the other sports began with "presidents" who, at some point, changed their title to "commissioner." (An old Soviet joke, circa 1930, tells of a grandfather who keeps referring to Stalin as "the czar." The young people upbraid him. "Don't call him a czar, he's the Commissar, only a comrade in authority." The grandfather says, "Look, if the Czar wants me to call him a Commissar, all right, I'll call him a Commissar." The old man can still recognize reality when he sees it.)

The commissioner of a league is still only the president hired and fired by the club owners to look after *their* interests. Structurally, within any single league or conference, president and commissioner are identical. A person is hired to carry out the wishes of the owners, in detail, to their satisfaction. He has no legal or practical powers beyond whatever they are willing to have him exercise. He has no ownership share, no "judicial" function and no enforcement machinery. He can rule "against" any member only if most of the others acquiesce in ganging up on that one, but he can never force anyone to do anything the group doesn't want. And he must do whatever the group insists on, even if he doesn't think it's a good idea.

In other words, the only "power" he really has is that of persuasion. He is hired to do what's best for the whole—the way the owners' group sees it. Presumably, they have confidence in his judgment and will go along with his decisions, but only when they are convinced he's right or they are relatively indifferent on that issue.

Nevertheless, this informal power can be immense in a skillful commissioner. Since he is a front man, a creation of and personification of a public relations necessity, a threat to resign—or even a public statement against an owner position—carries great weight in so public-relations dependent an activity as sports promotion. On the other hand, if he tries to do anything the group doesn't like, he either backs down or gets fired. It is, supremely, a matter of internal politics. He can lead those willing to be led by showing his ideas benefit them, but he must sound them out constantly to determine where they are willing to go. As his ideas turn out to be right (for them), they follow. If they don't, they dump him.

The position of Landis was unique because (1) he was given contractual powers in a moment of desperation, (2) baseball was alone on the major league scene, (3) the czarist myth fit perfectly and served the self-interest desires of Landis, the owners, the public and even the players, and (4) opposing it (as many owners wanted to) was too costly an effort during the boom of the 1920s, the Depression of the 1930, and the wartime of the 1940s.

The myth took hold, increasing the commissioner's prestige but also making him the target of every perceived flaw in the system. He was expected to "fix" everything anyone considered to be wrong, and his employers didn't mind having blame deflected away from them to him. The media and the public developed an unreasonable expectation of "justice" from him. But his ability to "spin" the news increased.

After Landis, no commissioner has had such practical power. And after the 1960s, when the players formed their own effective unions to protect themselves, all pretense of judicial function "representing everybody" evaporated, even though the media and the public clung to the myth.

A writer's relation to the commissioner also changed.

Landis made selected writers feel like insiders. All subsequent "czars" were clearly mere mortals, and being an "insider" was looked upon as being "a house man." And since commissioners were the obvious targets for blame or ridicule when anything went wrong, writers and commentators didn't hesitate to take potshots at them, convincing fans that they were inadequate "czars." They were still perceived as the "protectors" of the game, but as ineffective ones.

In the process, along with increasing prosperity, the commissioner's office expanded in size and scope, especially as negotiating television and other centralized contracts gained importance. And it automatically involved greater reliance on legal advice for decision making.

Up to the middle 1960s, the office remained compact. Established writers and columnists still had easy access to baseball's Happy Chandler and Ford Frick, football's Bert Bell and Pete Rozelle, basketball's Maurice Podoloff and Walter Kennedy, and hockey's Clarence Campbell. But the large majority of those writing about the subject, and commenting on radio and television, had no background or contact with the actual office; they simply accepted the inherited myth and went from there. What had been a position of accepted prestige became a focus for cheap-shot attack.

The next step was predictable and inescapable. A professional public relations core surrounded the commissioner, controlling his appearances and media relations. The royalty aura was restored and the informal contact disappeared except for a favored few.

Baseball chose William Eckert, a retired Air Force general with zero sports background, as a successor to Frick in 1965. He needed baseball insiders Lee MacPhail, John McHale and Joe Reichler (who left the Associated Press) to run things for him. Rozelle, an experienced top-flight publicity man himself, was ahead of the others in organizing his extensive central office, bringing in several former writers. Kennedy, who had been the basketball league's first publicity man under Podoloff, was followed by a Washington political insider, Larry O'Brien, who continued expanding the central office as the league membership increased.

When Eckert was first introduced to the press, in Florida in 1965, we asked him routine questions about background. What did he like to read in the newspapers at breakfast?

He cited page one, the sports section and comics.

"What's your favorite comic strip?" asked Harry Jupiter.

"I'd rather not single out any one," said the new Czar.

A new age had begun.

And next? Baseball's Bowie Kuhn had been the National League's lawyer for years, followed by Peter Ueberroth, who had just run the huge and unchallengeable bureaucracy of the 1984 Los Angeles Olympics. David Stern had been one of basketball's lawyers. Rozelle, when he finally retired, was succeeded by Paul Tagliabue, the league's lawyer. The current National Hockey League commissioner is Gary Bettman, who had been Stern's No. 2 man at the NBA.

Baseball followed Ueberroth with Bart Giamatti (a former Yale president) and Fay Vincent (Giamatti's hand-picked personal deputy), men with no baseball background at all, then went five years without a commissioner after firing Vincent before finally naming one of their own, Bud Selig (owner of the Milwaukee Brewers) to the post he had been filling informally.

What did all this mean to us writers?

It was easy to reach Frick by phone, since he had only two active assistants—Charlie Segar, a former writer we all knew, and young Frank Slocum, whose father had been an even more distinguished New York writer. We knew Podoloff and Kennedy from their league's infancy. The older writers knew the gregarious Bell before the National Football League became television's darling, and Rozelle, who knew the media business so well, surrounded himself with well-known sportswriters and publicity men from various parts of the country. They all, at that point, considered newspapers by far the most important outlet for their product, and responded to us accordingly.

Today, direct discussion between media people and a commissioner is rare. Formal statements, controlled press conferences and carefully managed "informal" appearances are the rule. And any illusion that they "represent" anything other than their owners is gone. Whatever we are told has been filtered through the public relations, marketing and legal arms of the office, and the quickest and surest way to please readers is to knock the commissioner for something he did or did not do.

So a dichotomy exists. In one sense, commissioners are important forces and the official spokesmen for the activities we cover. In another, they are less relevant than ever, as only one source—of a predictable nature—of information. Having said all that, they still deserve respect and acknowledgment of their position in any face-to-face contact, and personalizing criticism of their actions is still bad journalism (which can help career advancement). But for most occupants of the press box, the plain human interaction that existed 30 and more years ago does not include us, and has been transferred to television executives, business leaders who buy season luxury boxes and sponsorships, and appropriate politicians.

38

Others

In the days of press box supremacy, the world of sports sources was much more compact than it is today. All information is acquired from what someone tells you (in person or through printed material); there is no other way. We talked regularly to players, coaches and managers, club and college officials, league officers and commissioners, trainers, doctors, clubhouse attendants, road secretaries office secretaries, publicity people and, most of all, to each other. "Each other," of course, included broadcasters and photographers.

We still do.

But in recent times, people of a different type have also required frequent contact: Lawyers, agents, television executives at various levels, marketing experts, economists, advertiser representatives and union officials. How they affect the things we write about are less direct than the first group, but no less important and decisive. They also play a different role in the field. Players, club officials, etc., tell us more or less directly what they want to say. They certainly have their own "company line" and choose what to withhold, but their motives and agendas are usually fairly clear.

Lawyers and agents have different responsibilities. They speak for their clients, and their true agendas are not always so evident. It's not that they lie or purposely mislead us (although some do), but they have a legitimate obligation to advance the client's cause. To some extent, anyone who talks to the media is "using" us to get his or her point across, but agents and lawyers do this is to a greater extent, in a higher proportion of their contacts. So we have to learn their unspoken meanings. There's a profound difference between a player saying, "I don't want to play in that town," and an agent saying that the player doesn't.

Agents, however subtly or blatantly, are negotiating through the press. Lawyers, always aware of the implication of whatever they say, are in the habit of "making a record" for future use. So we have to be more careful about how we use their information, not knowing exactly at what stage their negotiation or case is at. The highly professionalized public relations people—who now have much greater input to the statements of commissioners, club officials, high-priced players and the rest of the organization—are also more adept at using the media. That's where the word "spin" came from.

So the sea through which sportswriters now swim is much larger than it was, with many more dangerous shoals and reefs. Dangerous, that is, if you and your editors are sticklers for confirming the accuracy of what you report. If you buy into the drama-over-narrative values of television, which most newspapers now adopt, the reefs and shoals are wonderful playgrounds in which to gain attention and (some hope) advance careers.

But in the interactions with all the different sorts of people described in this section of the book, a fundamental principle of journalism and information-gathering is always present: You must know and be able to judge the dependability of your source. Whatever you are told—the only way to learn anything—you must always weigh who's telling you, why, and for what ultimate purpose, if your "report" is to be valid.

Part Six

Teams

Every team develops a distinct culture, which changes only slowly over time unless there is a sudden major change in ownership. Tolstoy wrote, "Every happy family is alike. Every family is unhappy in its own way"— or something like that. (After all, he wrote it in Russian and I read it in English.) Since most teams lose most of the time, they are definitely not all alike. Winners are generally happy. Losers find alibis their own way.

Every club has its own culture, and one absorbs its coloration and mood from those who have spent most of their time with it. While with it (as a swing man), you may or may not be in tune with it, but you can't be unaware of it. It is rooted in the history, development and geography of each venue. Their present is always inseparable from their past, which must be described to make their current "feel" understandable.

So the experience of a writer in Detroit or Washington on Cleveland or Cincinnati is distinct from that of one in another city, but parallel in many respects, and those in two-team cities certainly knew how different were the atmospheres surrounding the Cubs and White Sox, Browns and Cardinals, Braves and Red Sox, A's and Phillies. And each sport, of course, had its own characteristics.

In what follows, I try to depict such feelings through very personal impressions tied to where I was, when I was, as one example of such auras. For the teams based in New York, the eras involved are roughly 1930 to 1975; for the teams in California, roughly from 1975 on. The Giants and Dodgers, naturally, straddle both.

Going back and forth among them makes you something of chameleon, but the essence of reporting is to be able to resonate with your surroundings.

39

Yankees

Aristocrats of the sports world.

That's how the Yankees have seen themselves since 1920, and how outsiders have perceived them. Their fans, vicarious participants in Yankee victories and status, take their privileged position for granted, as aristocrats do everywhere, and expect nothing less. To the rest of the population—all commoners—they are the focus of enthusiastic and (acknowledged or not, envious) hatred. "Break up the Yankees" was a slogan already popular in the 1930s. That sentiment, and much official baseball policy, is unchanged in the 21st century. (Until 1919, the Yankees were almost as much of a joke as the Mets of the early 1960s, but don't expect today's Yankee fans to know that.)

Four individuals created the dynasty. Jacob Ruppert, wealthy inheritor of a major brewery, was the owner. Miller Huggins, a little second baseman who had become manager of the St. Louis Browns, was the manager Ruppert hired in 1918. George Herman "Babe" Ruth, Boston's great left-handed pitcher who was playing outfield more often than pitching in 1919 and broke the home run record by hitting 29, was acquired by Ruppert in 1920. He paid Boston's owner, Harry Frazee, a Broadway producer who had many hits but was periodically wiped out by his flops, $100,000 (maybe more) for Ruth's contract, and gave Frazee a $350,000 personal loan. Ruth, as a Yankee, proceeded to revolutionize baseball by hitting 54 home runs in 1920, and 59 in 1921.

The fourth was Edward Grant Barrow, who had been Ruth's manager when the Red Sox won the World Series in 1918 and moved Ruth to the outfield in 1919. He'd been a young newspaper reporter and editor in Des Moines, a promoter of local teams, a minor-league club owner who discovered Honus Wagner, a major-league manager of the Detroit Tigers, a pennant-winning manager back in the high minors in Toronto, and president of the top-rated International League from 1911 to 1918, before going to the Red Sox. After the 1920 season, Ruppert hired him to be general manager with full authority for all baseball decisions.

With this group, the Yankees won six pennants in eight years (1921-28) and three World Series. Huggins died in 1929, and in 1931 Barrow and Ruppert made Joe McCarthy the manager, while Barrow also developed what would soon be the best farm system in the majors. Then the Yankees won eight pennants and seven World Series in 12 years from 1932 through 1943. Rupert died in 1939 and Barrow retired in 1945. That same year, the Ruppert estate sold the club, Yankee Stadium, the land it stood on, and the entire farm system for $2.8 million to Larry MacPhail (the managing partner), Dan Topping and Del Webb. They promptly adopted the top hat, symbol of aristocracy, as their defining emblem. MacPhail stayed only two years and front office operations fell to George Weiss, whom Barrow had nurtured as his farm director, and who was steeped in Yankee tradition.

So the Yankees we knew, in the post-Ruth period, represented Class with a capital K. They always wore ties and jackets (and hats, in those days) on the road. They played more bridge than poker. When Lou Gehrig's story was made into a movie, *Pride of the Yankees* was a natural title. They played in the most imposing of all ballparks, they considered winning a birthright, they signed more top prospects than any other team and their farm clubs tended to dominate their leagues. Their procession of superstars was unbroken—Ruth, Gehrig, DiMaggio, Mantle, not to mention Dickey, Ruffing, Gomez, Ford, Berra, Hall of Famers all. When Bucky Harris followed McCarthy as manager in 1947, he won the World Series for the first time since his rookie managerial season in 1924. Then Casey Stengel, considered a clown, took over in 1949 and won 10 pennants and seven World Series in 12 years. Then Ralph Houk won the next three pennants and Berra the one after that.

That made it 29 league championships in 44 years, a fact that overrode everything else about them. And in 13 of the other 15 seasons they were no lower than third.

In such a clubhouse, confidence was unbounded, but boasting and showboating had no place. They knew they were good, but they were supposed to be good. The veterans impressed that on all rookies and newcomers right away by word and example, generation by generation. Dizzy Dean (or someone) is supposed to have said, "it ain't boasting if you can do it"; the Yankees turned it around: "If you can do it, then you don't have to boast about it." And this wasn't merely a matter of behavior or style. It was a facet of concentration. You remain focused on the essential: Win it all, which is something (by definition) that only a team can do. The attitude is: Everybody here contributes, and if you don't contribute everything you can, that's MY money you're putting a risk. Shape up.

So Stengel's double-talk and Yogi's malaprops never impinged on the core, any more than Ruth's wild lifestyle did. In fact, the key element in establishing the dynasty came in the middle 1920s, when Barrow and Ruppert backed Huggins in the conflicts the Babe generated with his manager. When even Ruth could be brought into line, the lesson was not lost on everyone else. And they had fun, because winning, in and of itself, is fun.

Three stories about Ruth, stock material in countless biographies, illustrate the process. In 1927, after being brought into line by a $5,000 fine in 1926, he was holding out for a two-year contract at $100,000 per. It went on, wildly publicized, through spring training. Finally, Barrow and Ruppert got him alone.

"You want $200,000 for two years," said Barrow (the story goes). "How about $210,000 for three?"

Babe leaped at the higher number.

In 1930, his new contract called for $80,000.

"That's more than the President of the United States gets," someone observed, referring to Herbert Hoover's $75,000 salary.

"Well, I had a better year that he did," Ruth is supposed to have replied.

In the 1932 World Series, he presumably "called his shot" by pointing to the bleachers before hitting a home run off Charlie Root. He did point, but at what and with what meaning, no one knows. The story gained momentum only after a couple of days, and Ruth never denied it. But teammates insist it never happened. One asked him about it a few days later. Ruth laughed. "What kind of chump would I have been if I didn't hit it out?" But he knew a good story and didn't ruin it.

The Yankees I knew under Stengel thought he was nuts, but the aristocracy theme was so established that he couldn't (and didn't want to) shake it. DiMaggio, Henrich, Rizzuto and other older players were still there, and they indoctrinated newcomers to the clubhouse. Pete Sheehy, the clubhouse man—always a main force in any clubhouse—went back to the Huggins days. Stengel's first cry when they won that first 1949 pennant was "I couldn'a done it without my players," and he meant is as gratitude for being given the chance, not as a twisted boast.

Casey did make one innovation now pretty standard. He refused to discuss any possible line-up changes for the next day. "If I tell you I'm gonna do something and then I change my mind, you'll say I lied to you." Since he was a totally devoted platooner and used more than 100 different batting orders a season, his critics (of which he had plenty) had no comeback.

All this changed in 1964. Stengel and Weiss were gone, and under Ralph Houk the Yankees were even more formidable. However, Houk was moved into the front office, Yogi was made manager, and Dan Topping decided to sell the team in August. Webb had become less and less directly involved, the stadium and its land and the farm system had been sold off long before. The buyer was the Columbia Broadcasting System, taking 80 percent ownership with Topping remaining in charge as a hands-on minority partner. The Yankees lost the seventh game of the 1964 Series, fired Yogi and replaced him with Johnny Keane (their World Series conqueror with the Cardinals). They fell to fifth in 1965, fired Keane early in 1966, put Houk back in the dugout and finished last. Topping sold his remaining share and Mike Burke, a flamboyant assistant to CBS head Bill Paley, took charge of the ball club.

Weiss had started starving the farm system before he left. A draft of non-professional players, instituted in 1965 as an anti-Yankee measure, took away their advantage of having the most to offer a top prospect just because they were the Yankees. CBS, looking at the club as a corporate subsidiary, had no clue about how to produce a winner, even with Lee MacPhail brought back as general manager under Burke. In eight years, they were non-contenders seven times, touching second only in 1970. So in 1973 CBS sold them, at a loss, to a syndicate headed by George Steinbrenner of Cleveland. Soon Houk, Burke (who had brokered the deal) and MacPhail were out, and the volatile Steinbrenner era began. Instead of aristocrats, they became the famous Bronx Zoo, with a bewildering array of new faces, revolving managers, up-and-down fortunes, and various page-one scandals. After the 1973 season, Yankee Stadium closed down for two years to be rebuilt by the city in its present and (to me) less perfect form.

By then I was in California and out of daily contact with them, so I saw the "new " Yankees only at a distance. They went eleven years without another pennant until 1976, and after winning again in 1977, 1978 and 1981, 14 more before starting a new winning cycle in 1996. They kept promoting their heritage, and certain characteristics of it re-emerged in the late 1990s, but while that made them worthy of the tradition, it never re-created the old aura. Their fans became more arrogant and insatiable than ever, especially as New York itself, going through hard times, was no longer the "only place that counted." The rest of the baseball community made hating the Yankees a certification of mainstream sanity and virtue. The envy-based hatred had developed because they won so much more than anyone else. Now it fed on their being richer than anyone else as well.

In the 1990s, Buck Showalter and Joe Torre, with Gene Michael in the front office, brought them back to the aristocratic level. Their scouts used to have a rating system based on the highest they thought a prospect could go: Double-A, Triple-A, major league and—higher than that—Yankee. In my own mind, I've always distinguished "real Yankees" from others who just played (no matter how well) for the Yankees. I still think of Torre, coaches Mel Stottlemyre and Willie Randolph, Derek Jeter and Bernie Williams and others of that quality as "real" Yankees.

Their clubhouse became as uncomfortable for most media as everywhere else once Steinbrenner took over. It was probably at its loosest in the late-Stengel, Houk and Berra years before the winning stopped. But even then, the exposure of top newspaper brass to television's agenda-setting was making itself felt.

One night, probably in 1958, Whitey Ford had to leave an early-season game with shoulder soreness. I was still able, in those days, to penetrate the clubhouse while the game was still on. As an after-noon paper writer with the *Post*, I knew this would be my story no matter what else happened. Whitey, in street clothes, sat on a trunk and poured his heart out. He talked about his confusion and fears. How bad was it? Was his career in jeopardy? What could he ever do if not pitch? (He was 29 years old with a young family.) And of course, I thought, without him the whole pennant race picture would change, perhaps for years.

As it happened, the Yankees lost 2-1 because Bobby Richardson, the rookie second baseman, made an eighth-inning error. That was the dramatic moment on the telecast, which had no late information about Ford's condition.

I did a pretty good Ford story, which I had all to myself, and led my notes with Richardson and the ball game.

Jimmy Wechsler, the *Post*'s editor-in-chief and underdog-loving fan, confronted me the next day.

"Why didn't you write about the rookie whose error cost them the ball game? He must have felt awful."

"I thought the Ford stuff was more important, and I was the only one who had it."

"All the drama and excitement were about Richardson," insisted Wechsler. "We all saw that."

That's how early—1958—television started corrupting newspapers.

40

Giants

A generation gap separated the Yankee and Giants fans in New York, not so much as a matter of chronological age as of attitude.

When John McGraw took over the Giants in the middle of the 1902 season, they had been the only major league "New York" team for 17 years, with little competitive success in the last decade. He had them winning a pennant by 1904, and won 10 National League championships in 21 years, while running second eight times. He and his Giants "owned New York," he was by far baseball's most dominant (and aggressive) personality, and the team made the most money. He was dubbed "Little Napoleon" and worshipped by his fans, particularly the Broadway and Wall Street crowds. His players were lionized.

It's true that there had been a team in Brooklyn since the 1880s, but Brooklyn was a separate city until 1898 and of no concern to the "true" New Yorkers of Manhattan Island.

Theirs was baseball's most famous ballpark, the Polo Grounds, whose name had been transferred from 110th Street to 155th in 1888. When the American League transformed the Baltimore Orioles into the New York Yankees in 1903, the American Leaguers were strictly second bananas and, from 1913 on, tenants of the Giants in the Polo Grounds.

Then Babe Ruth came to the Yankees and the spotlight shifted.

In 1921, 1922 and 1923, there was a Yankee-Giant World Series. The Giants won the first two, the Yankees the third in their just-opened Yankee Stadium, a mile away across the Harlem River. Ruth's prowess turned a great many previously uninterested people into baseball fans. Even so, he didn't obliterate the McGraw charisma.

New York's traditional baseball fans were Giant fans, who never transferred loyalty to the Yankees. The early and hapless Yankees, much like the Mets of the 1960s, appealed to the sons, nephews and younger brothers of the established Giant fans, fed up with hearing about their seniors' legends, eager for something of "their own." When the Yankees suddenly became winners themselves, their defensiveness disappeared and the path to arrogance opened up. At the same time, the new fans Ruth was creating had no previous Giant loyalties and inbred fondness for pitching duels and bunts. The new game featured home runs flying over fences, and the Yankees gave them more of that than any other team. On top of that, the formation of Greater New York (in 1898) created borough loyalties. Brooklyn had its team, but Yankee Stadium became a natural magnet for the Bronx, and in Queens they could root for the Yankees and Dodgers in different leagues according to preference.

In short, throughout the 1930s, the creation of new Giant fans dried up while most new fans turned to the Yankees or Dodgers.

In terms of passion, however, the followers of the Giants were second to none. They had their own culture and history, and were more aware of their past (the glories of McGraw) than other fans. They didn't so much worship their best players as embrace them. They marveled at their skills and accomplishments, but weren't so concerned about having all others consider them "the greatest"; it was enough that they were Giants. They were beloved in a more personal way than Yankee heroes. From Christy Mathewson through Frankie Frisch ("the Fordham Flash") through Bill Terry, Carl Hubbell, Mel Ott and eventually Willie Mays, they were "ours"—to Giant fans—as family, not just association.

Horace Stoneham inherited the team in 1936 from his father Charles, who had acquired it in 1919, and running it was his only lifetime business. After World War II, his general manager was Charles (Chub) Feeney, his nephew. They mingled with their managers and players more closely than most ownerships did, filled their organization with ex-Giants, and they knew personally many more of their regular fans and ticket buyers than did their Yankee counterparts. They were closer to the center of the Toots Shor orbit, close to the football Giants and Fordham (their Polo Grounds tenants) and to their Broadway connections. In the clubhouse and on the road, they were much friendlier to their media people than were the aristocratic Yankees.

Yankees swaggered and flaunted it. Giants wallowed in affection.

And Giant history had a deep strain of just-miss. When McGraw won his first pennant in 1904, the Giants were denied a World Series because their owner, John T. Brush, would not participate in what looked like a boost for the fledgling Yankees (who didn't lose the American League pennant until the last day). In 1908, they were denied a pennant when a ninth-inning "victory" over Chicago reverted to a tie because rookie Fred Merkle failed to touch second to avoid a third-out force; when the race ended in a tie, they lost the make-up game. In 1912, they had a one-run lead in the 10th inning of the seventh game of the World Series, but lost. In 1916, they had winning streaks of 26 games (at home) and 17 (on the road), yet finished fourth. In 1917 they lost the World Series to the same White Sox who were good enough to lose the World Series on purpose two years later. In 1924, McGraw's last pennant-winning year, they lost the seventh game of the World Series in Washington when *two* bad-hop hits past third enabled the Senators to tie in the ninth and win in the 12th. In 1934, they were knocked out of first place in the last two games by the perennially sixth-place Dodgers, managed by Casey Stengel and inflamed by manager Bill Terry's pre-season quip, "Is Brooklyn still in the league?"

Giant fans knew suffering in a way Yankee fans never had.

Still, they held their own as a glamour team until after World Series losses to the Yankees in 1936 and 1937. They didn't finish first again for the next 14 years, while the Yankees won eight times and the Dodgers three. Finally, after Leo Durocher had made a shocking switch from managing the Dodgers to the Giants, they won their miracle pennant in 1951 on Bobby Thomson's homer. But the anti-climax was another World Series loss to the Yankees. In 1954 they actually swept Cleveland in the World Series and revealed Mays in his full glory, but it was too late to alter the new reality. Their attendance had sunk beyond repair and their status as No. 3 in the metropolitan market was ineradicable. Talk of a new stadium in Manhattan went nowhere, and their move out of town became inevitable.

Inured to disappointment but with unquenchable capacity for hope, the remaining Giant fans were less embittered than you'd suppose, and many retained their interest in the team transplanted to San Francisco in 1958. For a while, their games were radioed back to New York.

Their players were very proud of the club history. They really did hate the rival Dodgers, whom they faced 22 times a year. In their own way, they felt their team identity as strongly as the Yankees did. And they believed, down deep, in the superiority of the brand of baseball played in the National League.

In California, the near-miss syndrome became entrenched. In 1962, they lost the seventh game of the World Series (to the Yankees, who else?) when Willie McCovey's final line drive that would have turned a 1-0 loss into a 2-1 victory was just low enough to be caught. In the next four years, they lost close races to the Dodgers and Cardinals. When they finished first in the then still new Western Division in 1971, the Pirates knocked them out in the playoffs. When they got there again in 1987, the Cardinals knocked them out in seven after the Giants had won three of the first five. In 1989 they got to the World Series, against the cross-bay Oakland Athletics, only to have their first home game greeted by a major earthquake. When play was resumed 10 days later, they finished getting swept. Then they never got past the first round of the extended post-season playoffs until 2002, when they took a 3-2 lead in the World Series only to lose the last two games at Anaheim.

So to be a Giant fan is to love them, and to have plenty to love, but to have to display resilience far beyond the call of duty.

Charles Schulz, creator of the Peanuts comic strip, lived in Marin County and was a passionate Giant fan. Among his countless cartoons devoted to baseball, one of his most celebrated strips shows Charlie Brown and Linus sitting at the curb, looking glum, for three panels. In the fourth panel, Charlie says (sigh), "Why couldn't McCovey have hit it one foot higher?"

It's hard to imagine any other baseball team having that strong a grip on the national culture.

41

Dodgers

The idea that the denizens of Brooklyn were "always" crazy about their baseball team is a fine example of history being rewritten to fit later perceptions. Brooklyn entered the National League in 1890 and for 48 years its Dodgers were just a baseball team, passionately followed by the limited coterie of dedicated baseball fans but ignored by most of the populace, just as in any other city. That it was accepted as a symbol of local patriotism, to which Brooklyn's honor, fame and uniqueness were attached, was simply untrue.

Then two outlanders changed that overnight in the year 1938.

Larry MacPhail, a mid-westerner, was put in charge of a long-failing ball club. He brought in Red Barber, a southerner with an unmistakable drawl and regional vocabulary, to broadcast the games on radio.

MacPhail was a proven promotional genius. Barber was not only a genius in his field, but an originator of modern play-by-play baseball broadcasting. Whatever aspects he didn't actually invent, he had greater influence on all who followed him than anyone before him.

To put his games on the air, MacPhail had to break the agreement the three New York clubs had to not "give away their games for free" to potential ticket buyers through the new medium of radio. He understood, as the other two did not, that the "free" advertising was worth far more than any lost sales, and would produce a net increase in sales.

Barber, with his mellifluous voice and appealing personality, was above all a great teacher. He didn't just describe what happened, he made it make sense. He brought to life the drama of baseball, the identity of the players, the background and history of events, and the fascination of statistics. An entire population, hitherto casually interested or indifferent to baseball, was turned on. In particular, women—most of them homebound in those days—were introduced to this more exciting substitute for soap opera, and even more so school children. Games were played in the afternoon, conveniently just when school let out and before dinner.

Rooting for the Dodgers became universal in Brooklyn, and the myth of a special brand of fan loyalty was born.

Other forces converged. MacPhail quickly built a winning team. By 1941, it was able to win a pennant for the first time in 21 years. (The Yankees and Giants, in that interim, had won 18!) The manager, the brash and loud Leo Durocher, was a source of endless controversy and attention. And MacPhail, who had introduced night baseball to the major leagues in 1935 in Cincinnati (where he had first hired Barber), installed lights in Ebbets Field in 1938, opening the weekday door to working people and vastly increasing the radio audience. In their first night game, June 15, 1938, Johnny Vander Meer of the Reds pitched his second consecutive no-hit game, which ended with the bases loaded and Barber milking every ounce of melodrama out of the event. And in 1939, the first televised major league game was at Ebbets Field in August, although regular telecasts had to wait until after the war.

Before all that, Brooklyn baseball was eventful enough, but only rarely involving the whole borough beyond the baseball-fan segment. It was a hotbed of baseball clubs before full-scale professionalism took hold in the 1870s, playing a major role in baseball's early evolution. But it didn't have its own identifiable major league team until 1887, when it joined the American Association, which first challenged and then made peace with the original National League. It was promptly named "Trolley Dodgers," because its downtown Brooklyn ballpark was amid a maze of trolley car lines. In 1889 it won the pennant and lost to the Giants in a tumultuous World Series (the last of that primitive 1880s set), originating the inter-borough rivalry that would become legendary. In 1890, the National League players went on strike and started their own league (which lasted only one year) so Brooklyn moved into the National and won that pennant (but without a World Series to go to). By 1892, only the National, as a 12-team league, was left, and Brooklyn became a low-ranking member.

By the late 1890s, the team was owned jointly with the Baltimore Orioles, often the league champions under manager and part owner Ned Hanlon. In 1899, Hanlon and some of his best Orioles were shifted to Brooklyn and finished first. Then the league eliminated four teams, including Baltimore. Now called the Superbas (because a famous vaudeville troupe was known as Hanlon's Superbas), Brooklyn won the 1900 pennant. But in 1901, a new league called the American started to sign National League stars (including some from Brooklyn), and forced a joint agreement with the National by 1903. For the next 12 years, the team, now called the Dodgers again, finished no higher than fifth in the eight-team league. Its core of loyalists was vehement, but small.

They were now in the hands of a vigorous and true-believer owner in Charlie Ebbets, who went into hock to build a showplace of a modern stadium near Prospect Park, opening it in 1913. Two of the great Old Orioles were McGraw and Wilbert Robinson, the beefy catcher who was McGraw's business partner in Baltimore. When McGraw's Giants won pennants in 1911, 1912 and 1913, Robinson was McGraw's pitching coach and top assistant. But they had a falling out after the 1912 World Series loss, and Ebbets hired Robinson to become manager of the Dodgers in 1914.

Now began a different sort of legendary era. In 1916, the Robins, as they were now called, won a pennant, and another in 1920. And in 1924 they finished second. But the rest of the time, they lived in the second division: Never last, but sixth or seventh 12 times from 1922 through 1938.

These were the Daffiness Boys, referred to affectionately as Dem Bums. Robinson was no disciplinarian, and his players, who came and went with rapid turnover, made the most of it. Their misadventures, on and off the field, were well covered by talented New York and Brooklyn writers who knew good stories when they found them. Jokes about them got more attention than their lack of competitive success.

This was the team that wound up with three men on third, that had outfielders hit in the head by fly balls, and whose constant bickering made "zaniness" its trademark.

Babe Herman was a terrific hitter but erratic outfielder. On a long foul curling into the seats just short of the right-field wall, he raced at top speed from right center, threw his body over the railing, and just missed catching the ball while catching several bruises.

When he got back to the bench, Uncle Robby, instead of acknowledging the effort, growled, "Why'd you play so far off the line?"

"Why don't you go and f— yourself?" snapped Babe.

"That's it," said Robby. "You're out of the game." And for the next four days he wouldn't put him into the line-up.

Then the Dodgers found themselves in the home half of the ninth, one run behind, bases full, two out.

"Why don't you send Herman up to hit?" one of the players asked the manager.

"I'm not talking to him," said Robby. "You ask him."

So Babe went up and got the hit. And played from then on.

Robby retired after the 1931 season, and after two years under the too-serious Max Carey (who finished third and sixth), Stengel presided over his own continuation of the daffiness era in 1934-36 (finishing fifth, seventh and sixth).

One of his outfielders was Frenchy Bordagaray, who sported a mustache when facial hair was considered an absolute no-no.

"Shave it off," Stengel ordered.

Why?

"If there's gonna be a clown on this ball club, it's gonna be me."

But he couldn't stay mad at Frenchy. He sent him in to pinch run, and Frenchy promptly got picked off at second.

"What happened?"

"I was right on the base," said Bordagaray, "but tapping my foot. He got me between taps."

The core followers still loved their Bums, but the world at large didn't much care while Ebbets Field was deteriorating and attendance kept sinking. The banks had taken over a club headed for bankruptcy, and few of the faithful had vision of future glory.

Then came MacPhail, Durocher (made manager in 1939) and Barber.

MacPhail bought outstanding players right and left. The team went from third to second to first by 1941, and Barber's descriptions got the larger world's attention. Then the United States entered World War II and MacPhail departed after 1942 (when the Dodgers won 104 games but blew a 10-game lead and finished second). He was succeeded by Branch Rickey, who had built a dynasty (eight pennants) in St. Louis and had perfected the farm system format. With the war over, Ebbets Field refurbished, lots of night games and the revolutionary step of signing Jackie Robinson, the Dodgers became not only the pride of everyone in Brooklyn, but of liberal-leaning rooters everywhere.

These, then, became the Brooklyn Dodgers glorified in baseball lore. Rickey built a fantastic farm system. The team won six pennants, lost two pennant ties and was a contender every year from 1946 through 1957. Many of its top players, young and appealing personalities, lived in the Brooklyn neighborhoods and interacted closely with the community. The contours of Ebbets Field, so close to the playing field, bred intimacy. Pee Wee Reese, Gil Hodges, Jackie, Roy Campanella, Carl Furillo, Carl Erskine, Duke Snider, Don Newcombe, Preacher Roe, Billy Cox—all became true Brooklynites in spirit if not in year-round residence, just as Dolph Camilli, Pete Reiser, Whitlow Wyatt and Durocher had been in the pre-war group.

This younger group, more talented than its predecessors, was also better behaved. Gil Hodges, a solid and modest citizen, generated prayers in all the city's churches when he went hitless in a World Series. A practicing Catholic, he refused an airline meal including meat on a Friday, even after the Church had relaxed that requirement in the 1950s.

"You know, Gil, it's allowed now," a fellow Catholic told him.

"Not up here," said Gil. "Too near headquarters."

These post-war Dodgers are the ones immortalized—legitimately—in the many books that have been written about them. Their kinship to their community was probably closer than any other team achieved, even the Red Sox in Boston and Cubs in Chicago. Their media relationships were excellent, although stormy enough when the occasion warranted (and it often did). Their beat men and columnists, in the daffiness days had included such bright writers as Tom Meany, John Drebinger, Garry Schumacher, Roscoe McGowen, Tommy Holmes, Bob Cooke, John Kieran and Frank

Graham. A younger postwar group of Dick Young, Jack Lang, Harold Rosenthal, Sid Friedlander, Bill Roeder, Herb Goren and (briefly) Roger Kahn were even livelier while McGowen, Meany and Holmes were still going strong. The Yankees may have been the most victorious, the Giants may have had the more illustrious history, but the Dodgers provided the best stuff to read.

And, as befit daytime radio, they were a living soap opera, alternating great feats with major disappointments. The Jackie Robinson story contained conflict and controversy as well as social significance, the managerial and front office changes were dramatic and frequent, the victories always ended in World Series defeat until (at last!) 1955.

The home clubhouse under the right-field stands was much smaller and less luxurious than the ones at the Stadium and Polo Grounds, with only a thin wall separating it from the visitors' clubhouse, devoid of soundproofing. But the writers, generally speaking, were more cordially received there than in most others, and on the road, player-media socializing was closer than elsewhere. Rarely has a team "belonged" more completely to its community than the post-war Brooklyn Dodgers.

And O'Malley, when he replaced Rickey in 1951, was one of the few owners who would sometimes hang around the press room after games. It had been called Larry's saloon, after MacPhail, and when the war ended with Rickey in charge, the plaintive song (by Effrat) at the baseball writers' dinner was "Will the lights go on again, in Larry's saloon?" They did, and O'Malley exuded even more cordiality.

Then, in 1958—suddenly, unbelievably, incredibly, impossibly— the Brooklyn Dodgers became the Los Angeles Dodgers.

O'Malley had failed to promote the downtown Brooklyn domed-stadium he wanted, and had engineered the exodus. For this betrayal, Brooklyn has consigned him, for eternity, to the lowest circle of the Inferno, but in Los Angeles he became a hero. Almost everyone made the move, including broadcaster Vince Scully (but not Barber, who would wind up with the Yankees), the front-office people and almost all the familiar players.

And overnight, the character of the Dodgers changed. They went Hollywood on us.

The movie and television industry and its allied fields were full of transplanted New Yorkers and Brooklynites. Actors, directors, agents, studio big shots, nightclub entertainers and countless technical workers adopted the Dodgers with open arms. O'Malley's two top salesmen were Arthur (Red) Patterson, who had gone from *Herald Tribune* baseball writer to MacPhail's publicity man with the Yankees in 1946 to O'Malley's promotion head in 1954, and Harold Parrot, a Brooklyn born-and-bred newspaperman who had become a jack-of-all-trades for Rickey and had remained with O'Malley. They did a phenomenal job of selling the Dodgers to all segments of the fragmented Los Angeles population, using techniques of off-season sales and pre-game ceremonies that soon became standard everywhere.

For four years the Dodgers had to play in the 92,000-seat Coliseum, a football stadium ill-suited to the baseball field crammed into it, until the magnificent tailor-made Dodger Stadium was opened in 1962. By that time, the clubhouse and box seats and pre-game field activity were overflowing with the Hollywood crowd, an openly adoring local media, and the oil, banking and real estate operators who were the true Los Angeles elite. Scully's voice and artistry did for Southern California what Barber had originally done for Brooklyn, and more. Players were lionized, showered with freebies, and, as new blood arrived from the Rickey-built farm system, continued the team's success.

The new fans quickly put their own stamp on Dodgerism: Arrive just before game time, because the huge parking area at each level made that practical; leave after the seventh inning regardless of the score, to beat the traffic going home; and listen to Scully on portable radios while sitting in the stands to be clued in on every aspect of what they were seeing. Their players were not "bums," but "golden boys"; as time went on, more and more of them were native Californians to whom a laid-back climate was natural. In the clubhouse, writers were upstaged by Hollywood types: Actors, producers, agents, musicians. When Tommy Lasorda succeeded Walter Alston as manager, his office was overrun with the whole Frank Sinatra entourage, anyone with an attachment to Italian food, and the children of many of his players.

And in the press room, directly behind the press box in Dodger Stadium, you could enjoy the conversation of Jack Benny, Danny Kaye, Lauritz Melchior (the great Wagnerian tenor) and comparable showbiz legends, who shed whatever airs they might have put on elsewhere in the ultimate democracy of the old baseball press box.

Scully, whom we knew first as that kid from Fordham who was Barber's protégé, was now a deity, but also admirably resistant to celebrity syndrome. As they say, you can take the kid out of Brooklyn, but you can't take Brooklyn out of the kid.

He tells a story on himself that I like. At Fordham, he played in a game against Yale when George Bush Sr. was its first baseman. When he met the 41st President of the United States, he offered to send him a boxscore of that game. He found a *New York Times* story, by-lined by Louis Effrat, no less, mentioning Bush, a Yale regular, prominently. It had a single reference to Scully, who didn't start but entered the game as a reserve outfielder. Below the middle of the story, a paragraph begins:

"After Scully struck out...."

That was his only mention in *The Times* during his Fordham career.

In Brooklyn, O'Malley had charmed most writers until, by what they saw as an act of betrayal, he became the most detested of villains. (The betrayal was not simply the move, but his persistently misleading denials that it was coming long after it became clear that it was.) In California, he turned on the charm with nothing to oppose it, and emerged as a hero to the business community and local politicians as well as to a public suddenly given a major league team of established glamour.

Through the 1960s, I got to Los Angeles more often than most of the other New York writers, and O'Malley taught me about baseball economics.

"I lost $500,000 last year," he said. (That was real money then.)

"How is that possible?" I asked. "You drew 2.5 million and went to the World Series."

"We should have drawn 3 million," he replied.

When you didn't get more, that counts as a loss, right? Right.

42

Knicks

The New York Knickerbockers were formed, reluctantly, in 1946 when the Basketball Association of America was created. (Three years later, it changed its name to National Basketball Association after absorbing the older National Basketball League.) Big-city arena operators, who had business ties through the National and American Hockey Leagues, ice shows, the circus, college basketball double-headers and track meets, decided to form pro teams that could cash in on the reputations their collegians were creating and use them to fill empty dates.

Ned Irish, leasing Madison Square Garden, had created the college basketball bonanza in the 1930s and had risen to higher echelons of Garden management. He didn't have any empty dates, but he couldn't afford to let some outsider set up a New York franchise in a pro league that might succeed. So he went along and became president of the Garden-owned Knicks, counterparts of the Garden's hockey Rangers.

He hired Joe Lapchick, a legendary pro player in the 1920s and coach of the St. John's team that was one of Irish's Garden regulars, to be the coach, although Joe wouldn't be available until the following year (Neil Cohalan served as the first-year coach). Lapchick's reputation as "the big man" (6-foot-5) of the famous Original New York Celtics gave the BAA its biggest claim to major league legitimacy as it started to stock itself with recent collegians while most of the established pros remained in the smaller-town

National Basketball League in the midwest.

The arena-owned idea failed. Four of the original 11 teams folded after the first year, Chicago and St. Louis disappeared after 1950, and Washington soon afterwards. Only New York, Boston and Philadelphia remained as "big league cities" in public perception, defined by the 10-city baseball alignment that had been unchanged for half a century. Irish had only a handful of Garden dates available for the Knicks, who had to play most of their home games in the 5,000-seat 69th Regiment Armory on 26th Street. (Even the venerable Rangers had to play their playoff games on the road, dispossessed by the circus every spring.) Visiting teams labeled Rochester, Syracuse, Minneapolis, Fort Wayne, Indianapolis and Providence weren't going to sell tickets in New York, and didn't fill even the Armory. Irish found himself fighting a one-man guerrilla war within the league against the far less affluent owners about "how to be big league."

But a deeper problem prevented prompt acceptance of major league status. Most of the older and more influential writers, especially columnists, disliked basketball itself. Baseball was, of course, "our national game." But the other "manly" sports were boxing, football and even (in northern locations) hockey. Didn't basketball call itself a "non-contact" sport? How could you be forbidden to run with the ball without bouncing it, and why was a clean knockdown of an opponent a "foul"? And with height such an advantage, weren't the most effective players merely "glandular cases" instead of true athletes?

They called it "round ball" in derision, presumably to distinguish it from the oval shape of an honest football. The explosive popularity of the college game, triggered by the Garden double-headers, simply displayed their objections to it without changing their minds. They could accept its appeal to high school and college kids, but a pro major league? No way. They remembered that it had been tried and failed during the 1920s.

On top of that, it would use "playoffs." In baseball, only the two league champions met in a World Series; in the National Football League, only the two division winners in a championship game. Post-season playoffs were something the minor leagues invented to survive the Depression, adulterating the "true" reward of a full-season record. The National Hockey League had playoffs, but it had only six teams and Canadian origins, so it could be forgiven or ignored. At least hockey had body checks. And owners probably "made sure" each playoff final would go a full seven games, didn't they?

This version of macho thinking was widely acceptable in those days, even among the sedentary, heavy-drinking, often overweight and undoubtedly aging opinion makers whose columns were so influential. Facts were no impediment to their prejudices: In 1955-60, baseball's World Series went to seven games five times in six years, the NBA final only twice. So who was arranging what?

A younger generation—Young, Effrat, Lenny Lewin and a dozen others—didn't have such hang-ups, and had more of an inner-city background. They saw basketball for what it was, a full-scale test of *all* athletic abilities in which even the tall guys had to have agility and stamina, not only size. They covered a lot of the Garden games and didn't share the football religion. They knew the doubtful history of the pros, but were open to the possibilities of a new time. And the next age group—mine—had become basketball converts in high school.

So the generation gap reaction to the Knicks and the BAA had much in common with the coming of the Mets some 15 years later. We were in on the very beginnings of something, not being harangued about a history we'd never known, and it was "ours." The Garden, well aware its needs, knew how to cater to our receptivity. We were welcome in the dressing room, at courtside, in training camp, on the nearby road trips (but not the longer ones, on which the team went alone), in the playoffs and in the after-game gatherings at Leone's.

In this environment, team-media relations became more intimate than in the "established" sports. Above all, there were only 10 or 11 players and one coach to deal with, not three to four times as many people as in baseball and football. Then, at a courtside press table, we were much closer to the action than in other sports, and could actually talk to players and officials during every stoppage of play. We could see what actually went on in far greater detail than in other sports.

Finally, the college scandals in 1951 shifted attention to the pros in a way neither constituency could have expected, and the press-player intimacy became greater than ever.

More of us went on more road trips, including the long ones. We flew a lot (in 23-seat DC-3's) before the baseball teams did, and stayed in less luxurious hotels in smaller cities. When black players started joining the league, in the early 1950s, we were aware of the discrimination they faced in various cities, and unspoken quotas about how many a team would use. But that's the way things were in what was still a Jim Crow society, and within a team that was seldom an openly discussed issue. In many cases, a team did switch to an accept-all hotel even before the full-scale civil rights movement got rolling.

Lapchick's Knicks, from 1948 on, had few old pros and pioneered rotating seven or eight regulars in a running game. By 1951 they were good enough to go to the final round, only to lose the seventh game at Rochester. In 1952 they lost the seventh at Minneapolis, to the dominating George Mikan. In 1953, they won the first game of the final in Minneapolis, but lost the next four. In 1954, they led their division but got knocked out in a crazy round-robin preliminary round.

By that time, they had a solid following among New York basketball fans, and I, having moved to the *Post*, was with them on every trip.

Then the Knicks fell on hard times. Irish's second-guessing of Lapchick finally led him to resign in 1956 and go back to St. John's (where he won another NIT title). The Knicks finished last in their four-team division nine times in 10 years. Meanwhile, the Garden on Eighth Avenue and 49th Street, opened in 1925, was becoming obsolete and a new one was going up above Penn Station at 33d Street. With Irish more involved in corporate matters, Eddie Donovan, the general manager, was left alone to develop a winner. He finally succeeded. He drafted well, promoted Red Holzman from scout to coach, and moved into the new Garden in February of 1968 with a playoff team. Halfway through the next season, a trade for Dave DeBusschere provided the missing piece. Finishing third, they knocked off division-winning Baltimore in four straight before losing to eventual champion Boston (in Bill Russell's last year) in six. They were now the hottest sports property in New York.

Television had not paid much attention to the expanding NBA, but now that spotlight was turned on full blast. Intimacy was unraveling, the quote age was on us, and the league was finally big league in every respect. Frictions had begun that, by the mid-1970s, would make basketball life as harried as in all the other sports.

But first, a peak of glory was reached. In 1970, they finally won their first championship, routing Los Angeles (with Jerry West and Wilt Chamberlain) in the seventh game at New York. In 1971, they lost a seventh-game semi-final to Baltimore in New York. In 1972, they reached the final again but were beaten by the Lakers in five games. And in 1973, they earned a rematch, and beat the Lakers in five.

In the next 30 years they got to only two final rounds and lost both. And covering them was no longer the pleasure it had been in the first 25.

The intimacy established in the Lapchick years lasted until the championship years finally made it impossible in the expanding media spotlight. Four coaches who followed him—Vince Boryla, Fuzzy Levane, Carl Braun and Harry Gallatin—had known us while playing. Donovan knew us from his tournament appearances with St. Bonaventure before being hired to coach the Knicks. When he moved upstairs, Dick McGuire, whom we'd known from high school days, preceded Holzman. Red was certainly less flamboyant and more cautious in what he said than Lapchick, but equally accessible. And remarkably unassuming.

Poker was the game of choice whenever enough hands were available. Lapchick's enemies accused him of losing deliberately to let writers take his money, but in fact he was a rotten card player. On one return trip from Syracuse, we got on the train about 2 a.m. and the card players found an empty dining car instead of going to bed. We were due in about 10 a.m., so they played all night.

Entering the railroad yards in the Bronx, about 20 minutes from Grand Central Station, Lapchick was winning big. But some tie-up up ahead caused the train to sit still for about half an hour. They kept playing. By the time we finally got to Grand Central, Lapchick was out about 100 bucks.

"How the hell did he manage to have the train held up?" our chief skeptic wanted to know.

There are doubters everywhere.

Mets

If there is a heaven for baseball writers, it better be a perpetual version of what it was like to cover the Mets during their first three years.

It was 1962, the peak of the Kennedy Camelot era. The Yankees had been the only baseball team in town for four years, winning as always and climaxed in 1961 by having Roger Maris break Babe Ruth's record of 60 homers. The New York Mets and Houston Colt 45's were entering the National League, balancing the American's expansion of the previous year into Minnesota and Los Angeles. National League baseball, a New York fixture for 75 years from 1883 through 1957, was coming back.

Dick Young (*News*), Harold Rosenthal (*Tribune*) and Jack Lang (*Long Island Press*) had been abandoned by the Dodgers; Barney Kremenko (*Journal*) and Ken Smith (*Mirror*) by the Giants. Phil Pepe (*Telegram*), Len Shecter and I (*Post*) and the brightniks on *Newsday*—Stan Isaacs, Steve Jacobson, George Vecsey and Joe Donnelly—had been swing men in the three-team days. All of us had to share some sort of Yankee duty.

Now we had not only a new team in a new situation, starting from scratch, but also old associates in charge. Here was Casey Stengel, more garrulous than ever, as manager. And George Weiss, still aloof and whiney even without his Yankee arrogance, in the front office. And Lou Niss (former sports editor of the *Brooklyn Eagle*) as road secretary. And Tom Meany, of all people—as acerbic as he had ever been in print and frankly antagonistic to all the newspapermen he would supposedly serve—miscast as the publicity man. The broadcasting crew of Lindsey Nelson, Ralph Kiner and Bob Murphy overflowed with anecdotes and experience. And the roster included such familiar faces as Gil Hodges, Roger Craig, Don Zimmer, Richie Ashburn, Gus Bell and Frank Thomas. Rogers Hornsby and Red Ruffing, no less, were among the coaches.

In that kind of company, the laughs and conversational delights reached heights we'd never expected. We were at the Mount Everest of fun; that the home field was the familiar and moderately refurbished Polo Grounds only made the atmosphere feel more homey.

The Mets had been created unequal, carefully and deliberately, by the existing clubs. The expansion draft was designed to deny them any decent young prospects, and the National League teams had had an extra year to manipulate their farm system rosters to make sure none slipped through. Their on-field inadequacy was pre-ordained, plain to see and accepted on all sides. Therefore, there was none of the tension that goes with trying to win; these Mets couldn't, wouldn't and weren't expected to.

But they proved lovable from the start.

So many books have been written about them (one by me) that there's no point in retelling their story. You can, in Casey's favorite phrase, "look it up." Their young fans caught on right away, cheered their futile rallies, marveled at the original ways they found to beat themselves, ate up Casey's rhetoric, devoured the "negative statistics" Lang and the rest of us could generate from a club whose records were in our hands from Day One. Young dubbed them "The New Breed." Casey called his club "Amazin'!" and raved about "The yout' of America" and in burst of honesty after a defeat would declare, "We're a fraud; we trimmed the public again."

The writers—so exceptionally talented a group—enjoyed a creative freedom that serious pennant races didn't allow. The raw material for jokes and odd-ball descriptions was endless, and the new Met audience was responsive to the entertainment value of events and statements unencumbered by competitive expectations. When the New Breed started the practice of making and carrying signs, many of them truly clever, Weiss told the security forces to confiscate them, using the excuse that they blocked the vision of other patrons, but actually because he resented their irreverence. Young led our charge, in print, against this squelching of free speech and inspired fun, and Weiss not only backed down but eventually made a sign-carrying parade an official promotion. (Many of the larger ones were scrawled on bed sheets, so one of those in the parade read "The bed-sheet makers of American love the Mets.")

Casey never shut up or let up. Most of the players, who hated the situation they were in but couldn't do anything about it, never gave up trying while absorbing some of the mystique. One of the first Met games I attended, in early May (having started the season with the Yankees), was a drawn-out night game with the Cubs, still tied in the 10th inning, past 11 o'clock. As I left the press box to head for the right-field stands to be closer to the clubhouse when, if ever, it ended, a fan was leaving through the same aisle, and said to his friend, "I hate to leave—but I hate to stay." It was a perfect summation of the Met experience.

In 1962, the Mets lost 120 games, in 1963 only 111. In 1964, they finally moved into Shea Stadium, right next to the World's Fair in progress on the other side of the subway station. The Yankees that year won their fifth pennant in a row, while the Mets shaved their loss total to 109—and the Mets outdrew the Yankees by 30 percent, 1.7 million to 1.3.

But after that, the jokes started to wear thin, and as the Yankees also became losers, the charm of novelty disappeared. And the world turned nasty. Kennedy was assassinated after the 1963 baseball season was over, and Camelot was gone; 1965 was the year of urban riots; both the civil rights and anti-Vietnam movements were gathering steam, and Casey's broken hip forced his retirement. Covering the Mets became just another assignment in a less carefree time.

But those first three years put the lucky writers into a state of euphoria unknown in ordinary circumstances. You could write anything you wanted, any way you wanted, without ever running out of raw material for fun and games. You couldn't make things up like a player being traded for himself (Harry Chiti, a catcher); a first baseman (Marvelous Marv Throneberry) wiping out four runs in both halves of the first inning of a double-header by keeping the top half alive by interfering with a base-runner, then nullifying his own two-run triple in the bottom half by failing to touch second base *and* first base; Casey bringing in a relief pitcher from Yale (Ken Mackenzie) and telling him, "Okay, kid, make out they're Harvard"; a large crowd chanting "Let's Go Mets!" with two out in the ninth, two strikes on the hitter (Tim Harkness) and the Mets trailing 16-4; a 17-game losing streak almost entirely at the hands of the Giants and Dodgers; the fact that in their first season, they lost half a game in the standings before they played any (because their opener was rained out) and lost another half game after they finished playing (because the Giants and Dodgers had a three-game playoff for first place that counted in the standings).

After one all-night, plane-trouble-delayed trip from Milwaukee to Houston with an unscheduled stop in Dallas and a 90-minute bus ride through morning rush hour to the hotel, Stengel went to his room after informing Niss, "If anybody wants me, tell them I'm being embalmed."

You couldn't make this stuff up, but you couldn't miss it.

For me, a high point was spring training in 1964. It started with a pre-camp rookie camp. Then, when the regulars arrived, the exhibition schedule began with a three-day visit to Mexico City, facing two Mexican teams, before returning to Florida. On Friday night, the Mets lost because Harry (Suitcase) Simpson, who had once played for Stengel's Yankees, socked a home run. The next morning, a press conference was arranged to give the city's collection of foreign correspondents a chance to hear the famous Stengel.

"Do you think," one of these important journalists asked Stengel, eager to display his baseball sophistication and open the door to an alibi, "the altitude here (6,000 feet) bothered your players?"

"The altitude," replied Casey, "bothers my players at the Polo Grounds, and that's below sea level." (Which it really was.)

But the Mets did win the next two games, giving them a winning record in at least one country, and we had to get up at 5 a.m. Monday for the journey back to St. Petersburg. We'd been briefed to be sure to not pack our passports in our luggage, but one person did, and that caused a three-hour delay. That person was Edna, Mrs. Stengel.

Casey was so furious and embarrassed that he refused to say a word to her on the flight to Miami, during the change of planes to

St. Pete, and on that flight. Finally, it was evening, and we were on the bus that would take us to the hotel, and Casey decided it was time to make up. He jumped off, was gone for 10 minutes, came back and said to Edna—his first words to her in more than 12 hours—"I checked on your bags and they've got all three of them on the bus."

Said Edna: "There's four."

Those were the days, my friend. But we knew better than to think they'd never end.

The sudden rise of 1969 was truly miraculous, although it had been built by astute farm development, wise trades and the installation of Hodges as manager for 1968. The Super Bowl triumph of the Jets (which we'll come to in a later chapter) was a one-day shocker, but the baseball saga unfolded over seven months. Around Labor Day, when I picked them up in Los Angeles towards the end of a road trip, I congratulated Hodges on having them in third place, an unprecedented and almost inconceivable height. He was slightly miffed. "We're not out of it," he said, "I still think we can win it." If anyone else had said it, I'd have shrugged it off as routine bravado or political correctness, but I knew Gil well enough to see he simply meant it. And if that's how he felt, I'd better re-adjust my own frame of reference.

The ultimate World Series victory, in a sense, spoiled everything.

Losing could no longer be cute, while winning could not be guaranteed. The Mets had morphed into just another baseball team, with ups and down. And some downs hit hard quickly. Johnny Murphy, the old Yankee who had presided over building the team, died suddenly at Christmas time. Late in the 1970 season, Hodges had a serious heart attack and although he was able to resume managing in 1971, he dropped dead at the end of spring training in 1972, just as the players were going on strike for the first time. Yogi Berra replaced him an manager, Willie Mays was obtained from the Giants (because Mrs. Payson could pay him when Stoneham no longer could), and another miracle finish put them in the 1973 World Series, which they lost in seven games to Oakland.

With M. Donald Grant taking charge at the top as Mrs. Payson's financial advisor, and a series of new managers after another dismissal of Berra, the climate upstairs and in the clubhouse was no longer media-friendly, and by 1980 there was new ownership as well. The Mets fell into a close approximation of the biblical cycle of seven lean years followed by seven fat years. The first seven had been lean indeed. Then, from 1970 through 1976, they were lower than third only once. From 1977 through 1983, they were last seven years in a row. From 1984 through 1990, they finished first or second every year and won the 1986 World Series. From 1991 through 1996 they never got above .500. Then they were contenders for five straight years, losing the 2000 World Series to the Yankees, before sinking to fifth in 2002.

The 1960s were now ancient history, the media scene—as well as the rest of the world—had changed completely, and the old lesson was demonstrated again: A miracle is miraculous because it happens only once.

Football Giants
and Jets

New York's three greatest ethnic groupings, up to World War II, were the Irish, the Italians and the Jews. They shared interest in all sports, but by the 1950s the Jews felt closest to basketball and the Italians, since Tony Lazzeri and Joe DiMaggio had come on the scene, to baseball. The Irish, originally most prominent in baseball, had begun to shift to football, drawn to the success of Notre Dame and other Catholic colleges and the growing National Football League's New York football Giants. (You always had to say "football Giants" to distinguish them from the baseball team.) And the pros became an increasing element in the equation.

The football Giants had strong ties to other Irish community members. Tim Mara, a successful and respectable bookmaker in days before pari-mutuel betting machines, bought the New York franchise in the primitive NFL in 1925 for $500, on the theory that a New York franchise in anything at all was worth a $500 investment. His sons, Jack and Wellington, became football junkies and eventually the active operators of the team. One of their early publicity men was Ned Irish, who emerged as a Madison Square Garden big shot. Their landlord at the Polo Grounds was Charles Stoneham when McGraw was still the main man, and Horace and the Mara sons grew up together. Connection to Fordham University was also strong, since it was the college football tenant and Wellington was a student there. Notre Dame had produced "subway alumni" by playing Army in New York every year (at the

Polo Grounds at first and then at Yankee Stadium), and the original appeal of the NFL's Sunday games was to football fans who lacked personal identification with any particular college power. Football rooting requires a type of fervor analogous to patriotism, which high school and college affiliations provide automatically, but this is easily transferred to a local city identity.

Through the 1930s, the football Giants produced contenders and championship teams under coach Steve Owen, excelling in defense. Fine rivalries developed with the Chicago Bears, Green Bay Packers, Washington Redskins and Brooklyn (football) Dodgers. Pro football was still definitely second to college football in impact, but a fan base was being built.

Owen had strong ties to the local colleges. Lou Little, a leader of the national coaches' association, was enjoying a decade of success at Columbia. Fordham's coach was Jim Crowley, one of Notre Dame's original Four Horsemen, later succeeded by Fordham alumnus Ed Danowski, who had been a successful Giant quarterback. Arthur Daley, who became the only regular sports columnist on *The New York Times* after John Kieran retired, was married to Tim Mara's daughter, so Jack and Wellington were his in-laws. Joe Sheehan, of *The Times*, was a major contributor to Giant game-day programs (a perfectly honorable arrangement in those days).

So the Maras, running a family business, had close relationships with the baseball Giants and the Polo Grounds, Madison Square Garden, the city's two top college football powers as well as Notre Dame, and even with Don Topping, who had owned the football Brooklyn Dodgers before he acquired baseball's New York Yankees.

Nobody could be more thoroughly inside New York "insiders."

For all that, the football Giants were a minor member of the New York scene until after World War II, when the advent of television began lifting pro football to the status it finally attained. Then they climbed, by 1960, to a position higher than baseball's. The fact that the television networks were based in New York, with their executives in such constant contact with the New York happenings, was more than a coincidental benefit. The football Giants had only a moderate following while leading their division five times in the 1930s, and also went to the championship game in 1941 and 1944 (losing both times) under the shadow of the war. But when they got there again in 1946 (but again losing), attention jumped to a higher level, and in the 1950s they began battling the spectacular Cleveland Browns for the division title. In 1956, they moved into Yankee Stadium (because the baseball Giants, unknown to the public, had already decided they would have to leave town) and won the NFL championship by beating the Bears, 47-7. Within a year, the baseball Giants and Dodgers were gone and the football Giants were New York's sports elite on a par with the Yankees and above anyone else. In the 1960s, when the Mets started up, the Yankee dynasty ran out and the Knicks and Rangers were going nowhere, the Giants finished first or second in their division seven times. Now, in Shor's and Leone's, Charlie Conerly, Frank Gifford, Kyle Rote and a dozen teammates were as big as Mickey Mantle, Whitey Ford and other top Yankees, not just in Downey's. Their season-ticket waiting list was in the thousands and their supporters the most passionate in town. When it came time to rebuild Yankee Stadium in the 1970s, they were able to get their own stadium in the Meadowlands complex across the river in New Jersey.

The shift from baseball to football dominance is illustrated by the following incident:

When the Yankees were at a low point in the late 1960s, they made their history a chief selling point. Frank Messer, a broadcaster brought in from Baltimore by Lee MacPhail, was in his first Yankee Stadium season and wanted to score points with his new employers. In a pre-game interview with Bob Shepard, the legendary public address announcer, he asked:

"Bob, you've been here all these years, what's the one thing that stands out most in your memory? Roger Maris's 61st homer? Don Larsen's perfect game? Something Mickey Mantle or Yogi Berra did? What one thing?"

"Well, I really can't pick anything out," said Shepard. "There have been so many. All the ones you mentioned and more."

"But there must be one that stands out," Messer insisted. "Maris? Larsen? Allie Reynolds' second no-hitter? Something."

"Honestly," said Shepard, "No single thing stands out."

Messer wouldn't let it go. "There must be *something*."

"Well," said Shepard, giving in, "the time Pat Summerall kicked that field goal in the snow..."

He was referring to a key last-second victory over the Cleveland Browns.

Messer gulped and changed the subject.

(Messer also excelled as a restaurant critic. He called one in Tampa the best steak house anywhere. "They give you a martini *this* big.")

In their pre-war years, the football Giants were media-friendly and unabashedly loyal to their loyal supporters. Then, as the NFL evolved into the bureaucracy-dictatorship mode under the Pete Rozelle-television industry alliance, they became no more or less easy to deal with than any other NFL team. They, like so many others, had progressed from family business to corporate partnership and technological sophistication, even though, as of 2003, Wellington was still there and many of his sons were now involved. Time does march on.

In Yankee Stadium, starting in 1956, game day was more social than at the Polo Grounds. On a pre-game sandwich spread, celebrity ticket holders mixed with the writer and advertising contingents. The football press box off the mezzanine was right in front of the main season-ticket box holders (like Toots) and we could mingle going and coming. During the game, writers who had now become NFL experts chattered like their baseball counterparts (often the same individuals). Norman Miller, who moved from the United Press to the *Daily News*, was so prone to identifying an upcoming "key play" that we had to ration him: No more than four key plays a game. But we would join him in calling out "G.F.P." whenever the Giants got possession in "good field position."

NFL Sundays had become just as thoroughly a social event as Yale-Harvard Saturdays had been in the decades before the war.

● ● ●

The Jets are a different story entirely.

The success of the 12-team NFL in the 1950s built up tremendous pressure for other cities, enjoying population explosions, to seek admission. As usual, the existing insiders resisted diluting their shares of the whole, so the outsiders decided to form a new league in 1960, the American Football League. They had three basic ideas for survival: (1) be on television, (2) have the NFL label and (3) force a merger by competing for top players. No. 1 meant that it had to include teams in New York and Los Angeles because that was where TV executives who made decisions and largest existing audiences were based.

Lamar Hunt of Texas was a leader of this movement. Barron Hilton, the hotel man, was ready to put a team in Los Angeles, but New York meant finding someone to buck all those Mara alliances. A brash broadcaster named Harry Wismer was willing to try it.

The Polo Grounds, sitting empty since the baseball Giants left and waiting to be torn down for a housing project, could be rented. A relatively cheap roster could be assembled. Wismer's talent was fast-talk persuasion. He got the project off the ground, hoping, like the rest, to cash in eventually through television and NFL inclusion. In effect, he was following Tim Mara's line of thought: A New York franchise in anything had to be worth something.

He called the team "the Titans," to parallel the Giants. It got minimal attention in the Big Town (as Ring Lardner had once named New York), and he was looked upon by many as a clown. But the Titans did play the 1960 season in the Polo Grounds, and when baseball decided to expand in 1961, the projected New York Mets, promised a new multi-purpose stadium in Flushing, could play there also until it was ready. And when it was, the football team could move there too, with the city as landlord.

By November of his third season, Wismer could no longer pay his bills and the league had to take on financial responsibility for the franchise. By March, he was in bankruptcy and the club was bought for $1 million by a five-man syndicate headed by Sonny Werblin, who had important connections in the television, performer representation and advertising spheres. Werblin became a key player in the AFL's success.

The team finished its fourth season at the Polo Grounds, having gone 7-7, 7-7, 5-9 and 5-8-1. Shea Stadium would be ready in 1964, so Werblin changed the name to Jets, to rhyme with Mets and associate it with the hottest word in the transportation industry. He also had a hand in achieving a new television deal. The league had begun with a five-year contract worth about $10 million with ABC, then very much the weakest of the three networks. The NFL had settled on CBS, so NBC badly need a pro football rival. In January 1964 it signed a $36-million, five-year agreement starting in 1965, with another $6.7 million for the championship and all-star games. Now the league had a sound financial base. Just four weeks before, Werblin had shaken up the sports world by signing the top college quarterback, Joe Namath of Alabama, to a "$400,000 deal," the largest sum ever offered any collegian in any sport, at a time when the top baseball stars were in the $150,000-a-year range. That $400,000 number got everyone's attention, and certainly helped close the NBC deal, even though it was actually a multi-year agreement including stretched-out bonuses.

Werblin's Jets promptly began setting AFL attendance records at Shea. By 1966, an agreement to merge with the NFL was reached, ending the salary wars and making a Super Bowl and a common draft possible. By 1967, the Jets were finishing only one game behind division leader Houston. In 1968 they went 11-3, beat defending champion Oakland in the AFL title game, and upset NFL champion Baltimore in Super Bowl III in Miami in January. That made Namath, who had "guaranteed" a Jet victory the week before, a national hero and settled the argument about AFL teams being unable to compete in a combined NFL.

The impact of that one game can't be over-emphasized. The NFL people, from the start, had sneered at the "inferiority" of the AFL and saw the economic necessity of merger as a lamentable sell-out of their artistic integrity. Vince Lombardi's Green Bay Packers had scored lopsided victories in the first two Super Bowls, and the Colts had annihilated the Cleveland Browns, 34-0, in the 1968 NFL championship game. So Baltimore was installed as an 18-point favorite over the Jets.

One of my sidelines at that time was a brief sports commentary segment on a weekly news show at Channel 13, the "educational channel," as we called it before PBS was a familiar designation. The question hanging in the air was, how badly would the Jets be embarrassed?

I'm not sure whether or not I already knew of Namath's boast, but I did know a little about football reality. I said (in effect), "I have no idea who's going to win, but there's no reason why it shouldn't be an even battle, and 18 points is ridiculous. The reason is simple: For seven years, all these teams have been drafting players from the same pool of talent and exposing them to the same amount of training and experience. I've just covered the Colts wiping out the Browns from the same league. Any football game can turn out that way on any particular day. But to assume there's some inherent difference in the talent level of two finalists is just silly. If you must bet, by all means take 18 points."

So when Namath made good, it paved the way for agreement (in May) on how to realign into a single league with two 13-team conferences—and everybody had that valuable NFL label. CBS and NBC took a conference each, and in 1970 ABC jumped in with its *Monday Night Football* idea. The ascendancy of pro football was secure.

For the players, the five years of competition for stars was a bonanza, as salaries reached heights no one had imagined. (College signing bonuses went as high as $711,000.) And it was certainly a good deal for all three networks to market that NFL identity. But it was also a bonanza for the writers, who were treated better and catered to by both leagues in the fight for favorable publicity. Access and accommodation were the rule in those days, and many a wannabe baseball writer was converted to the football religion, with its much easier once-a-week life pattern.

The purpose of the merger, of course, was to shut off salary escalation, which it did. It also gave the league complete control of access and press box management, in which its bureaucratic instincts and partnership with television took over. Football writers, never having enjoyed the self-government the BBWAA had exercised from 1920 on, have been meekly accepting whatever restrictions the NFL adopted, because (1) covering football had acquired so much prestige and (2) they couldn't do anything about it anyhow. As time went on, the basketball and baseball people learned that they could be just as controlling, and the freedom of operation we had in the 1950s and 1960s is in the dust bin of history.

Which is my book's theme.

45

Niners and Raiders

SAN FRANCISCO 49ERS

LEONARD KOPPETT

MEDIA

7 (6,3,2,1)   009

Football's only other two-team metropolitan area that still exists, beyond New York, is the San Francisco Bay Area. The Los Angeles AFL team, after one year, became the San Diego Chargers. The Cardinals left Chicago to the Bears by moving to St. Louis in 1960 (and then to Arizona). The Los Angeles (originally Cleveland) Rams had the transplanted Raiders as neighbors from 1982 through 1994, although the Rams had already moved south to Anaheim. Then both were gone in 1995, the Rams to St. Louis and the Raiders back to Oakland.

So the San Francisco 49ers, who started out in the All-American Conference in 1946 and moved into the NFL in 1950 (along with the Cleveland Browns), have shared the area for 22 years with the Oakland Raiders after they were formed in 1960, and again since 1995.

The Niners and Raiders have had dramatically different characteristics, histories and fan bases. In 1946, the Niners gave Northern California its first taste of "major league" sports, although in a new and not yet fully accepted league, while Los Angeles obtained the NFL Rams, league champions in Cleveland the year before. Football could do this because once-a-week games could be scheduled with train travel reaching the east. In 1950, when the All-America Conference folded, the new Cleveland Browns, its perennial champion, and the Niners, its perennial runner-up, joined the NFL. The baseball Giants didn't come west until 1958 and the basketball Warriors not until 1962, thanks to the development of jet planes.

So the Niners generated the special affection conferred on those who were the first to give the area higher status. Just as the Giants had their strongest roots in New York's Irish community, the Niners strongest ties were to San Francisco's important Italian community, because the team's owners, the Morabito brothers, Vic and Tony, were so much a part of it.

Their home field was Kezar Stadium, in the middle of town at the edge of Golden Gate Park, remarkably intimate even though it could hold 60,000 (but averaged about half that most of the time). There were four major papers in town, lots of radio stations and many suburban papers, so its media monopoly had to be shared only with Stanford and Cal college teams. Their rooters far outnumbered their customers, and their style—wide-open offense, not always effective defense—appealed to everyone. Love is not too strong a word to apply to the feeling of San Franciscans for this team.

Their competitive success was sporadic. From 1951 through 1954 they had winning seasons under Buck Shaw, their original coach, whose roots were down the Peninsula in Santa Clara. Then they were essentially a .500 team for the next 15 years. The closest approach to a title was in 1957, when they tied for their division lead but lost a playoff to Detroit, before 60,000 at Kezar, 31-27 despite a 27-7 lead in the third quarter. Finally, under Dick Nolan, they made the playoffs in the expanded NFL in 1970, 1971 and 1972, losing each time to Dallas.

In 1971, they moved into Candlestick Park, built for the baseball Giants in 1960 but now expanded (over Stoneham's objections) to 60,000-plus for football. But three losing seasons followed and attendance dwindled. Tony Morabito had died during that exciting 1957 season, and Vic in 1964. Lou Spadia had been running the club for the heirs and it was time to sell. Al Davis, running the Raiders across the bay, helped find a buyer.

The new owner was Eddie DeBartolo, son of a self-made millionaire in Youngstown, Ohio. He chose Joe Thomas, an NFL veteran, to be the operating head. It was a disaster. The Niners and their followers had always been "family," in the strongest sense, steeped in San Francisco tradition, closely involved with Stanford,

Cal and Santa Clara coaches and players as well as alumni, and not too demanding of victory. Thomas tried to wipe out all these old associations, snubbing 49er alumni, and to impose his own football concepts. He discarded the successful and popular 1976 coach (Monte Clark), antagonized the media and—to nail it down—produced 5-9 and 2-14 seasons with attendance dipping to 30,000.

Young Eddie didn't take long to acknowledge his mistake. He had plenty of money at his disposal, and a burning desire to win and be popular. He went directly to the media to promise better things, fired Thomas, hired Bill Walsh away from Stanford, and proved willing to spend whatever it took to find and satisfy good players. Walsh had languished for years in assistant roles before displaying brilliant success in two years at Stanford, featuring the most attractive kind of wide-open offense and a most un-football-like charming personality. Rebuilding Niner traditional associations began immediately.

Walsh started with another 2-14 season, but came up with Joe Montana, who had been passed over at least twice by all other clubs in the 1979 draft. A 6-10 season followed, including five defeats by a touchdown or less in a mid-season eight-game losing streak. In 1981, with Montana installed as the regular quarterback, the Niners went all the way to a Super Bowl victory after a 13-3 regular season.

In a flash, a new mob of "49er Faithful" sprang up. Season-ticket buyers gobbled up all 60,000 seats and formed a waiting list of 10,000. They dwarfed the number of the real Faithful, the true followers of the team for 30 years, and thought all history began only when Walsh and Montana arrived. We'll come back to them in a moment.

Meanwhile, the Raiders had a very different beginning. When the AFL was formed, it put a franchise in Minneapolis, but it never got started. Before the first season opened, it was awarded instead to Oakland (over Atlanta). The team played on a high school field and its first three seasons were 6-8, 2-12 and 1-13. Its impact on the Bay Area was zero.

In 1963, Ed McGah, one of the original investors, emerged as principal owner and hired Al Davis as head coach and general manager. Al produced a 10-4 record the first year, one game behind champion San Diego, had a losing year in 1964 and finished one game behind San Diego again in 1965.

At that point, the league made Davis its commissioner, and within months he brought the NFL to its knees and the merger table by offering huge contracts to top NFL quarterbacks. With that done, he returned to Oakland as managing general partner and very hands-on boss, the only owner in football with such extensive technical football knowledge.

Back in 1964, Oakland authorities had decided to build a multi-purpose stadium to attract a major league baseball team. It was ready in 1966 and the Raiders moved in on a 15-year lease.

The 1966 Raiders finished second to Kansas City (which went on to lose to the Packers in the first Super Bowl). Then they went 13-1 and lost to the Packers in the second Super Bowl. They were 12-2 in 1968, losing the AFL championship game to the Jets, and 12-1-1 in 1969, losing the AFL title game to Kansas City, who went on to win Super Bowl IV.

By now they had established a passionate following in East Bay. Oakland's relationship to San Francisco is not unlike Brooklyn's to Manhattan, and the winner Davis had built appealed to the local population, more blue-collar than the San Francisco crowd. Now included in the NFL, the two teams could be compared for local rivalry purposes. And the aggressive imagery Davis preferred—the Raiders had an eye-patch pirate-like emblem and the stark colors of silver and black—went along with a reputation for "rehabilitating" winning players who had been in trouble else-where. In the 1970s, the Raiders finished first six times and second three times and won the Super Bowl after the 1976 season, while the 49ers were gradually sinking to the bottom. The Raiders were selling out every game and clearly had become the area's elite.

However, in 1968 Oakland's pursuit of a baseball team succeeded, and the one-time Philadelphia Athletics, after 13 years in Kansas City, moved into the Coliseum. They immediately cut Giant attendance in half and, as the favored tenant, interfered with the early season Raider home schedule. Winning three straight World Series in 1971-1973 gave the A's even greater prestige than the Raiders. Then came free agency in baseball, in 1977, and the A's were undone.

The Raider lease was up in 1981. Davis wanted luxury boxes and a better break in scheduling. Baseball wanted the A's to move to

Denver, and was ready to kick in half the $4 million cost of refurbishing the Coliseum. But the Rams, in 1980, had abandoned Los Angeles to move 30 miles south to Anaheim, home of Disneyland, and the city-owned L.A. Coliseum, seeking a new tenant, was making Davis a better offer. The Oakland authorities, afraid of losing both the A's and the Raiders as tenants, concentrated on the baseball team (soon bought by the Haas family of San Francisco, who pledged to keep it in Oakland) and resisted the terms Davis wanted.

So Davis opted to move to Los Angeles. The city, county and NFL office tried to stop him, but an anti-trust suit, activated as soon as the L.A. Coliseum had a prospective tenant, prevailed. In quick succession, the 49ers won the Super Bowl while the Raiders had their first losing season in 16 years, and when the Raiders opened 1982 in L.A., the season was marred by a seven-week player strike. After the Raiders won the Super Bowl again in the 1983 season, their move to Los Angeles started to go sour.

In the Bay Area, the Raiders had been a symbol of success and the Niners a symbol of failure. After their 1981 Super Bowl, the 49ers failed to make the playoffs in the strike year of 1982 even though the playoffs had expanded to 16 teams. But they did in 1983, and that started a record-breaking run of 16 consecutive seasons of at least 10 victories, while the Raiders, never getting the promised improvements in the L.A. Coliseum, drifted into mediocrity. Raider media relations in Los Angeles were bad from the start.

By now, you can see the pattern.

Walsh, his success based on having complete control of the football operation, began to cut the media out of the "family" loop soon after his first Super Bowl. In the old Redwood City practice facility, in those first two losing years, we were welcome in every corner of the small building, including the coaches' dressing room and the upstairs offices. Then an adjacent quonset hut was built for media purposes, and the NFL-style arms-length relationship gradually took hold. In 1988, the practice facility was moved to an 11-acre, specially designed (and beautiful) complex in Santa Clara, where "security" arrangements were strictly observed. The press had adequate space, with designated desks for regulars and press conference facilities, but wandering around was out, contacts were by appointment, and informality was a thing of the past.

Walsh had been noted for his charm and openness at Stanford and, at first, with the Niners. But he believed—correctly—that "satisfying" the media was less important than creating the atmosphere and rigorous scheduling needed to maintain winning teams. An us-against-the-world psychology is a strong element in football success, more so than in other sports. The Redwood City facilities had certainly been outgrown, and the sumptuous new quarters were excellently designed. But contact with the ever-expanding media horde had to be carefully and constantly controlled. Walsh stepped down as coach in 1989, after a third Super Bowl, but later returned as an "advisor" with varying degrees of power. George Seifert, his top assistant who succeeded him, kept the same operational methods in place and kept winning. The organization maintained success for an unprecedented duration, so Walsh's judgment was correct. But for us, it was less pleasant, more constrictive and at times the word "fascistic" would be tossed around.

Davis, who certainly deserved his reputation as a control freak, made enemies right and left, but at the same time generated tremendous loyalty among many of his troops. His dealings with media were strictly reward-punishment types. If you're for us, you're welcome; if you're not, we're not going to go out of our way to make things easy for you, and we're going to let you know it. Increasingly involved in lawsuits after 1980, and the target of all kinds of retaliation from the NFL central office and many fellow owners, Davis made himself less and less available as time went on, and lived by his most famous motto: "Just win, baby." It took until January 2003, but he did get back to the Super Bowl, although the Tampa Bay Buccaneers spoiled the return.

I had moved to California in 1973. That was still a time of cordiality towards the press, and, of course, I had *The New York Times* imprimatur. So my first contacts with Walsh and Davis were all entirely positive. By the time the climate started to change, I was out of the line of fire of daily coverage. I still admire both, but if I'd had to work around them in the conditions that developed later, I wouldn't have liked it. They entered the press box era toward its very end, and adjusted to a different world—in my opinion—inevitably and correctly. But it doesn't contain the kind of fun my profession used to consider the natural order of things.

Meanwhile, the Johnny-come-lately 49ers fans, who thought the world began in 1981 and that they were entitled to a Super Bowl every year, could never accept Montana's departure (in 1991) and became terribly spoiled. Around the turn of the century, they were losing and the Raiders were winning. What goes around, come around.

"Front-runner" is a term of disapproval in the sports world. Few places, however, have raised front-running to the high art it is in the Bay Area.

46

Oakland A's

When I first covered an A's game, in 1949, Connie Mack was still their manager, they were based in Philadelphia and their home field was called Shibe Park. After they moved to Kansas City in 1955, I'd visit there with the Yankees, all too cognizant that once a Yankee farm club had played there. When Charlie Finley became their owner in 1961, I was fully exposed to his unusual ideas, like the mechanical rabbit that popped up behind home plate to give the umpire fresh baseballs; sheep grazing on the hillside behind the right-field fence; promoting a yellow baseball (which Larry MacPhail had tried in 1939); phoning his managers in the dugout during a game; and getting more mileage out of baiting the Yankees than anyone else did. I also got blow-by-blow descriptions of his conflicts with Kansas City authorities over plans for a new ballpark.

When the Oakland people showed up at the 1964 All-Star Game in Cleveland with models of the stadium they were going to build, Charlie was taking about moving to Louisville "even if I have to play in a cow pasture," or Seattle or Dallas or somewhere else. But Oakland? No. But in December of 1967, in Chicago, at an owners' meeting that I covered, he chose Oakland and was voted down. Then another vote was taken, the Yankees switched from no to yes, and it was done, with a vague promise of a future expansion team for Kansas City. Minutes later, irate phone calls from the mayor of Kansas City and Missouri's powerful U.S. Senator Stuart Symington told baseball officials they'd better get a new team into Kansas City immediately or else, using the magic word "antitrust." Red-faced, they hastily announced this would happen in 1969.

The fallout was widespread. A baseball league must have an even number of teams so that every team can have an opponent every day. If the American League was going to have Oakland *and* Kansas City, it needed a 12th team also. It turned out to be Seattle rather than Dallas. (After one year, the Seattle Pilots became the Milwaukee Brewers.) That pushed the National League, which didn't want expansion at all, to add two teams to also make 12. It chose San Diego and Montreal, triggering the largest one-year expansion baseball has ever had, creating two divisions within each league and a pre-World Series playoff. No single franchise shift had such far-reaching consequences for baseball since the American League's entry into New York in 1903.

The term usually applied to Finley was "maverick," but he was crazy like a fox. He was putting together a terrific team, using (and discarding) a dozen of the best baseball brains around, and he always finished in the black by skimping on expenses and keeping salaries low, as the reserve clause made possible.

When he got to Oakland in 1968, he took away exactly half of the San Francisco annual attendance without adding much to the area total despite his own victories. That first year in Oakland, the A's finished over .500 for the first time in 15 years. Then they finished second in their division twice, first five times in a row and second again in 1976, winning three straight World Series in 1972-74.

Their turmoil was non-stop. In his first 10 years, Charlie changed managers 11 times. When Dick Williams led the team to its first two World Series triumphs, players fought with each other in the club-house. The third came under Alvin Dark, whom Finley had hired and fired in Kansas City. He fired him again when they lost the 1975 playoff to Boston. When Chuck Tanner took over in 1976, the beginning of free agency started Finley on dismantling the club and suing commissioner Bowie Kuhn for trying to stop him.

By this time, the drain on Giant attendance forced Stoneham to sell the team his family had operated for 56 years. He sold it to Toronto, which would have left Finley with the whole Bay Area to himself, but instead San Francisco found a local buyer (Bob Lurie). The A's went to the bottom and both clubs continued to struggle.

In 1980, when Finley tried to sell his team to Denver, complicating the Raider situation, he hired Billy Martin and actually let him manage without interference. With a non-star roster, Martin lifted it from seventh place to second in one year, and finished first in the strike-split season of 1981, getting to the second round of the playoffs before being eliminated by the Yankees. When the Haas family (of the Levi Strauss jeans business) saved the team for Oakland, Martin was the main asset they bought because he had made it attractive enough to buy.

Covering these teams was no picnic for the writers. San Francisco was down to two papers, the once mighty *Oakland Tribune* was starting its death throes (a different company, ANG Newspapers, uses that name today), and football was taking over. The Giants were basically writer-friendly, but unsuccessful and increasingly testy. Their press box was too small and too open to political and other local big shots, carrying on a tradition established by the 49ers at Kezar. Finley fought with the media the way he fought with everyone else, and the Oakland working press facilities were abysmal, worse than Candlestick's. The NFL example, the escalating player salaries, and the ever-increasing influence of television combined to lessen "the power of the press" in an area that had no long-term big league traditions to fall back on. Walsh and Davis were showing how to utilize the press without fawning on it, and the baseball operators learned to follow suit.

We come full circle to the difference between the press box of old and today's. The "western" world is much more homogenized than it used to be. The physical characteristics of airports, fast-food outlets, street traffic, high-rise skylines, luxury hotels and shopping malls are very much alike in large cities across America and Europe. And the cultural imperialism of American movies, pop music, casual dress, eating habits and constant mobility—all cross-fertilized by European and other influences incorporated into "American"— are a topic of widespread complaint (but just as wide acceptance) elsewhere. Pizza and chow mein are more American than Italian or Chinese, while the instant hamburger and Coke are consumed worldwide.

More places look alike, feel alike and make one behave alike regardless of geography. Individuality is diminished; its loss often lamented by the very people who have abandoned it. Gadgets are universal and affect life the same way everywhere. Need I say more than "television" and "mobile phone?"

Sports, as always, reflect the culture they're part of. The physical facilities for media workers in the new ballparks and stadiums are certainly superior to what used to be—and less distinct from one another. But the functions they serve are radically different. The press box was essentially for daily newspaper writers whose tasks and needs were similar and well defined, with radio booths tacked on one way or another. Its population did not fit today's idea of diversity. It was male and white, a relatively small number with a high incidence of men who knew each other well, with essentially the same concerns about the work they had to do. By and large, they were people of a common background and social class for all their individuality, living within the cultural parameters of that time. The generation gap was much smaller, and slower changing, in terms of taste and familiarity, than it has since become.

Today's media have a greater variety of needs and purposes. The newspaper writers need phone connections at their seats for laptops that have replaced typewriters, and perform the transmission function without telegraphers. There are as many various news services and statistical services and independent dot-com writers needing outlets, as there are newspaper people. Radio stations, often using more than one person, augment the "extra" population—all legitimately. But they tend to cluster around their own specialties, and the box-wide interaction among (and often within) the different groups is less than it was.

The "rights holders," radio and television stations carrying play-by-play and paying the club, have their own separate quarters, often on a different level. But the press box also contains a whole crew of public relations people. Space for a complex scoreboard operation, involving half a dozen people and bulky equipment, has had to be carved out of what used to be press box space.

Finally, the difference in travel has added to the diffusion. In the train-travel days, the time on board brought writers and players together in club cars and dining cars. The main train stations had more distinct character than today's airports. Hotels had lobbies. Now clubs fly charters that usually don't include writers, who may even use a different hotel in some cities. And in the old press boxes, most of the time, more than half the occupants were the traveling writers of the two teams. Now more than two-thirds of that population are non-travelers.

It all adds up to one major degree of separation, an atmosphere intensified by all the above. The media, to the clubs, are an enemy— one that must be dealt with and tolerated peacefully, but not part of the family—against whom one must be constantly on guard. Those who felt that way in the past—and plenty did—kept it to themselves most of the time because their employers saw "the press" as essential. Now that the employers don't, or at least not to a comparable degree, mutual suspicion is out in the open. And the press box has moved from a particular culture to merely a work place.

Part Seven

Games

Post-Season and All-Star Games

The underlying concept of league play is that every victory has the same value, as distinct from non-league games, which have none. That made the World Series or a National Football League championship game, and all-star games, special events on an even more glamorous plane than the championship season.

Playoffs changed all that.

No one ever referred to the World Series as "post-season" (nor, for that matter, training camp exhibition games as "pre-season") before 1960. It was something that stood by itself. Each team was completely accepted as a true league champion, a pennant winner, whose accomplishment would not be diminished by being the World Series loser. The winner had an additional special honor, but the loser didn't have to apologize, and spent the next season identified as the "defending champion."

But playoffs are elimination tournaments. The regular season is merely a way to qualify. In baseball, each league produces a pennant winner, but it's not necessarily the team that had the best season, just the one that went furthest in the playoffs. In football, basketball and hockey, division winners are quickly forgotten; what counts is how far they get towards the Super Bowl, the NBA final and the Stanley Cup final. Then, that winner is the one and only true "champion," an extension of the "No. One-ism" so successful taught the public by the advertising industry the last 50 years. So a team like Buffalo, so good that it could reach the Super Bowl four straight years (which no other team has ever done), is held up to ridicule for losing those four individual games instead of being admired for accomplishing what 29 rivals never did.

And the World Series loser has become similarly downgraded in a way that was not true for the first half of the 20th century. The opinion-makers on television and in print keep talking about the need to win a championship to establish a player's greatness, as if an individual rather than an entire team can ever "win" one. But no one thought to downplay Ty Cobb or Ted Williams because they "never won a World Series," or a football coach who never won "a national championship." Number One-ism was not always America's religion.

But hockey had its Stanley Cup playoffs from the beginning, and the NBA took on the same system because its original owners were familiar with hockey. Football adopted it when the league grew beyond two divisions, and baseball when each league broke into divisions.

Purists (which many commentators like to present themselves as) may scoff, but make no mistake: Playoffs are a truly great promotional invention. Fans love them because the excitement of facing elimination is far more intense than fluctuations of daily league standings, and getting into the playoffs is a triumph in itself. They vote not only with their feet but with their pocketbooks, and playoff games sell out most of the time. And while they lower the "importance" of regular season games, they don't diminish season ticket sales because these entitle the holders to buy playoff tickets, which become harder to get because of demand (and at higher prices).

What develops, then, is "the second season," which basketball and hockey fans recognized early on as superior entertainment. The actual play is different: Most competitive (because only the better teams got in), more fiercely fought (for playoff money and pride), more intense (under the threat of elimination) with less strategic compromise for the sake of "tomorrow."

That jibes with the trend of the times, to think of sports as primarily entertainment and not simply competition. The playoffs are what television really wants, with the regular season only a lead-in it has to buy to get the playoff rights. And television wants to maximize the ratings of its "show" by going into prime time. So we have World Series games at night, even on weekends; a Super Bowl starting at 6:30 p.m. eastern time; basketball playoffs including excessive off-days to add extra weekends, and west-coast games running well past midnight in the more populous east. And we have college football games, in longer schedules, almost every day of the week, not just Saturdays, obviously damaging to the regularity of routine and classroom work college life should provide. And college basketball tournaments proliferating during Christmas vacation and leading to the March Madness NCAA tournament that now has 64 teams.

All this the purists deplore, but there are few purists among promoters and ticket buyers. For every purist turned off, there seem to be two or more new customers eager to be turned on.

So the demise of the old press box and its aura is simply one aspect, and a minor one, of a different world. Whether it's better or worse—an opinion anyone can have—it is what it is, leaving us with only two choices: Ride along or "stop the world, I want to get off."

All-star games have gone through the same evolution, but without the boost that higher stakes give playoffs. At first, such games (starting in the 1930s) were the epitome of sports glamour: The best facing the best on one field at one time. The first 15 years of the NBA all-star games were exciting the same way. But then there were two leagues for a while, and expansion created four divisions, and the east-west pairing became less compelling. In football and hockey, with their dependence on reckless and violent contact for effectiveness, all-star games don't have as much credibility. But the baseball games began to lose their luster in the late 1950s when for four seasons an ill-advised method of boosting pension-fund revenue by having two a year was tried, just as expansion was getting started. The squads became too diluted and in the late 1990s, when inter-league regular-season play began and a reorganization of Major League Baseball eliminated the independent league offices, any real sense of rivalry between them evaporated.

At the same time, starting in the 1980s, side events (like a home run hitting contest) grew into a two-day festival and, of course, the game itself went under the lights in prime time. The NBA, far better at self-promotion, turned their all-star extravaganza into a three-day festival on a weekend, including shooting contests, a rookie game, an old-timers game, and more.

All this was in line with the metamorphosis from "pure sport" to "entertainment." So was the in-game practice of deafening music, scoreboard-led cheering and greeting announcements, saturation with ads, and 15 minutes or more of promotional ceremonies instead of fielding practice before a baseball game.

It works, as attendance records prove. But in a strange way, it has also made the World Series and its counterparts something of an anti-climax for everyone but the actual winner. Part of that is just passage of time. No matter how dramatic the events of a 95th World Series may be, they don't fix themselves in the public imagination for future retelling the way the events did when there had been only 10 or 20 World Series to that point. The sheer volume of today's sports overloads the memory of even the recent past, while the totality of the past grows ever larger.

48

Football and Basketball, Then and Now

Baseball—the game, not the business—has been essentially unchanged for a century. In 1901 (National League) and 1903 (American League) fouls up to two strikes in any at-bat began to count as strikes. That was the last fundamental change baseball playing rules ever made. There have been other changes, like the designated hitter, but that's a line-up rule, not a different way to score runs or record outs. Ground rules and scoring rules have changed, ballparks have changed their dimensions, and new ballparks, each with a different layout, have multiplied. But the basic rules of play have remained the same.

Football and basketball have not had such historical stability and it has affected the way reporters cover them.

By 1905, mass-attack football was so violent (with numerous fatalities) that the President of the United States, Theodore Roosevelt, ordered the colleges to clean it up or else. New rules permitted passing the ball forward. By 1920, this was a potent but subsidiary weapon, and in the early 1930s still restricted: The ball had to be thrown from at least five yards behind the line of scrimmage and an incomplete pass into the end zone was still treated as a touchback. Then the pros got rid of the five-yard rule, and their game used more crowd-pleasing passes than the colleges. By loosening restrictions on substitutions, the pros paved the way for offense-defense specialization, increasing the pace of play. The colleges followed, half-heartedly, but from 1965 on, also allowed unlimited substitution and, therefore, two-platoon football. This doubled the number of players you had to use, and maximized the talent in both directions. What had been primarily a ground game became an aerial circus, and everyone concerned liked it that way.

By the 1950s, the football had been made slimmer to make it easier to throw (and harder to drop-kick but easier to place-kick with a holder). Hash marks were adopted to keep the start of a play away from the sidelines. The goal posts went up to the goal line, then back to the end line. There used to be a 15-yard penalty for "coaching from the sideline" and a substitute couldn't join the huddle for the first play, lest he carry instructions. Now coaches call every play, and in the pros communicate with the quarterback by radio (in his helmet) between plays. Overtime tie-breakers were devised to avert tie games.

In the old game (pre-1960 or so) a reporter could chart every play and concentrate on a few scoring drives to tell his story. A pencil and notebook would do. Now the official scoring crew supplies play-by-play and statistics and the reporter keeps only the notes he needs to amplify those details, so that he can spend more time watching (including replays on television) than scribbling. But it is harder, not easier, to get the truly significant details right of a much more complicated game.

Basketball, in the 1920s, allowed one player to take all his team's free throws and, until the mid-1930s, there was a center jump after every score. That gave such an advantage to the taller center that it was abandoned, letting the team scored upon put the ball in play from out of bounds. That, in turn, created a running instead of a static style of play, and set off basketball's popularity with spectators. But two inherent problems remained in what was an artificially invented game. Fouls and violations were so subjective that officiating was too often seen as unsatisfactory, and the team could foul deliberately to yield one free throw point to get a chance score a two-point basket. Since the team behind could do that to try to catch up, the leading team (late in the game) would foul first to prevent that.

The pros found the answer: A time limit within which you had to shoot and hit the basket, and a limit on team (as distinct from only personal) fouls, making every foul after that a chance to make two points. The NBA arrived at that in 1954, the international bodies a few years later, and the colleges not until the 1980s. Then a three-point basket was added.

When I started to cover basketball in the 1940s, scores averaged in the 50s or less per team, and I could keep my own play-by-play scorebook. As the game became faster and higher-scoring, you couldn't afford to look down to record a score because the most important moment in the change of possession was the pass in to start a fast break. So, as in football, we became dependent on the scorer to distribute typewritten play-by-play and statistics, letting us see more and taking notes on what we wanted to amplify from the supplied material. It made us better reporters.

The issue here is what I consider the fundamental rule of journalism. In order to "get it right," in context as well as fact, you have to learn enough about the subject you're covering to understand what's significant and what isn't. And you can't learn that unless you're able to watch the game.

In football, of course, every fan and writer considers himself an expert on X's and O's, able to draw up plays and understand them.

Lou Effrat, covering a football Giants game for *The Times*, was sitting next to Joe Sheehan, his *Times* colleague who was editing the game program but not working that day. Louie, involved in a conversation, missed what happened when Tuffy Leemans ran off-tackle for a five-yard gain.

"What was the last play?" he asked Joe, meaning, "Who carried for how many yards?"

Joe, always glad to be helpful, grabbed a pencil and quickly sketched the offensive and defensive alignment.

"It was a single-wing right," he said, "the guard pulled, the end blocked down on the tackle, the fullback faked into the middle, the wingback decoyed left..."

Louie never asked him again.

Racetracks

One venue we worked at was different from all the rest: Racetracks.

We loved them.

This was the period after pari-mutuel machines had replaced bookie stalls and before off-track betting shops existed. Outside of Nevada, a few riverboats and off-shore cruises—and, of course, the stock market—you couldn't bet legally outside the confines of a racetrack. Gambling, as we've already discussed, is endemic in sports, which wouldn't exist (commercially) if they didn't provide an outlet for that urge. Informal (and technically illegal) betting was universal. No school or place of business lacked access to a bookie and any two or more people could bet among themselves, but ball-parks and arenas contained big signs saying "No Betting Allowed." At baseball games, those who liked to bet on every pitch would gather in the bleachers or in the left-field stands and use hand signals, not unlike the activity on the floor of the stock exchange. In arenas, lobbies and courtside, verbal exchange was simple.

But at the racetrack, betting was not only legitimate, it was acknowledged as the reason for being there at all. And just as the sports promoter's concern was providing adequate sight lines for his customers, the track's management focused on making the bettors comfortable. Eating and seating arrangements were ample, the betting windows were easy to reach, odds boards were visible wherever you were, and the passage of time was divorced from ordinary life. Its demarcations were the post time of each race, all outside concerns were wiped from your mind, and the one or two minutes each race lasted seemed interminable. Einstein's idea about time being relative was demonstrated daily at the racetrack.

For the affluent, it was recreation at its best, relaxed and stimulating at the same time, and a place for social interaction. For the ordinary horse player, ranging from disciplined watchers of their budget to hopeless addicts who may have been ruining their lives, it also provided congenial surroundings. Everybody was in a good mood, polite to strangers, shrugging off the last loss, perpetually hopeful of having the next winner. Whoever you came across was worth listening to because he or she (and she's were plentiful) might have a tip on an upcoming race. The hint might be inadvertent, indirect, open to interpretation or real information, but what did you have to lose by hearing it?

So writers, working or not, got out to the track as often as they could, on the road as well as at home. If you had to cover the races that particular day, the work was easy: The results were in front of you, the charts were supplied directly to the paper, and all the readers wanted to know was who won and what the payoffs were. If the racetrack was your beat, you did your work early in the morning, hanging around the barns, and mingling with racing people at lunch. Then you wrote whatever you wanted about the unlimited supply of interesting personalities, unusual stories, anecdotes and occasional hard news, without the constraints on graceful prose that game details impose.

To top it all off, the press box, in the roof of the grandstand at the finish line, often had a betting window all its own.

Thoroughbred racing was always a daytime affair. The harness tracks operated at night. In my set, all the famous, endlessly repeated stories featured Effrat's misfortunes. I will mention only some I witnessed personally.

At Aqueduct one day, Louie had a sure thing going in the daily double, the winners of the first two races. But he also had to write an advance for a big weekend race. Hurrying to finish before post time, he got immersed in what he was writing and looked up suddenly, realizing he had just missed the deadline for betting on the first race, which meant he was also shut out from the double.

Sure enough the horse he would have bet on won.

The second half was going to be a long shot. He could still double his usual bet and make out okay. But in finishing his story, he also missed the second race post time. The long shot won. The double paid $1,100.

Joe Trimble, of the *News*, had the same plan as Effrat, and they'd discussed it.

"Well, I guess we had a good day," said Joe, putting the $1,100 in a envelope, sealing it, and putting it in his pocket.

Lou had to admit he missed out.

As the day wore on, Louie had three other winners, but blew his profit on a long shot in the last race. Trimble spent the rest of the day sitting on his winnings. On the way home, Louie started berating Trimble.

"What you did is a disgrace," said Effrat. "You had $1,100 of the track's money to play with, and you should have run it up onto the thousands. You're a dummy. You know nothing about how to bet."

"Louie," asked Trimble, "how'd you make out?"

"Lost about a hundred."

Trimble shook his head. "You lost a hundred, I'm sitting here with $1,100 in my pocket, and *you're* telling *me* how to bet?"

Once we were in Cleveland, following a close pennant race, when the game was rained out early. One of the Cleveland writers, Frank Gibbons, had connections with the local track—Thistledown, nothing like the big league New York tracks—so we piled into two cars and went out there. As we arrived, the horses were on their way to the starting gate for the third race. Going through the turnstile, our host conferred briefly with a track official, and said to us, "No. 5, but hurry, it's almost post time." We scattered to different windows and just did get our bets down. No. 5 won in a breeze, evidently with some cooperation from the others, which gave him a five-length lead out of the gate. He paid about $12 for $2, and some of us bet a lot more than $2.

Louie looked morose.

"Didn't you get you bet down?"

"Yeah, but I had No 1."

"Why? Gibby told us No. 5."

"I know, but the guy at the window said No. 1 and looked like he knew something."

Didn't he think Gibby "knew something?" But Effrat was Effrat.

In Chicago, a part owner of the Washington Senators, who had befriended us, invited us out to the trotters one night as guests of the owners and president of the track, in their box. The winks and nods made it clear that No. 7 in the fifth race was the one to back. Louie, the master handicapper, studied the form sheet and said he liked No. 5 better, but agreed the track owner's party must "know something." No. 7 was going off as the favorite, but why be greedy about a sure thing?

Louie and I were sitting in the back of the box at a small table. I invested $10. Louie had a stack of tickets in front of him, so he must have bet $100. Down the stretch came No. 7, neck-and-neck with long-shot No. 5 in a photo finish. The box was thick with tension.

"I've got No. 5," Louis confessed, softly, not wanting to insult our hosts.

The scoreboard flashed 7, 5, 2, posted in that order, bringing cheers.

Then it flashed "OBJECTION."

Then "APPEAL."

Finally "OFFICIAL: 5, 7, 2."

Groans. Louis, out of politeness, kept still, but had won at least a thousand bucks.

Except for one thing.

In the confusion, a waiter had swiped his tickets off the table.

If I hadn't been there, I would never have believed his story.

This was the man whose defining remark (remember?) came when his horse dropped dead in the stretch: "I bet him to *live!*" It was said that four of the horses he had bet on dropped dead, and that finally owners would offer to pay him not to bet on theirs. Obviously, he must have cashed many tickets over the years, because he remained solvent somehow, no matter how often he tapped out on a particular day. We called him "Tap-out Louie."

Dick Young, his lifelong friend, had the best explanation.

"Horses talk to Louie," he said. "But they lie."

Part Eight

Summing Up

50

Ethics
and
Responsibilities

One of the greatest changes in American journalism between 1950 and 2000 is in the realm of what constitutes acceptable ethical practices. Many things we now consider unethical, or at least questionable, were once looked upon differently. The watershed of the change was the Watergate scandal that brought down President Richard Nixon, on the heels of the entire Vietnamese experience and the social and civil rights upheavals of the 1960s. Newspaper management, responding to its own editorial page criticism of government misbehavior and importance of "the appearance of conflict of interest" whether actual or not, began to worry about its own "appearance." A "purer than Caesar's wife" syndrome took hold.

The sports section became a primary target. A no-hit game was a major event, therefore a big story. If the official scorer, who preserved it by deciding between hit and error, was a reporter covering the game, was that a conflict of interest? Every day his decision affected his "relationship" to players he had to "interview." Our paper is supposed to report—not make—the news. How can we allow the reporter to be "part of the story?" Assuming he's perfectly objective and incorruptible, don't we still seem hypocritical in demanding a higher standard of officials?

So no more scoring assignments for our reporters. Especially since they get a fee (then about $25) from the league they're supposed to cover.

This got carried to greater lengths. *The New York Times* decided their theater critics should not vote for awards like "play of the year." Could sportswriters still vote for Most Valuable Player (whose prestige was based on the fact that it was only writers affiliated with baseball doing the voting)? What about the universal practice of writing stories for game programs, which clearly involved "getting paid" by the promoter, who could favor one writer over another and certainly wouldn't use a "negative" story? What about outside work in general, for other publications or radio and television? Did the "independence" of the reporter and the paper appear to be adulterated?

Most of all, what about the practice of a ball club paying the travel expenses of a writer so that its road games could get publicity back home? Wasn't he under pressure to write favorable stories and soft-pedal negative ones? How could that be tolerated?

Weren't all these some form of "bribery"? Including free tickets?

Such issues permeated the newspaper business in the 1970s. Not every paper came to the same conclusion on every point, but an underlying general agreement was reached. The "adversary relationship" between reporter and subject must be demanded, made clear and flaunted. The time-honored practice of simply running a press release (on some routine announcement, like appointment of a business executive) became taboo; it had to be reworded. And any official pronouncement by a manager, coach or club official ought to be regarded with suspicion by any "tough" reporter.

We didn't think that way in the 1950s. Stanley Woodward of the *Herald Tribune*, regarded as the strongest and most visible sports editor of his time, met some of these questions head on in his book *Sports Page*, published in 1948. After describing how some papers (the smaller and less affluent ones) still accepted a club's hospitality while larger ones had begun paying their own way, he zeros in on where the ethical issue lies, and how little effect it has in practice. He says (Page 142):

"When we changed policy and started paying our own expenses, it made no difference to the writer. He went on as before, only now the ball club sent a bill to his office which the sports editor okayed and passed for payment.... Everything was the same except the bookkeeping. I can't say the departure had changed baseball writing an iota. It was always generally honest and critical. It has become neither more honest nor more critical. Long ago the ball clubs stopped trying to control the writers they transported."

What worried him was that the publisher would use the added expense of paying for road trips as an excuse to cut personnel and other coverage.

The point here is that the "integrity" of the writer depends entirely on the writer, unrelated to who pays the costs of meals, travel and hotels as long as it doesn't come out of the writer's pocket. All sports travel has always been the responsibility of the employer—the paper—whatever form it takes. Whether I hand in an expense account (for meals, incidentals, etc.) to my paper, or simply sign hotels tabs and accept the train or plane accommodations assigned to me and have the club bill the paper, it makes no difference to my relationship and attitudes. That doesn't mean some writer can't be a "house man" and curry favor with the club and players, or another can't be unreasonably hostile. But who's paying the bills has nothing to do with it. It's the individual's character that determines his behavior and what he chooses to write.

The same applies to outside writing, and scoring. The only currency a writer has is his reputation for objectivity. His (or her) name is on the story wherever it appears and the need to protect your own integrity greatly outweighs the (invariably small) dollar value of such pieces. The same goes for minor publicity jobs, even in the same sport. Your connection is known to everyone who matters, so any "angling" of your newspaper stories discredits you.

In those days, the vast majority of working reporters, even on the biggest papers, were not being paid enough to live decently—especially not in proportion to the prominence the paper was giving them. They had to do outside writing—presumably their chief marketable skill—to get by. And their papers not only knew but welcomed the system. They could keep talent at a cheaper rate, and the talent would be more willing to stay at that rate.

As for being "tough," an antagonistic or unjustified criticism is no more "honest" than unearned praise or avoided embarrassment. The bedrock journalistic ethic is "get it right"—factually, in context, drawing only sound conclusions from the circumstances.

Athletes and promoters are not government officials dispensing tax dollars, patronage and punishment, backed up by the judicial and coercive power of the state. It's entertainment of a totally voluntary type for participant and follower. The admirable American journalistic tradition of "watchdog" applies to government and other socially powerful entities, not blindly to accounts of ball games, movie reviews, comics and (need it be said?) the content of advertisements. There has to be a sense of proportion about any kind of blanket rule. Ethics depend on conscience, not formulas.

Also, in those days, society had a different view of what was legitimately private and what was "fit to print," including certain words. Compare only the press treatment of the private affairs of Presidents Roosevelt and Kennedy to that of President Clinton. In sports, also, the line of what was considered fair comment was drawn in a different place then now—despicably in something like the silent toleration of discrimination, more reasonably in the areas of sex, personal vices and off-field events.

Today's media world is entirely different. What used to be seen as "tabloid sensationalism" is now routine television and newspaper fare. Media people themselves, as well as the subjects of their attention, accept the "watchdog" idea of an antagonist relationship as a starting point. The (to me) oxymoronic phrase "investigatory journalism" became popular through Watergate. Investigations are conducted by detectives, policemen, prosecutors, congressional bodies, scientists and accident analysts, all of whom have some official standing for pursuing that investigation, who eventually "write a report." A "reporter" finds out what investigations have revealed and transmits the information to the public. An "investigator" and a "reporter" can't be the same person, if only because the investigator knows what he's looking for and hopes to get evidence, while a reporter is supposed to report, without preconceptions, on something that has already been determined.

Ethical posturing is being used today, in sports media, to advance careers, draw attention, justify self-serving and self-aggrandizing activity and place oneself on a higher level than competitors. It is also a favorite device of writers and commentators eager to issue holier-than-thou pronouncements on moral issues they either don't know much about or violate themselves. Before expressing condemnation and outrage directed at an athlete who gets his lift from greenies (amphetamines) slipped into his coffee before a game, one should consider how many performers (including news anchors), housewives, advertising executives and long-haul truckers seek equivalent energy boosters? To write blithely about a need for "drug-free baseball" in a total society that is anything but drug-free is not a display of high moral or ethical standards, only a sure way to get nods of agreement from a large audience.

Most media people today, especially the younger ones, sincerely believe that ethical standards today are higher than they once were, and have been taught that in many journalism classes. I want to be on record disputing that view. Different? Certainly. Higher? By what measure? Lower? In many respects. One thing I can report as a fact, from personal experience: We were definitely less pretentious about it then.

51

Styles
(Of Writing
and Behavior)

In one my other books, I observed that when well-educated, highly-literate sportswriters spend a lot of time in contact with pro athletes, the writers start to talk like ball players rather than the other way around.

The same goes for dress codes, attitudes and behavior patterns. Among the athletes, the veterans set the tone that rookies learn to adopt, and the traveling writers follow along. This is natural, since most of the writers, most of the time, are in the same 20-to-40 age group as the players, and writers who are still there at older ages have formed their habits in their younger days.

Before World War II, men in the large cities of the east and midwest always wore ties and jackets, hats, and overcoats in cold weather. That was considered decent public appearance in offices, on the street and in the ball park, and players, whatever their backgrounds, tended to abide by those customs while traveling. There were exceptions, of course, but they were noted as that: Exceptions.

In the decade after the war, hats started to change or disappear altogether. The hat of all trades was the fedora (with a press pass stuck in the reporter's hatband in all movie clichés), but the stiff, round straw hat was common in summertime and derbies were frequently worn. Look at crowd shots in newsreels from the 1930s to get the picture. Then sports jackets became more numerous than three-piece suits, and before long vests were becoming an unnecessary rarity, replaced by sweaters if warmth was an issue. Where the climate justified it, fur and hunting caps were worn, and the new sheepskin-lined canvas overcoats. Very few athletes or writers tried to be fashion plates, however, and their taste in clothing could be best described as ordinary. The amount spent on wardrobe was not dramatically different in the two groups.

In the 1960s, "suits" was turning into a derogatory synonym for office workers, especially of the executive class. Any matching of pants and jacket or sweater became acceptable in hotel lobbies and restaurants on the road, and in airports.

Then the players started making much more money, and two trends diverged. For most of the population, greater and greater informality became proper, broadening the opportunities for individual choice. For those who could afford it, tailored high fashion was available to *really* express individuality. Fur, leather and all sorts of other materials were displayed, on long coats and short jackets, with high or wide lapels. Elaborate accessories, including jewelry, went along with new hairstyles (even spats made a brief comeback). Facial hair, considered taboo from the 1920s on, was in evidence everywhere. What the Sixties Revolution had done, of course, was make appearance a conscious "statement."

Before long, it was every man and women for himself and herself. In the ball park and everywhere else, any kind of jeans or slacks with any kind of sports shirt, sweater or zipper jacket, and every variety of mustache, beard and hairdo is seen without comment. In the stands and on the street, replicas of sports uniforms (with names and numbers), team caps, warm-up jackets and sweat suits are used as daily clothing. The press box occupants, in all their variety, reflect the new social norms, just as they always had.

To me, the strangest development was everyone's willingness—even eagerness—to be a walking billboard for someone's commercial product: A team, a city, a soft drink, a shoe company, whatever. T-shirts with messages, front and back, proliferated. This led me to surmise the following imaginary historical incident:

Gutenberg has invented the printing press and is seeking financing. He explains to a skeptical investor how movable type works.

The investor says, "That's very interesting, but what good is it? How can you make money with it?"

Gutenberg replies, "We'll make shirts! We'll get rich!"

Writing and reportorial style have also moved with the times.

Up to the 1940s, flowery language and far-out adjectives mingled with shameless clichés on most sports pages. The approach to big games was what we later called "life and death" exaggeration, as distinct from the "fun and games" approach my own generation favored. The quality of writing, in literary terms, was generally pretty low and careless, for all the brilliance that the best talents produced.

After the war, thanks largely to the G.I. Bill, the proportion of Americans with exposure to higher education exploded. Newspapers (and professional radio announcers) started paying more attention to proper usage. More careful editing lifted the level of writing—less jargon, fewer outrageous metaphors, not as many clichés—as fewer surviving papers served a better-educated population.

Over all, today's sports pages are better written—in the literary sense—than they were 50 years ago. But the change in content and purpose is much greater. Our idea, then, was "get the story, tell it as clearly as you can, avoid being wrong, look for the most interesting angle, don't worry about stenographic reproduction of quotes." Today's formula is "make (not just get) the story, be entertaining at whatever cost to accuracy, aim at getting the reader's attention (which will draw attention to you), and move up the ladder as fast as possible." We considered jokes and funny lines seasoning on our staple diet of passing along information. Today, jokes are an end in themselves, ostensibly serving the interests of entertainment and self-promotion. The difficulty is that good joke-makers have a rare talent, as Jim Murray and a few others did, and admiring imitators can't do it 90 percent of the time.

We used to be gratified if someone told us "that was a good story you had yesterday." What today's writers want to hear is "that was a great *line* you had yesterday." There is a difference. We paid, by and large, to the tradition of an informative lead paragraph in the inverted-pyramid approach to construction: Main things first, then the secondary elements, then amplification in the same order. Now stories start with attention-getters, quotes or little descriptive essays, with the result mentioned eventually, almost incidentally. Once a cynical remark, "never let a fact get in the way of a good story," has become an accepted instruction in many quarters.

Also accepted are attitudes once universally criticized. Boasting, taunting and insult ("trash talk"), once considered "bad sportsmanship," are now "self-expression" and admired for their originality if entertaining enough. To congratulate teammates, as visibly as possible, for every positive play or part of a play, has become the proper "good teamwork" response. And writers, starting with the chipmunk generation, like to tell each other how good they are in a way previous generations would have found embarrassing or gauche.

This is not "better" or "worse" in any objective sense. It's simply the tenor of the times. People grow up accustomed to the friendly joshing, bad grammar, careless pronunciation and general inanity of local television news, and accept the same from newspapers struggling to maintain readership in a television-dominated age.

And, as I've mentioned so often already, different concepts exist concerning what is legitimately private, what kind of words are suitable in a "family newspaper," how accurate (no matter how vapid) quotes are supposed to be, and a general preference for negative criticism (justified or not) over the positive (even when clearly more prevalent). Differing value systems produce differing styles.

Quotes, in my opinion, are the bane of today's journalism. They make what people say more important than what people do, and rarely capture in print the true meaning and flavor of words that, when delivered, involved tone of voice, body language, unspoken assumptions and context of situation. The tape recorder and microphone, unambiguously, get the exact words. Then these are picked up and repeated endlessly everywhere with or without relevance or completeness.

Our old approach was more cavalier. We did make up quotes. They were icing on the cake of information, and one of Yogi Berra's books is appropriately called *I Really Didn't Say Everything I Said*. (Yogi certainly produced wonderful Yogi-isms, but their pattern was too easy to reproduce and to ascribe to him.) But when we did it, we knew the people we wrote about well enough to know what they thought and would say about a certain situation. We knew this on the basis of many conversations about the subject at hand, and felt it was perfectly all right to have a manager say, concisely, "We need another left-handed hitter," without actually calling him again to hear him utter those exact words. Could we be wrong? Sure. But not getting at the true import of exact wording without comparable background knowledge is just as wrong. We did it only when we were experienced enough to be pretty sure we were right enough not to be misleading.

That's why I preach to historians that they shouldn't draw conclusions about some situation just on the presence or absence of newspaper quotes, without other corroboration.

Moe Siegel was one of Washington's best known, most appreciated writers and broadcasters for more than 40 years. A man with a terrific personality, who could speak Yiddish with a heavy southern accent, he was a true wit, recognizable and welcome on the sports scene all over the world. An ultimate Washington insider, he had great contacts and really knew his stuff, especially on baseball and football.

Once he had to write a pre-season analysis of the Washington Senators, whom he'd covered for years. He went through player by player, including a lot of quotes from the manager, Joe Kuhel. The desk called back.

"Moe, you've got Kuhel saying all these things about players, but don't you remember? He's no longer the manager this year. Ossie Bluege is."

"Oh yeah, that's right," said Moe. "Give all the Kuhel quotes to Bluege."

With all due respect to everyone involved, and to ethical theories, I still believe that Washington's sports public was as well served then as it is now. Every era lives within its own parameters.

52

Statistics

Obsessive attention to quotes has damaged the quality of sports reporting to some degree. But excessive use of statistics, if not checked, may turn out to be a fatal malady.

Only since the advent of the hand-held calculator, followed by the incomparably greater power of the computer, has the danger of overuse become acute. As fascinating and persuasive as statistics can be, their nature must be understood properly by those who employ and disseminate them. Most writers and broadcasters don't think through what a particular statistic may or may not mean, and are either unaware of its flaws or don't care whether they make sense or not.

I'll discuss this in terms of baseball, the most statistics-infected game, but my argument applies to all the other sports too.

To have validity as useful information, statistics must:

Cover a large enough number of truly comparable cases.

Define explicitly exactly what has been counted.

Have a large enough historical record for that item to determine when a particular statistic is out of the ordinary.

That record must be complete for the category at issue.

Whatever the numbers say, they must be interpreted correctly.

They can never predict, only record past events.

As a record of events created by living, fallible and inconsistent human beings, sports statistics are *not* the same thing as "probabilities."

Manipulating mathematically the numbers produced by sports statistics is more likely to produce misleading rather than illuminating conclusions.

Too many statistics, used too often, become soporific and sap the vitality of the significant ones.

Let's consider those points one by one.

No. 1: Averages are just that, something divided by something in a sufficiently large sample. If you get 100 hits in 300 at bats, that's .333 and impressive. If you get two hits in six tries, that's also .333, but it doesn't mean the same thing. Difference is size is difference in kind.

Ron Fairly, an outstanding and highly intelligent hitter, was broadcasting San Francisco Giant games when Brett Butler played centerfield and led off. Brett's speed and bunting ability gave him a lot of infield hits without much power, and he usually hit above .300. Fairly respected his all-around ability, but not the high batting average.

"If you took away his bunts and dribblers," complained Ron, "he'd be hitting .260."

"Sure," I'd say. "And if you took away his outs, he'd be hitting 1.000."

You can't "take away" things in an average.

No. 2: What's being counted here are hits, defined as "reached base safely on a batted ball without the aid of a fielding error." That stat doesn't distinguish between line drives, bloop singles, slow or tricky grounders, long drives caught by a great play, bunts or home runs; it counts only hits and official times at bat.

The worst example of an unreasoned statistic is the current "pitch count," publicized universally only in the last 20 years or so. It's always cited as "96 pitches, 59 strikes, 37 balls." By convention, every pitch batted fair is assumed to be a strike and every foul ball—even if it doesn't count after two strikes—is also treated as a strike. All of which is just plain silly. The correct statistic should say, "96 pitches, 32 hit fair, 27 strikes (called or swung at and missed) or fouls, 37 balls." It would be no harder to do, nor take up too much extra room in the boxscore. You can bet that the pitching coaches, who kept these charts before the media did, don't consider fence-rattling doubles "a strike," and know which fouls would have been balls if taken. But "59 strikes" is just misinformation.

No. 3: We consider .300 a good batting average, a lower than 3.00 earned run average a good pitching record, a .600 winning percentage enough to contend for (if not win) a division title. Why? Are .299, 3.10 or .595 significantly different? Not at all. We just know that 100 years of accumulated records show most "good" hitters go above the convenient round number of .300, and most of the lesser hitters don't. What makes an easy classification does not necessarily reflect any reality.

But we also have to know something about that history. Before 1920, in the "dead ball" era, 20 homers in a season was fabulous and 30-game winners not unusual. In 1930, when the entire National League hit above .300 and Babe Ruth had raised the homer run record to 60, batting averages had a different meaning than in 1968, when only one player in the entire American League hit .301 and won the batting title. Raw numbers are informative only when compared to other relevant numbers.

No. 4: Any comparison, to be valid, can be made only if *all* the instances of that feature are recorded. You can't be selective (as in the Butler-Fairly example) in choosing which items to compare. Unless you know what's "normal," you can't tell what's "unusual," and you can't define normal unless you have a complete record of all the instances in question.

No. 5: Combining the first four points enables you interpret correctly what the statistic really represents. Merely listing things in order, or subjecting them to sophisticated math like "regressive analysis," is like dividing by zero or dealing with infinity: You can get almost any answer you want with enough manipulation.

Consider an engineer. He starts by knowing what he wants to find out: Will this bridge or building stand up? He then uses math to calculate whether his material and techniques will succeed, or whether his design is impossible. But he doesn't try to conclude from the math what his goal should be. He just confirms its possibility.

A sports statistician who starts by knowing what he wants to prove can almost always find some numbers to back up his pre-conceived conclusion. But to believe that the statistics will some-how reveal what no one knew before is a denial of the real world—of statistics and of play.

Nos. 6 and 7: The reason sports statistics can't predict

performance is that they don't deal with the fundamental element of their compilation: They don't count the same thing. It's the adding apples and oranges fallacy in a subtle form. It shows up most often in "lifetime" matches. Suppose a hitter is 1-for-10 against a particular pitcher. That's too small a sample to be conclusive. But suppose he's 8-for-80. That's a sizeable sample—but it must cover, of necessity, several seasons, and neither the hitter nor the pitcher is exactly the same player he was three years ago. And you'd also better know if he was 2 for the first 60 but 6 for the last 20.

"Probabilities" must be drawn from identical instances. The probability of rolling a seven with two dice is one-sixth because each die is assumed to be balanced and is a physical object following the laws of physics. There are 36 possible combinations and six of them are sevens. It won't happen in every 36 throws, but over time the odds are real. But physical actions on a ball field are never "the same," even if the identity of the individuals is the same. There are too many unpredictable variables. The statistical record can suggest more or less chance of success, and is a very convincing argument when used. But in real life, a tactical decision by a manager is like the engineer's. He knows what he thinks of this hitter's chance against that pitcher this day in this circumstance. The statistic may confirm his opinion, but it didn't form it. His opinion is based on the mix of what he's seen (about a swing or a pitch's behavior), what he knows about the players and their condition and tendencies, how today's conditions differ from other times, *and* the statistic. All this is about guessing right or wrong, but it's not about "probabilities." The real probabilities are only two: You'll win or you'll lose.

We are inundated with statistics merely because they have become available. Press box notes, running to many pages, contain such gems as "So-and-so has hit safely in four of his last six games," or " So-and-so is in a 2-for-21 slump," as if five games can be a "slump." Does anyone bother to find out how often the best hitters have a stretch of 2-for-21? Or 11-for-21? (Combine those into 13 for 42 and it comes out to .310.) Then there's the silliest of all clichés, "on a pace for." A player with 11 homers in his first 27 games is said to be "on a pace for 66 homers." Isn't it obvious enough that home runs (and most other things) occur in irregular spurts? When Toronto Blue Jays' George Bell hit three home runs on opening day in 1988, was he on a pace for 486, but for only 243 the next day? (He finished with 24, although the year before he had hit 47.) It's a little less silly, but still sheer speculation, if you play the pace game after mid-season. When Mark McGwire lifted the home run record to 70 in 1998, he had 65 with four games left, which projected to a final 66 or 67. But he actually hit five in the last three and wound up with 70. "Pace" is a figment of mathematician's imagination.

No. 8 and 9: What's misleading about statistics is the fact that we are still counting only the things we started counting 100 years ago. But those things are the not crucial elements in winning, which is much more complicated and the only thing the team is really trying to accomplish. We could count more relevant items (like the number of men on base for opportunities to drive in runs), but since we didn't, we can't form the necessary backlog to establish "norms." Statistics experts can only manipulate the figures they have available. The real-life manager doesn't need numbers to feel that Joe comes through more often than Sam with men on base; his eye and experience have told him that.

Many studies have tried to prove the uselessness of the sacrifice bunt. How? By showing that a man on first with none out leads to more scores than a man on second with one out. But that's not the choice the real-life manager is making, and it's an illogical comparison. Does a man on first with one out produce more runs than a man on first with none out? No. But the only time a manager orders a sacrifice is when he believes the batter is likely to leave the man on first there. He's not "giving up an out," he's trying to gain 90 feet. If he thinks his batter can advance the runner some other way (with a hit), he doesn't order the sacrifice. But the only record we have of sacrifices is of those actually tried. So that's not a random sample subject to "probabilities."

This is the crux of the limitations of statistics. In the real world, there is no such thing as a "game situation"—two men on, one out, eighth inning, score tied—in the abstract. There is only the actuality of Joe on second, Jim on first, Bill at bat and George pitching, on this day in this park in that moment's weather conditions—and the manager's estimate of the capabilities of each player at that moment against that pitcher.

In the 1950s and 1960s, as I moved through the *Post* and *The*

New York Times, I acquired a reputation as a statistics pioneer. Such subsequent gurus as Bill James cited me as an inspiration (because few other writers were using statistics the way I was). But I had neither the interest, nor the ability, to use them the way a later generation did in devising Sabrmetrics to "evaluate" performance and strategy. (Sabrmetrics is the name devised for statistical studies originating in SABR, the Society for American Baseball Research, to which I belong.) It's flattering, but I played no role in paving the path they followed.

What I did do was more in keeping with my times. We kept our own record of daily games, pitchers, home runs, streaks and so forth, not because they weren't being provided (as they were starting to be in the 1950s) but because that's how we fixed in our minds the salient features of the games we were covering. It was more like writing out words in studying a foreign language, to help memory, than like creating an archive.

My approach to statistics, taught me at a tender age by Bob Harron and Homer Cooke, was to use their persuasiveness to buttress some idea I already had from observation. To cite Sandy Koufax's strikeouts, low-hit games and victories meant more than simply saying "he's the greatest," or quoting someone saying it. But I didn't form my opinion of Koufax from "the numbers he put up." I got it from watching him get people out and hearing what they (and his teammates) had to say about it. Numbers are so convincing—because they seem so dispassionate and "factual"— that I could use them to make a point if I could find the right ones. I learned two good habits. If the numbers did *not* reflect the idea I had in mind, I could drop the idea (or at least rethink it) and not use them. And when I could use them, I didn't waste them on what we now call "trivia," but only to emphasize some point in a significant way.

When too much information is available, it becomes noise, which blots out information. An early computer age phrase impressed me: GIGO, standing for "garbage in, garbage out." If the input is flawed or incomplete, manipulating it won't produce a more sensible answer.

The other way statistics may choke us to death is their sheer volume. Not only can we count and record 10 times as many things as we used to—pitches, offensive rebounds and blocks, minutes on ice, yards per every type of play and field location—but there are now more than 120 major league teams creating these statistics instead of 42 we had back in the 1950s. The boxscores, league standings, and team and individual statistics generated by them eat up space at the expense of written words. The romance and drama that make spectator sports distinct from other types of entertainment can be instilled in fans only by words—written or spoken—and not by numbers.

53

The Unknown Future

Where is the press box headed? What will be its role and layout 20 years from now? Predicting the future gives you only two options: Make pure guesses, or chose some trends to extrapolate.

I have little faith in the second option.

At the New York World's Fair of 1939-40, the most popular exhibit was "The World of Tomorrow." After standing in a long, long line, you were seated in a moving chair which carried you through an immense panorama of a future metropolis full of soaring towers with connecting cross-walks, automated roadways at several levels, underground delivery facilities, and hover cars in the air all around.

That future was defined as 1960.

Didn't happen. Hasn't yet.

I was already an avid reader of science fiction and by 1969, when men first reached the moon, I'd read dozens of stories about that much anticipated giant step for mankind. Hundreds had been written, involving every imaginable plot complication and some remarkably accurate depictions of the technology and physics involved. However, I don't know of a single story that focused on (or even mentioned) the most striking aspect of this hazardous and world-changing occurrence when it actually took place in real life. No one predicted that it would be, by design, an absorbing television event watched worldwide by millions in their homes. It was perceived as a show, not as an exploration. Nor do I know of a story that assumed we'd reach the moon successfully and, without finding anything wrong or having other trouble, never go back to it.

So I avoid making predictions. My annual answer to "who will win this Super Bowl game or World Series?" is "one or the other." What's the future of the press box? I have no idea.

I do know several things about the present, however.

The internet and computer communication in general are in their infancy. Whatever they evolve into, press box facilities and mores will have to accommodate them better than they have so far.

The laptop makes possible communication and instant research we never even dreamed of. Its potentialities will continue to change the way reporters, publicity people and offices interact, and press box routines will reflect them.

Intimacy that grew up in a much smaller, homogenous universe will never return. Diversity of personnel and functions will create their own habits and standards.

The economics of new stadiums and arenas alter the value of every square foot of available space. The present size and location of press boxes is simply too valuable, in luxury-box terms, to last. Most of the new buildings (the last 30 years) have either left it out of the original design (to be shoe-horned in later) or drew up an arrangement so an ample part of the space had to be taken away before long. The situation becomes most acute in post-season events. World Series overflow used to be addressed by temporary tables in upper-stand seating areas behind home plate, giving the same view as the press box. Now the bulk of the press (and radio) corps is placed out in left field and even in the bleachers. Space allotted to "rights holders" is inviolate. No one else matters as much, and gets less accordingly.

The same overcrowding factor produces less clubhouse access and more formal press conference settings. This changes the culture of the press box worker. Exactly how? We'll find out, but change it will.

But the bottom line—a phrase not used so universally 40 years ago—is that newspapers are a smaller part of life today, with less influence and less reach. The press box, in its heyday, was geared to the needs and importance of major local papers. When their importance diminished, so did the impact of their representatives and the need to cater to them.

The rise of the press box paralleled the development of large-scale commercialized spectator sports. It made possible the impact that radio and television could use for their purposes. It created, magnified, disseminated and established the romance and detail that made sports so appealing, and indoctrinated children in their formative years to that kind of pleasure, creating lifelong addictions. It did so as an integral part of the complex culture that marked America through most of the 20th century, one that always did change rapidly but took off in radically new directions during the last quarter of it. The scene now would not be what it is without the press box having been what it was. But this is now and that was then.

Today's fans enjoy sports in different ways than fans did a generation and more ago. They grow up with television, have less patience and a shorter attention span, and experience a much greater tapestry all year round, not just "in season." Fewer feel as intensely about any particular game, team or person; many more are exposed to the high points of all. But that doesn't mean they enjoy it any less. They simply respond differently to a different time and different conditions, in accordance with different tastes, attitudes and way of life. Every indication is that more and more people, worldwide, are being attracted to this form of recreation, and getting more access to it. The existence of future fans is not in question. The nature of their response will be whatever suits them. And promoters will react to that.

To talk about that, you'll have to turn to someone who is part of this time. I've tried to tell you what it was like in my time.

What's here should be enjoyed in its own terms. What's gone need not be mourned, but can be respected for what it was in its own context. If you're old enough, you can dwell on some memories; if not, you can use this as raw material for imagining, if you care to.

But I can tell you this: It sure was great fun while it lasted.

Index